CW00552074

The
Apostle Paul
and the
Christian Life

The
Apostle Paul
and the
Christian Life

Ethical and *Missional Implications*

of the *New Perspective*

Edited by Scot McKnight
and Joseph B. Modica

B
Baker Academic
a division of Baker Publishing Group
Grand Rapids, Michigan

© 2016 by Scot McKnight and Joseph B. Modica

Published by Baker Academic
a division of Baker Publishing Group
P.O. Box 6287, Grand Rapids, MI 49516-6287
www.bakeracademic.com

Printed in the United States of America

All rights reserved. No part of this publication may be reproduced, stored in a retrieval system, or transmitted in any form or by any means—for example, electronic, photocopy, recording—without the prior written permission of the publisher. The only exception is brief quotations in printed reviews.

Library of Congress Cataloging-in-Publication Data
Names: McKnight, Scot, editor.
Title: The apostle Paul and the Christian life : ethical and missional implications of the new
    perspective / edited by Scot McKnight and Joseph B. Modica.
Description: Grand Rapids, MI : Baker Academic, 2016. | Includes bibliographical references and
    index.
Identifiers: LCCN 2015037180 | ISBN 9780801049767 (pbk.)
Subjects: LCSH: Christian life—Biblical teaching. | Bible. Epistles of Paul—Criticism,
    interpretation, etc.
Classification: LCC BS680.C47 A66 2016 | DDC 227/.06—dc23 LC record available at http://lccn
    .loc.gov/2015037180

Scripture quotations labeled AT are those of the author.

Scripture quotations labeled ESV are from The Holy Bible, English Standard Version® (ESV®), copyright © 2001 by Crossway, a publishing ministry of Good News Publishers. Used by permission. All rights reserved. ESV Text Edition: 2011

Scripture quotations labeled KJV are from the King James Version of the Bible.

Scripture quotations labeled NIV are from the Holy Bible, New International Version®. NIV®. Copyright © 1973, 1978, 1984, 2011 by Biblica, Inc.™ Used by permission of Zondervan. All rights reserved worldwide. www.zondervan.com

Scripture quotations labeled NRSV are from the New Revised Standard Version of the Bible, copyright © 1989, by the Division of Christian Education of the National Council of the Churches of Christ in the United States of America. Used by permission. All rights reserved.

In keeping with biblical principles of creation stewardship, Baker Publishing Group advocates the responsible use of our natural resources. As a member of the Green Press Initiative, our company uses recycled paper when possible. The text paper of this book is composed in part of post-consumer waste.

16 17 18 19 20 21 22   7 6 5 4 3 2 1

Scot McKnight dedicates this volume to
James D. G. Dunn
Emeritus J. B. Lightfoot Professor of Divinity,
University of Durham,
and Fellow of the British Academy,
who teaches about and dwells in the Spirit.

Joseph B. Modica dedicates this volume to
William V. Crockett
Professor Emeritus of New Testament,
Alliance Theological Seminary, Nyack, New York,
who teaches well by his scholarship and life.

μιμηταί μου γίνεσθε καθὼς κἀγὼ Χριστοῦ. (1 Cor. 11:1)

Contents

Acknowledgments

We want to thank Bob Hosack, executive editor at Baker Academic, for his encouragement for this project, along with our copy editor, Ryan Davis, and project editor, Tim West. All three editors improved our book significantly.

Our contributors did exceedingly well with the task at hand: to imagine what the apostle Paul thought of the Christian life—a bit of a daunting but necessary task for those committed to following Jesus in the twenty-first century. We thank our contributors for their skillfulness, for their diligence in meeting deadlines, and for their friendship.

We dedicate this book to our mentors (Scot McKnight—James D. G. Dunn; Joseph B. Modica—William V. Crockett), who have taught us much about the apostle Paul and modeled for us what it means to live the Christian life.

Introduction

SCOT MCKNIGHT AND JOSEPH B. MODICA

One of the greatest double-play combinations in baseball history is Tinker to Evers to Chance.[1] These three players led the Chicago Cubs to four pennants during their tenure.[2] They were the glue that held the infield together and in many ways the entire team. As many of us know, especially one of the coeditors of this volume (whose initials are SMcK), the Cubs have waited very patiently for their chances to return to the World Series.

With all such combinations there is a rhythm and sequence. As one briefly reflects upon the origins and impact of the new perspective on Paul (NPP),[3] one immediately thinks of an imaginary double-play combination of Stendahl to Sanders to Dunn. It appears that the three worked assiduously with one another, almost like teammates, even when the contribution perhaps was unknown to the one who followed. Granted, there are always contributing factors to any "new" movement, but for now we'll very briefly consider the three contributions to this so-called NPP double-play combination.

1. The trio has been immortalized in the 1910 poem "Baseball's Sad Lexicon" by Franklin Pierce Adams. They were elected together to the National Baseball Hall of Fame in 1946.
2. From 1906 to 1910.
3. For a basic introduction of the new perspective on the apostle Paul, see Kent L. Yinger, *The New Perspective on Paul: An Introduction* (Eugene, OR: Cascade, 2011), and Michael B. Thompson, *The New Perspective on Paul*, rev. ed. (Cambridge, UK: Grove, 2010). See also Mark Mattison's very resourceful website: www.thepaulpage.com.

Krister Stendahl, with his influential article "The Apostle Paul and the Introspective Conscience of the West,"[4] is in many ways the agile shortstop who begins the double play by handling well the ground ball. Stendahl warned against interpreting the apostle Paul through the theological lens (i.e., guilty conscience) of the Protestant Reformer Martin Luther. As Magnus Zetterholm rightly observes about what light the NPP shed on interpreting Paul, "The problem Luther wrestles with—how to find a merciful God—was not Paul's quandary. Paul's main interest was precisely the relationship between Jews and non-Jews."[5]

What can one say about E. P. Sanders's landmark book *Paul and Palestinian Judaism*, except that it is essential reading for any serious interpreter of the New Testament? What Sanders did was reinterpret and recontextualize for modern-day readers what constituted first-century Judaism(s). Perhaps the most enduring contribution of Sanders is the understanding that Judaism was not a works-based religion emerging from human effort but one emerging from divine election and the obedience expected of those who were already in the covenant. The implications for Paul simmered on the topic of Sanders's reevaluation of Judaism. Sanders's classic definition of Judaism as "covenantal nomism" has now redefined a generation of New Testament scholars, even if not all have bowed the knee to the idea.[6] His contribution was a herculean paradigm shift, to borrow Thomas Kuhn's concept. Sanders took the toss from Stendahl, stepped on second base, and began to pivot his throw to first base to complete the double play.[7]

Here is where we find James D. G. Dunn, affectionately known as Jimmy, playing first base. Dunn completes the double play with his groundbreaking lecture in 1982 entitled "The New Perspective on Paul."[8] He established specific interpretive language to Sanders's methodology for the apostle Paul while agreeing with Sanders's general thesis about covenantal nomism. Dunn's

4. See K. Stendahl, "The Apostle Paul and the Introspective Conscience of the West," *Harvard Theological Review* 56 (1963): 199–215, reprinted in his *Paul among Jews and Gentiles and Other Essays* (Philadelphia: Fortress, 1976), 78–96.

5. See Magnus Zetterholm, *Approaches to Paul: A Student's Guide to Recent Scholarship* (Minneapolis: Fortress, 2009), 98. Zetterholm's book is essential reading for anyone interested in the historical approaches to the apostle Paul.

6. "Covenantal nomism is the view that one's place in God's plan is established on the basis of the covenant and that the covenant requires as the proper response of man his obedience to its commandments, while providing means of atonement of transgressions" (Sanders, *Paul and Palestinian Judaism* [Philadelphia: Fortress, 1977], 75).

7. In part 2 ("Paul"), Sanders recognizes the contribution of Stendahl (ibid., 435–38).

8. See James D. G. Dunn, "The New Perspective on Paul," *Bulletin of the John Rylands University Library of Manchester* 65 (1983): 95–122. Also see the reprint of the above article in Dunn, *The New Perspective on Paul* (Grand Rapids: Eerdmans, 2008), 99–120.

language involved seeing "works of the law" as "badges" or "boundary markers"[9] that the apostle Paul, according to Dunn, opposed when critiquing Jews and Judaism. Instead of seeing "works of the law" as attempts by humans to earn favor with God in order to be saved, Dunn located this expression in the debate between Paul and those who thought gentiles needed to adopt the "works of the law" if they wanted to be fully acceptable to God and full members in the "Israel of God." In retrospect, Sanders does not spend much time with the apostle Paul in his book (exceedingly much more with Palestinian Judaism); it is Dunn who is actually responsible for using Sanders's observations in interpreting the apostle Paul's letters.

We are well aware that at times standing at first base were others—not least N. T. Wright, who in his massive studies has given his own twist to the NPP in what he at times has called the "fresh" perspective on Paul—but it is more than fair to say that Dunn's contribution was to turn the relay throw of Sanders into an out.

What we attempt to answer in this book is this question: How did the apostle Paul understand the Christian life? We believe that a new-perspective reading of Paul—however that might be understood today—offers much to an understanding of the Christian life, so we have assembled a collection of essays from new-perspective scholars. We are very fortunate to have two of the major players (not to overuse the baseball analogy) contribute to this volume: Professors James D. G. Dunn and N. T. (Tom) Wright.

Likewise, we recognize and value the contributions of the old perspective, but we have not yet encountered how a particular old-perspective reading of the apostle Paul unpacks one's understanding of the Christian life. Sometimes an old-perspective reading of Paul can simply get "stuck" with the implications and aspects of individual salvation or chase the whole of Paul's thought through what is often called the *ordo salutis*. Of course, individual salvation is important. Moreover, it seems that a new-perspective reading of Paul offers a fresh and a rich approach as one grapples with the apostle Paul's understanding of the Christian life.[10]

9. Dunn interprets "the works of the law" that Paul opposes in Galatians primarily as circumcision, but elsewhere they would include food laws (clean and unclean) and the Sabbath observance.

10. As one might imagine, there are detractors (or modifiers) to the new perspective on Paul often attempting to move beyond the established polarities. See Francis Watson's *Paul, Judaism, and the Gentiles: Beyond the New Perspective*, rev. ed. (Grand Rapids: Eerdmans, 2007). Watson argues that the old and new perspectives are too entrenched and that his proposal presents "a *forward* rather than a *backward* step." Douglas Campbell and others have espoused an apocalyptic approach in contrast to the new perspective. Interaction with the many and innovative approaches to Paul of Campbell and others is beyond the scope of this introduction. Again,

The strength of this volume and the new perspective overall is its emphasis on *ecclesiology*—life in the church (McKnight and Gombis); *pneumatology*—life in the Spirit (Mitchel); *missiology*—life in mission-in-the-world (Wright); *Christology*—life in Christ (Dunn); *soteriology*—a "saved" life (Cohick); *ethicality*—a moral life (Longenecker); and *sanctification*—a holy life (Leach).

---

these approaches are laudable in the current debate about how best to read and interpret the apostle Paul. But are they helpful in providing a holistic vision for reading and understanding all of Paul's letters? Thus, what is the *best* prism through which to read and interpret *all* of Paul's letters?

1

The Christian Life from the Perspective of Paul's Letter to the Galatians

JAMES D. G. DUNN

P aul's letter to the Galatians is of particular interest in any attempt to characterize the Christian life as seen or intended by Paul.[1] Not only does it focus on what is the key question here—What is it which makes a person a Christian? What is the central feature, for Paul, of being a Christian?[2]—but, exceptionally in Paul's letters, it is in Galatians that Paul

1. I have not attempted to refer to other literature in what follows (which, if as complete as this mini-exposition of Galatians requires, would have extended the essay beyond the word limit), but, of course, I draw intensively on my principal contributions on Galatians (*The Epistle to the Galatians*, Black's New Testament Commentary [London: Black, 1993; Grand Rapids: Baker Academic, 2011], *The Theology of Paul's Letter to the Galatians* [Cambridge: Cambridge University Press, 1993], and *Christianity in the Making*, vol. 2, *Beginning from Jerusalem* [Grand Rapids: Eerdmans, 2009], 720–46), in which participation in the exegetical debate is of course central. Perhaps I should also mention my collected essays, *Jesus, Paul and the Law: Studies in Mark and Galatians* (London: SPCK; Louisville: Westminster John Knox, 1990), which includes the essays "The Incident at Antioch (Gal. 2:11–18)," "The New Perspective on Paul," and "The Theology of Galatians." I use the translation of Paul's Greek as given in my *Galatians* commentary.

2. In his letters, Paul himself never uses the term *Christian*. But arguably it had already come into currency prior to Paul's active ministry and in Antioch, from which Paul began his evangelistic ministry (Acts 11:25–26; 13:2–3). There are only three uses of the term "Christian" in the New Testament—Acts 11:26; 26:28; 1 Pet. 4:16.

gives a clear account of his own conversion (Gal. 1:13–17). So after drawing attention to the weight of authority he sought to invest in the letter, we will then look at Paul's account of how he himself became a Christian, and then at the way he had to fight to define and defend what he regarded as the fundamental factors which constituted or qualified a person to be counted as "Christian."

In fact, two words stand out in Paul's talk of the Christian life in Galatians—*pistis*, "faith," and *pneuma*, "spirit." *Pistis* occurs twenty-two times, a higher proportion of usage than in almost any other New Testament writing.[3] And *pneuma* appears more intensively in Galatians 3–5 (fourteen times) than almost anywhere else in Paul, though not with quite the intensity of Romans 8 and 1 Corinthians 12 and 14. These basic statistics, almost alone, would be sufficient to indicate that faith in Christ and the gift of the Spirit are central to Paul's understanding of the Christian life. And this first impression is quickly confirmed by a closer look at the text.

The Unusual Opening of the Letter

Paul begins his letter in his usual style by introducing himself as "Paul, apostle."[4] Notable, however, is the elaboration he adds before he mentions to whom the letter is sent (Gal. 1:2b). In other letters he elaborates the initial self-introduction as "apostle of Christ Jesus" and more.[5] But in Galatians Paul can hardly restrain himself, going on immediately to indicate that his apostleship was "not from men or through a man, but through Jesus Christ and God the Father" (1:1). For him thus to disrupt the normal polite convention of an epistolary introduction is very surprising.[6] Paul's sensitivity on the point is self-evident and striking. Evidently he felt his apostleship to be at issue, a status and authority he has to make clear as he determines to call his Galatian converts to account. And it quickly becomes clear that he is writing to make fresh claim to his apostolic authority in order to give what follows the weight he wants it to have.

The further addition Paul makes following his usual "grace and peace" benediction (1:3) is also a departure from his usual letter opening—the

---

3. Only in 1 Timothy is usage higher (nineteen times).

4. Cf. Rom. 1:1; 1 Cor. 1:1; 2 Cor. 1:1; also Eph. 1:1; Col. 1:1; 1 Tim. 1:1; 2 Tim. 1:1; Titus 1:1. The exceptions of 1–2 Thessalonians and Philippians are noticeable. It was with Galatians that Paul felt it necessary, probably for the first time, to emphasize his apostolic commission and authority.

5. 1 Cor. 1:1; 2 Cor. 1:1; also Eph. 1:1; Col. 1:1; the Pastoral Epistles.

6. Even the most elaborated self-introduction, in Rom. 1:1–7, has nothing of the character of self-defense and insistence on status which we find in Gal. 1:1.

formulaic, Christ "who gave himself for our sins in order that he might rescue us from the present evil age" (1:4). Anyone who was familiar with Paul's normal and more typical epistolary introduction might well pick up the implication that the conduct and policies he was about to rebuke were too reminiscent and typical of the "evil age" from which the gospel had rescued them.

Most noticeable of all, however, is Paul's still more striking departure from common courteous convention in what follows. For the normal convention, as we see in other letters of his, was to continue the opening greeting with a word of thanksgiving and prayer on behalf of those addressed, as in what is probably Paul's earliest letter, 1 Thessalonians (1:2–3): "We give thanks to God always for you all, making mention of you in our prayers, constantly remembering your work of faith" (AT).[7] But in this case Paul has no time for such niceties. So far as he is concerned, there is nothing to give thanks to God for in what he has heard concerning the Galatian churches. Having restrained himself thus far, evidently with some impatience, Paul can hold back no longer and turns abruptly to his primary concern in writing.

> I am astonished that you are so quickly turning away from the one who called you in the grace (of Christ) to another gospel, which is not another, except that there are some who are disturbing you and wanting to turn the gospel of the Christ into something else. But even if we or an angel from heaven preach to you a gospel contrary to what we preached to you, let him be accursed! As we said before, I now also say again: if anyone preaches to you something contrary to what you received, let him be accursed! For am I now trying to persuade men, or God? Or am I seeking to please men? If I were still trying to please men, I would not be the slave of Christ. (Gal. 1:6–10)

The issue is clear, and the reason for Paul's departure from normal epistolary convention is clear too. There were those who had come to the communities/congregations which Paul had established in Galatia and who were, in Paul's view, preaching a *different* gospel from the one to which the Galatians had first responded. As the letter unfolds it becomes clear that what these others were trying to achieve was for the Galatian believers to be circumcised (5:2–6). The fierceness of this opening rebuke, totally usurping the usual epistolary pleasantries, makes the passage exceptional in Paul's letters.[8] The nearest parallel in intensity of opposition comes later in the same letter, where Paul

---

7. Cf. Rom. 1:8–10; 1 Cor. 1:4–7; Phil. 1:3–11; Col. 1:3–6; 2 Thess. 1:3–4; Philem. 4–7.
8. Particularly noticeable, indicating the intensity of Paul's feeling, is the repetition of the curse formula ("let him be accursed") in verses 8–9.

wishes that those who were insisting that the Galatian converts should be circumcised "would castrate themselves" (5:12)![9]

What was at stake here, in Paul's view, was whether this new faith in/commitment to Jesus (the) Christ meant that gentile believers were converting to Judaism. Was belief in Jesus (the) Christ simply a first step to becoming a Jew? Paul was clear that the answer was no! It was the incomers (to Galatia) insisting that the Galatians' belief in/commitment to Christ was only a first step to becoming a full proselyte which so infuriated Paul. In response, and outrage as nowhere else, Paul insisted that *pisteuein eis Christon* was a full response to the gospel of Christ. To insist on anything more as equally fundamental was to diminish and deny the fundamental character and role of faith. All this becomes clear as the letter progresses.

Paul's Conversion

In responding to this threat to his gospel, as to his Galatian converts, Paul's first instinct was to tell, or remind the Galatians of, his own testimony and in doing so to correct false rumors about his relation to the center of the new movement and its chief authorities (Gal. 1:13–17).

He points out, or reminds them, that he had previously been a strong advocate of the views he now contests. His earlier life had been "in Judaism";[10] he was a zealot for the views and policies he now resists, a violent persecutor of the followers of the Jesus whom he now seeks to serve (1:13–14). His conversion from such zealotry had been an act of divine grace, when God "revealed his Son in me,"[11] which came to Paul primarily as a commission to preach the Jesus whose followers he had persecuted, and to preach him among the gentiles (1:15–16). Since there is no indication elsewhere in Paul's writings that he had had any doubts or anxieties about his role as persecutor,[12] it is hard to grasp the extent of the (total) upset and transformation in what mattered to him, which was occasioned by his conversion.[13]

9. Paul's opposition to the would-be Judaizers in 2 Cor. 10–13 is intense (cf. particularly 2 Cor. 11:12–15), but nowhere as crude.

10. It is of interest, but also significant, that it is only in this letter that Paul uses the term *Judaism*. But the "Judaism" he is referring to is the ardent Judaism of the zealous Pharisee; Paul still thought of himself as a Jew (Gal. 2:15).

11. This comes across as a very personal encounter, but elsewhere Paul's reference is more in line with the Acts accounts (1 Cor. 9:1; 15:8).

12. Cf. Phil. 3:5–6: "as to the law, a Pharisee; as to zeal, a persecutor of the church; as to righteousness under the law, blameless."

13. Should we speak also of transformation of character? Galatians 5:12 and 2 Cor. 11:12–15 suggest not!

That after his conversion Paul spent three years in Damascus and (significantly) Arabia suggests a lengthy and penetrating rethinking of his priorities and goals. It was evidently also of importance to him to insist that he did not consult with anyone whom the Jerusalem authorities would recognize, nor did he return to Jerusalem during that time (1:16–17). His insistence that even when he did go to Jerusalem three years later, he stayed with Cephas for only a fortnight (otherwise seeing only James of the Jerusalem leadership, 1:18–19), suggests that there were those who wanted to maintain his dependence on and subordinate status to Cephas and the Jerusalem apostles.[14] The fact that he adds a solemn oath—"What I write to you, please note, before God, I am not lying" (1:20)—assuredly indicates (or confirms) that for Paul, the God-given character of his gospel and its degree of independence from the Jerusalem leadership (including, of course, those who had been Jesus's own closest disciples) were the unarguable givens of his apostleship.

That Paul continued in effect to narrate his own biography as a disciple of Jesus Christ, commissioned directly by him, indicates what he saw to be of first importance in writing this letter. After that short visit to Jerusalem he had been absent from Jerusalem for another fourteen years.[15] During that time he had preached in Syria and Cilicia, with some success and the warm approval of the churches of Judea (1:21–24). Only after fourteen years had he and Barnabas gone up to Jerusalem, under divine authority (2:1–2), and there successfully resisted the attempt by some Jewish believers to insist that their uncircumcised (gentile) companion (Titus) be circumcised (2:3–6). The backing of the pillar apostles (James, Cephas, and John) was of particular importance in their recognition of a legitimate (noncircumcision) gentile mission, even while they continued to prosecute an equivalent mission among the circumcised (2:7–10).[16]

This degree of concord was shattered by "the Antioch incident" (2:11–14). Presumably as a result of the advocacy of "certain individuals who came

14. This is one of the clearest points at which the author of Acts (Luke) softens the strength of Paul's claim to dependence directly on Christ rather than on the Jerusalem leadership (Acts 9:23–26), as again in his account of the Jerusalem conference (cf. Acts 15:6–21 with Gal. 2:1–10)—Luke evidently wishing to present a Paul not only in accord with but also dependent on Peter, James, etc., in contrast to Paul's own account of the relationship.

15. Whether the "fourteen years" should include the three years of 1:18 or be counted in addition to that three years (totaling seventeen) is one of the chronological problems which Galatians poses and which has never been satisfactorily resolved.

16. Whether James was accounted an apostle (cf. 1:19) and whether Paul was accounted by the Jerusalem "pillars" as an apostle (2:8) remain ambiguous, perhaps as a result of the intensity of feeling with which Paul wrote. Similarly with the "me"/"we" contrast in 2:9—Paul is so insistent on his own commissioning that the status of Barnabas's commissioning is again left ambiguous.

from James," Peter and the other Jewish believers, who had been accustomed to eating with gentile believers, withdrew from table fellowship with and "separated" themselves from these gentiles because they "feared those of the circumcision" (2:11–12). One can almost hear the sob in Paul's voice when he adds that "even Barnabas"—his close companion and fellow missionary during that first mission (2:9)—"was carried away with their hypocrisy" (2:13). Paul could not agree that this was what the gospel demanded—that Jewish believers should refrain from table fellowship with gentile believers. So he confronted and rebuked Cephas/Peter[17] publicly on the issue. Such policy and practice, Paul argued, was *not* in accordance or straight with the gospel. The gospel did *not* compel gentile believers to "judaize" (2:14). It was this confrontation, following his experience of the total transformation of his own principles and priorities, and following too the previous agreement in Jerusalem, which made Paul realize that the believers in Galatia had to be told even more firmly that participation in Christ and the church of those who believed in Christ was by faith alone.

The Centrality of "Faith" in Galatians

We should be grateful for the Antioch incident since it seems to have been the confrontation which caused Paul to dictate (in his letter) one of the clearest and most emphatic statements of the gospel, of what he understood to be good news.

> We are Jews by nature and not "Gentile sinners," knowing that no human being is justified by works of the law but only through faith in Jesus Christ, and we have believed in Christ Jesus, in order that we might be justified by faith in Christ and not by works of the law, because by works of the law shall no flesh be justified. (Gal. 2:15–16)

I put "Gentile sinners" in quotation marks since I infer that Paul was echoing (or quoting) the reason which some of the Jewish believers gave for separating from the gentile believers. Gentiles were outsiders, outside the covenant which YHWH had made with Israel. So how could Jews have fellowship with gentiles, even gentile believers, sitting and eating at the same table? Paul's response does two things. First, it strips the gospel to its central and definitive

---

17. The variation of Cephas (1:18; 2:9, 11, 14) and Peter (2:7–8) is intriguing: the former perhaps indicating Paul's view of Cephas as a prominent Jerusalemite, the latter as a fellow missionary.

character: what the gospel demands of would-be respondents is faith in Jesus Christ. And second, it warns that any addition to that fundamental demand undermines and destroys its fundamental character. To demand "works of the law" in addition to faith, as a necessary expression of faith, was to destroy the fundamental role of faith. "Works of the law" were not an essential addition to or expression of faith—without which faith could not be regarded as real faith. By "works of the law" Paul would certainly have been thinking of the two confrontations just described in the earlier paragraphs of Galatians 2 (circumcision and food laws).[18] The Jerusalem leadership had accepted the point so far as circumcision was concerned (2:1–10). But under pressure to remain true to another distinctive feature of Israel's covenant relation with YHWH (Israel's food laws), Peter and the other Jewish believers in Antioch had in effect said that belief in Christ alone was inadequate, insufficient. To function as part of the covenant relationship with YHWH, one had, in effect, to recognize that this covenant relationship was only with Israel—Jews alone were the people of God, so that the dietary laws which Israel had accepted and which distinguished Israel were integral to that relationship, and those who sought the benefits of that relationship had therefore to accept these rules as well.

This was where Paul drew the line. Becoming a member of the people of God (Israel) was not primarily what the gospel was about. Rather, the gospel was primarily about being related to God through Christ—being a member of Christ. To be justified before God, only faith in Christ was required. To require any more was to undermine that central gospel affirmation. As Paul goes on to show, faith would express itself in many ways, some of which could be regarded as "works"—baptism being an obvious and prime example (3:27). But to allow any "work" to be regarded as of equal significance—even baptism, or love-inspired actions (5:6)—would be to diminish the fundamental role and significance of that yielding and committing of oneself to God (faith) from which all else sprang. The point was so important for Paul that in this initial statement (2:16) he underlines the point by repetition—faith in Christ and not works, faith in Christ and not works.[19]

18. He would presumably include "special days, and months, and seasons, and years" (4:10) among the "works of the law" which he had in mind, but the immediate reference of 2:16 is to circumcision (2:1–10) and food laws (2:11–14).

19. The point has unfortunately been obscured by those who insist that *pistis Christou* should be translated as "the faithfulness of Christ"—thus losing the very point which Paul makes, and which by his very repetition he makes more emphatically: "not from works of the law, but through faith in Jesus Christ; and we have believed in Jesus Christ precisely so that we should be justified by faith in Christ and *not* by works of the law."

This emphasis on the gospel being received and coming to its full force through faith is one which Paul hammers home by repetition throughout chapter 3:

3:2: "by hearing with faith [*ex akoēs pisteōs*]"

3:5: "by hearing with faith [*ex akoēs pisteōs*]"

3:6: "Just as Abraham believed [*episteusen*] God, and it was reckoned to him for righteousness"

3:7: "those of faith [*hoi ek pisteōs*]"

3:8: "God would justify the Gentiles from faith [*ek pisteōs*]"

3:9: "those of faith [*hoi ek pisteōs*]"

3:11: "The righteous from faith [*ek pisteōs*] shall live" (cf. Hab. 2:4)

3:12: "the law is not from faith [*ek pisteōs*]"

3:14: "we might receive the Spirit through faith [*dia tēs pisteōs*]"

3:22: "in order that the promise might be given from faith [*ek pisteōs*] in Jesus Christ to those who believe [*pisteuousin*]"

3:23: "Before the coming of this faith [*pistin*] we were held in custody under the law, confined till the faith [*pistin*] which was to come should be revealed"

3:24: "in order that we might be justified from faith [*ek pisteōs*]"

3:25: "But faith [*pisteōs*] having come, we are no longer under the custodian"

3:26: "For all of you are sons of God, through this faith [*dia tēs pisteōs*], in Christ Jesus"

When it is so obvious that "those of faith [*hoi ek pisteōs*]" are precisely those who "believe" as Abraham believed (3:6–9), I find it most puzzling that the alternative view, that *pistis* should be understood as the "faith(fulness)" of Christ at any point in the argument, has gained so much traction among exegetes. To me, I must confess, it seems quite obvious that Paul is arguing for a "faith alone" (*ek/dia pisteōs*) understanding of what reception of the gospel involves, as against the "faith plus works" which he saw Peter and the other Jewish believers at Antioch demanding of gentile believers. The danger which he saw threatening his Galatian converts, and the reason for the shrillness of the letter, led him to make his point and repeat his point over and over, in chapter 3 in particular. So it should be no surprise that Paul underlines his point so forcibly in 2:16 and repeats himself so regularly, as in 3:22. Those who think that Paul, the good stylist, would not repeat himself, as in 2:16 and 3:22, have fallen into the trap of treating the letter as a dispassionate treatise, rather than one in which Paul's indignant passion determines the repetition by which he tries to drive home his point—"by faith alone."

The intensity of Paul's argument should not be allowed to cloud or diminish this central point which he wanted to make. Paul goes on to argue, somewhat convolutedly, that the seed of Abraham to and for whom the promise had been made was primarily Christ (3:15–16). So those related to Christ, who belonged to Christ, and who were thus "in Christ," were thereby Abraham's offspring and heirs according to the same promise (3:28–29). The law, which came in well after the promise to Abraham (430 years later), did not alter the terms of the original promise (3:17–18). The law's role was as a "custodian" (*paidagōgos*) pointing the way forward to faith in Christ. But now that "faith" had come, the custodian no longer had the same role (3:23–25). The immediacy of relationship with God through Christ which faith in Christ makes effective is not to be qualified and hedged around by commands which had only a limited role in the divine purpose. The laws, particularly regarding circumcision, table fellowship, and holy days (4:10), had such a limited role and should not be regarded as equally important as the basic gospel call to believe. There should be many outworkings of that faith, but "in Christ Jesus neither circumcision counts for anything, nor uncircumcision, only faith operating effectively through love" (5:6).

For many this could be a disturbing conclusion. Surely faith in Christ will be expressed in particular ways, with particular outworkings. Yes, says Paul, that is true. *Love*, love of neighbor, says it all—through love serving one another (5:13–14). But that love commitment cannot and should not be focused on particular ritual acts, so that these acts become not so much an expression of that love but become equally as important as that love. Love, the unconditional love, the unconstrained love shown by Christ, is the model. To demand that it be expressed only in particular ways, only be recognizable if expressed in particular religious forms, was to make such expressions as fundamental as faith. As a result, the fundamental role of faith would be compromised; the commitment to God through Christ, which was an active faith, would become obscured, sidetracked, perverted, and its character as the primary bond of the believer with God through Christ would be lost to sight—as, Paul feared, was happening in the Galatian churches.

So faith in Christ is the one essential to the establishment and continuance of the relationship with God through Christ. For the convert, that would be expressed through baptism—baptism in water as the counterpart and expression of being baptized into Christ (3:27).[20] But it would run counter

---

20. It should not be lightly assumed that "baptized in Spirit, into Christ" was for Paul simply synonymous with baptized in water, into the church. But what should be noted is that it was

to Paul's primary concern in this letter if baptism was seen as a "work" demanded in addition to faith rather than as the expression of faith. So it is not surprising that in Galatians the only mention of baptism is in the verbal phrase "baptized into Christ," where it is the immediacy and directness of the commitment to Christ thereby expressed, rather than a rite of entry into the church—which as such could so easily become yet another "work" to be required in addition to faith. To make clear the sole primacy of faith—faith, yes, as expressed in baptism and "working through love," but faith as the sole means and medium through which the justifying relation with Christ is established and sustained—was Paul's principal concern in writing to the Galatians, and that should never be forgotten or downplayed. That the Christian life, as "Christian," is a life of faith, faith in Christ, from start to finish, is the primary message of Galatians.

The Gift of the Spirit as the Counterpart to the Primacy of Faith

If Paul's emphasis on faith—we might properly say faith alone—is so clear in Galatians, it is equally noticeable that the gift of the Spirit is almost as important for Paul in the same letter.[21] Indeed, it is somewhat surprising that in the history of interpretation, though for understandable reasons, much greater emphasis has been given to the importance of "justification by faith" in Galatians than to the gift of the Spirit, since the former appears relatively seldom in Galatians, though, of course, at crucial points in the argument.[22] But it was evidently of more importance for the Galatians that they had received the Spirit, and Paul evidently shared their sense of that importance—shown in the way he turns to the gift of the Spirit at the crucial point in the development of his argument, as also in the repeated emphasis on the point in chapter 5.

> You foolish Galatians! Who has bewitched you—you before whose eyes Jesus Christ was openly portrayed as crucified? This only I want to learn from you: was it by works of the law that you received the Spirit, or by hearing with faith? Are you so foolish? Having begun with the Spirit are you now made complete with the flesh? Have you experienced so much in vain? If it is indeed in vain. So I ask again, he who supplies the Spirit to you and works miracles among you, is it by works of the law or by hearing with faith? (Gal. 3:1–5)

---

the former which was fundamental for Paul (Rom. 6:3; 1 Cor. 12:13; Gal. 3:27), whereas he was less concerned about the latter (1 Cor. 1:13–17).

21. *Pistis*—twenty-two times; *pneuma*—eighteen times.

22. *Dikaios*—3:11 (Hab. 2:4); *dikaiosunē*—2:21; 3:6, 21; 5:5; *dikaioō*—2:16 (3x), 17; 3:8, 11, 24; 5:4.

Paul, having calmed down somewhat as he put the argument he so wished might have been more effective to Peter in Antioch (2:15–21),[23] now renews the forcefulness which he had expressed in 1:6–9: "You foolish Galatians!" (3:1). Here the focus is on the impact and success of his gospel in the Galatians' own experience. The argument is not in terms of justification but on the proof of a positive relation with God in the here and now—that is, through the gift of the Spirit. This tells us something which has proved considerably controversial in church history: that the gift of the Spirit to the Galatians was something they had experienced. They, or Paul, did not have to argue the following: you have believed; you have been baptized; therefore you have received the Spirit— whether you experienced anything or not. Their experience of the Spirit was something to which Paul, and they, could refer directly. What that experience amounted to—whether, for example, they spoke in tongues as evidence of Spirit reception (as in Acts 10:44–48)—we cannot say. Certainly Paul does not say, though it is true that the fruit of the Spirit in 5:22–23 include at least some emotive features. But the point in 3:1–5 remains that Paul's question, "How did you receive the Spirit?" was one which he evidently expected to make sense to them and to be answerable by them with reference to their experience. The fact that he could link the same question to their experience of miracles (3:5) carries the same implication.

So, then, the fact that the transformative power of the Spirit was the divine response to faith, to faith alone, means that for Paul the gift of the Spirit had the equivalent role from the divine side in the event of becoming Christian as faith had on the human side. And not just in becoming Christian, but in being Christian—as Paul makes clear in the rest of the letter. "By faith alone" could be matched by the equivalent phrase "by Spirit alone" as the heart of Paul's gospel. The outworkings of each should never be allowed to diminish or confuse the primacy of each.

Equally striking is the way Paul sums up his argument that the defining model for justification by faith is Abraham (3:6–14). The promise to Abraham, that the blessing given to Abraham would be shared by the gentiles (3:8–9), was not contradicted or made conditional by the law. For Christ, by his death, had brought redemption from the curse of the law, that is, redemption for all who fell under the law's curse because they fell short of the law's demands, "in order that to the Gentiles the blessing of Abraham might come in Christ Jesus, in order that we might receive the promise of the Spirit through faith"

23. The fact that Paul does not indicate that in Antioch Peter gave a satisfactory response to his rebuke (2:11–14)—in contrast to the success of Paul's equivalent stand in Jerusalem (2:5–10)— suggests that Paul's stand in Antioch was unsuccessful, *not* backed by the Jewish believers.

(3:14). Again the model which Abraham provided was not only, or not simply, the model of justification by faith, but the model also of receiving the gift of the Spirit.[24] Again we have to infer that this was the primary feature of the gospel Paul preached so successfully to the Galatians—the gospel summed up as the Spirit given to those who believed. Later church history would have tended to shy away from such a summing up of the Christian gospel, but would Paul have done so? Even though the "manifestation of the Spirit" (1 Cor. 12:7) certainly caused problems in the church in Corinth (1 Cor. 14), Paul still insisted that the Spirit was the living breath of the body of Christ (1 Cor. 12:13).

In the next phase of his argument (Gal. 3:15–4:7) Paul plays on the twin theme of sons/seed/children of Abraham[25] and sons of God.[26] The argument is somewhat strained, but effective nonetheless. Since the promise to Abraham was to his "seed" (singular), its primary reference is to the one person, Christ (3:16). The consequence is that those "in Christ" can also be counted as Abraham's seed.[27] For "if you are Christ's, then you are Abraham's seed, heirs according to the promise" (3:29). The mission of Christ, indeed, had precisely that objective in view—in order that we might be adopted as God's sons (4:5).

> And in that[28] you are sons, God sent the Spirit of his Son into our hearts crying "Abba! Father!" Consequently you are no longer a slave, but a son. And if a son, then also an heir through God. (Gal. 4:6–7)

Here again, as in 3:14, the gift of the Spirit is the climactic point in the argument. The proof that the promise made through Abraham has been fulfilled, the proof that the Galatians are indeed "sons of God," is precisely the gift of the Spirit. This climactic place of the gift of the Spirit, here as in 3:14, underlines just how important the gift of the Spirit was in Paul's understanding of how the gospel came to effect in human lives. Here again, as in 3:4, it should be noted, Paul is thinking of the reception of the Spirit as an

---

24. Regrettably the Reformation picked up and majored on the first of these models, whereas the latter proved too disturbing.

25. Sons (*huioi*)—3:7, 27; seed (*sperma*)—3:16, 29; children (*tekna*)—4:28, 31.

26. Gal. 3:26; 4:6, 7.

27. Gal. 3:14, 26, 28.

28. The more immediately obvious translation of *hote de este huioi*—"because you are sons"—could be taken to imply that the two divine actions, adopting as children and the giving of the Spirit, were temporally separated—sonship and later, consequently, the gift of the Spirit. Paul's point, however, is rather that sonship and Spirit are two sides of the same relationship: it is precisely the gift of the Spirit which effects and constitutes the sonship, as expressed in the "Abba, Father" cry of the Spirit thus given.

experience. Whether the Spirit's entry into and work within a life was manifested by speaking in tongues, as so often in Acts, Paul does not say. Here (4:6) the experience was or included an intense impulse to cry out "Abba! Father!"[29]—that is, something at least of a reproduction of Jesus's own sense of sonship.[30] And Paul will produce more evidence of the Spirit's presence in and action through the Galatian believers in the rest of the letter. They already had the evidence of an intimate relationship with God through his Spirit, so that the urgings of those who were unsettling them, by insisting that the Galatian believers needed also to take on particular requirements laid down by the law ("works of the law"), could be ignored and should be rejected.

An interesting feature of the next phase of argument (4:8–5:1) is that reference to the Spirit comes once again as part of the climax of the argument (4:29)—as 3:14 was part of the climax of 3:1–14, and 4:6 was integral to the climax of the argument in 3:15–4:7. As in 3:15–18, the argument of 4:21–31 is somewhat strained[31]—the allegory (4:24) of the different lines of descent from Abraham (Gen. 15:16; 21:2). The line from Sarah is the line of promise, of freedom, whereas the line from Hagar is the line of flesh, of slavery.[32] The contrast between the two lines of descent is summed up in the phrases "born in accordance with the flesh" and "born in accordance with the Spirit," a contrast which Paul applies to the current situation ("so also now," 4:29). For Paul the important factor was that the "slave/free" antithesis blends neatly into his characteristic "flesh/Spirit" antithesis. To think that the line of promise through Abraham was a line of natural descent ("in accordance with the flesh") was to misunderstand the unnaturalness of the promise (Sarah long barren, 4:27). No, the promise was more obviously to be seen as linked to and dependent on the supernatural work of the Spirit ("in accordance with the Spirit").

This turning of the tables on those who were Paul's fellow Jews is astonishingly dramatic, running counter as it does to the more obvious reading of the Sarah/Isaac story. The line of descent from Abraham through Sarah is characterized by promise and freedom (4:23), a promise prior to and independent of the law subsequently given (3:15–18), and fulfilled in those likewise born of the Spirit (4:29). In contrast, the natural or fleshly descendants of Abraham are to be identified more with Abraham's offspring through Hagar, the slave. The law has become antithetical to the promise,

29. As in Rom. 8:15, the verb *krazein*, "cry out," indicates not a filial murmur of quiet piety but a cry of some intensity, whether of feeling or volume.

30. *Abba*—Mark 14:36; Rom. 8:15; Gal. 4:6.

31. The strain is most evident in v. 25: "This Hagar-Sinai is a mountain in Arabia."

32. "Promise"—4:23, 28; "free"—4:22, 23, 26, 30; "flesh"—4:23, 29; "slave"—4:22, 23, 30, 31.

as those who insist that the promise cannot be fulfilled apart from the law need to understand.

Paul makes the argument with some intensity, his frustration barely restrained:

4:11: "I am afraid that perhaps I have labored for you to no avail."

4:19: "My children, over whom I am again in the pain of childbirth until Christ is formed in you . . ."

4:30: "What says the scripture? 'Throw out the slave girl and her son; for the son of the slave girl will never inherit with the son of the free woman.'"

But it is in the following paragraph (5:1–6) that his indignation boils over:

For freedom Christ has set us free. Stand firm, therefore, and do not be subject again to a yoke of slavery. Look! I, Paul, say to you that if you are circumcised, Christ will benefit you not at all. I testify again to everyone who is being circumcised that he is obligated to do the whole law. You have been estranged from Christ, you who are seeking to be justified by the law; you have fallen away from grace. For we by the Spirit, from faith, are awaiting eagerly the hope of righteousness. For in Christ Jesus neither circumcision counts for anything, nor uncircumcision, but faith operating effectively through love.

This is the first time Paul makes it plain what it is that those he refers to as "troublemakers" (5:12) were doing: they were insisting that if the Galatians really wanted to share in Abraham's inheritance, they would have to be circumcised, that is, become full proselytes. So far as Paul was concerned, to insist on such a policy was effectively to put Christ and the law in sharp antithesis. It is the same point as in 2:16: to add anything to faith in Christ as equally essential was in fact to undermine and deny the sole essentialness of faith—was indeed to cut them off from the grace which came only to and through faith. Here again the gift of the Spirit is, for Paul, the medium of that grace, the divine corollary to such faith. The issue of circumcision only confused that basic point—the faith/Spirit nexus at the heart, and alone at the heart, of all relationship with God. That relationship of course expresses itself in attitude and action—"faith operating effectively through love." But to regard particular expressions of that love as equally integral and fundamental as the central faith/Spirit nexus would be to deny and undermine its fundamental centrality.

This critically central point for Paul is so easily lost to sight. Some actions and commitments are such obvious expressions of the faith/Spirit nexus that they can easily be regarded as equally fundamental—in effect as important as the faith/Spirit core of the gospel itself. Examples are not hard to itemize:

- Some forms of churchmanship, where *bene esse* (well-being) becomes confused with *esse* (being)
- Some forms of discipleship or lifestyle
- Some secondary beliefs (*adiaphora*) raised to the level of essentials

This was what the "troublemakers" were doing in Galatia, in Paul's view. By insisting that heirs of the promise to Abraham had to be circumcised as Abraham had been was to confuse and undermine, distract and depart from the most important aspect of the promise made to Abraham—God's Spirit given to those who believe. Those who insist that to be real Christianity, its expression and disciples must be marked in particular ways by particular forms of churchmanship and particular lifestyles, have badly missed the fundamental point which Paul makes, with no little intensity, in this letter to the Galatians. There is no way of being Christian, according to Galatians, other than faith-and-Spirit working through love. In the imagery which Paul uses elsewhere, the Spirit is the first installment and guarantee of the righteousness reckoned to those who believe (5:5).[33]

The importance for Paul of the gift of the Spirit to those who believe is underlined later in the same chapter:

> I tell you, walk by the Spirit and you will not satisfy the desires of the flesh. For the flesh desires against the Spirit, and the Spirit desires against the flesh; for these are opposed to one another, to prevent you from doing those things you want to do. But if you are led by the Spirit, you are not under the law. And the works of the flesh are plain. . . . But the fruit of the Spirit is love, joy, peace, patience, kindness, goodness, faith, gentleness, self-control. Against such as these there is no law. And those who belong to the Christ Jesus have crucified the flesh with its passions and desires. (Gal. 5:16–19, 22–24)

Walking by the Spirit (5:16) was for Paul clearly different from walking according to the law, different from a discipleship determined by rules of ritual. The law thus insisted on (the law of "works") is actually less effective in controlling the desires of the flesh, despite what the law actually rules out (5:19–21). To be led by the Spirit may seem to throw off the constraints of the law, but only in the case of such conduct as is integral to the life of

---

33. *Aparchē* ("first fruits")—Rom. 8:23; *arrabōn* ("first installment, pledge")—2 Cor. 1:22; 5:5; Eph. 1:13–14.

the Spirit. The life of the Spirit is not displayed in works of the law, but in "love, joy, peace, patience, kindness, goodness, faith, gentleness, self-control" (5:22–23). To confuse that "fruit of the Spirit" with (required) obedience to the law of circumcision and the laws that regulated table fellowship was to misunderstand the way God works through his Spirit in the lives of those who believe. It is the Spirit, not the law, which conquers the passions and desires of the flesh. This is the heart of Paul's resistance to the would-be Judaizers in Galatia: that the works of the law are actually less effective in restraining and conquering the works of the flesh than is the gift of the Spirit. So, for the gift of the Spirit to be linked with or tied to works of the law was actually to counter and restrict the fruit of the Spirit, to make being led by the Spirit less rather than more easy. The Christian life, for Paul here, is more distinctively marked by the fruit of the Spirit, and not by works of the law.

All this is again a disturbing conclusion for those who think of "walking by the Spirit" and being "led by the Spirit" as essentially disrupting to good order in church and worship. Such a conclusion would be all the more striking if indeed Paul wrote Galatians from Corinth, where what we might describe as excessive liberty of the Spirit may have already been evident (1 Cor. 12–14). Or perhaps we should regard the firm advice of the Corinthian chapters to be something of a reaction on Paul's part against what he might have come to regard as a too unconstrained reliance on the experience of the Spirit. But a close reading of these chapters in 1 Corinthians indicates more of a qualification of the earlier advice than an abandonment of it. The fact that Galatians, somewhat remote from the main theater of Paul's mission (the Aegean), was preserved presumably indicates that its relevance and importance within the wider range of Pauline churches were never really doubted. Paul's reputation as the apostle of the Spirit remained unquestioned and undimmed.

In fact, Paul's focus on the Spirit does not diminish as he begins to draw his letter to a close. Indeed, he sums up his exhortation, with his passion more constrained, by a simple summary reference to the Spirit: "If we live by the Spirit, let us also follow the Spirit" (5:25). As the gift of the Spirit is the fundamental element in becoming a Christian, so the life of the Christian can be summed up as following the Spirit. It is not that the gift of the Spirit marks the beginning of discipleship, a discipleship which then can be hedged around with various constraints of law and tradition. It is rather, for Paul, that the gift of the Spirit, even when unconstrained by law, will not find expression in conceit, provocation, and envy (5:26). No, the life of the Spirit will be expressed in mutual concern, self-awareness of one's own vulnerability to temptation, a willingness to bear another's burden (6:1–2). Paul thus expresses his confidence in the Spirit as well as his unwillingness to constrain the life of the Spirit by rules, practices, and traditions which may be determined by the law but which run counter to "the law of Christ."[34] If Paul can so sum up his exhortation to the Galatians in terms of "living by the Spirit" and "following the Spirit," it is something of a tragedy that his exhortation sounds so strange and even dangerous to so many since then.

Apart from the final benediction (6:18) Paul has one other (double) reference to the Spirit, in which he sums up and reinforces his earlier plea to the Galatians: "Those who sow to their own flesh shall from the flesh reap corruption; but those who sow to the Spirit shall from the Spirit reap eternal life" (6:8). In so saying, Paul confirms that for him the most important aspect in the process of becoming a Christian was the fact that he and they had received the Spirit. It was the entrance of the Spirit into their lives which made the vital difference and departure from a life dominated by self-service. It was the work of the Spirit in their lives which ensured the inheritance of eternal life. Beside that, everything else was secondary. And anything which distracted from or confused that central offer and promise of the gospel was a corruption of and distraction from the gospel. If the Christian life began with the reception of the Spirit, then it was also to be lived in accordance with the Spirit.

Conclusion

The Christian life as portrayed and argued for in Galatians is thus as distinctively Pauline as Paul's own coming to faith. It was the same immediacy of relationship with and commissioning by the risen Christ which marked out Paul's understanding of the Christian life. Many good things would flow directly from the immediacy of that relationship (the fruit of the Spirit), but to identify any particular "work" as an essential mark of the Spirit, any particular ritual obligation as an essential condition for having the Spirit, would be to misunderstand and cloud the essential faith-Spirit nexus at the center of Paul's gospel and theology. The plain fact is that we do not and will not understand Paul's theology and gospel unless we recognize this fundamental nexus of faith and Spirit at its heart. Equally

---

34. It is noticeable that Paul did not feel constrained in talking about "the law of Christ" even though he had posed Spirit and law in such opposition earlier in the letter. Presumably he was thinking of the Jesus tradition summed up in 5:14; that Jesus had summed up "the whole law" in the single commandment "You shall love your neighbor as yourself" meant that Paul could equate the law of Christ with the preeminent fruit of the Spirit (5:14, 22).

important is the point which he insisted on so strongly in this letter: that any additional requirement which clouds or distracts from or undermines this fundamental base of the divine-human relationship is to be resisted with all strength as destructive of the gospel. We most honor Paul when we take his angry denunciation in Galatians 1:6–9 as seriously as he himself no doubt intended.

2

The New Perspective and the Christian Life in Paul's Letter to the Ephesians

Lynn H. Cohick

"Come and follow me." This is the call, this is the charge Jesus spoke to his first disciples that rings down through the ages, a call unto salvation, and a challenge to walk in imitation of his holy life. Paul, apostle to the gentiles, heeded the call to follow and pursued the commission to walk as Jesus Christ walked. He wrote to his churches that they too must live in newness of life.

Yet what seems at first to be so simple can become complex—namely, the connection between right belief, indeed salvific belief or faith in Christ, and holy living. In popular preaching, the noble goal of maintaining faith alone as the center of a believer's right relationship with God has at times, and often inadvertently, led to minimizing the necessity for holy living. One reason for this separation of "faith" and "works" is the concern that human effort is equivalent to human striving, which is tantamount to human pride. Scripture (both Old Testament and New Testament) warns against pride;

however, Christian exegesis has created a *typos* of the prideful human and equated this image with the first-century historical Jew.[1] In a second interpretative move, the exegete then assumes that Paul, in presenting the gospel, argues against this prideful Jew and the Judaism that encourages human pride and effort.

A reexamination of Judaism at the time of Jesus and the apostles suggests that many Jews in the first century pursued a life of holiness out of gratitude to God for being members of his chosen people. This explanation of Second Temple Judaism is developed in what is called the new perspective on Paul (henceforth NPP), and it impacts the study of the New Testament inasmuch as the claims of Christ and about Christ are seen within this milieu. The historical reconstruction of Second Temple Judaism stands on its own; however, because Paul speaks comparatively and contrastively about the gospel and the Judaism of his day, the NPP plays an important role both in understanding Paul's claims and in reconstructing his assumptions and presuppositions about God's redemptive work.

This essay will study the Epistle to the Ephesians through the lens of the NPP and with discipleship in mind. Paul's soaring language in Ephesians lifts the listener up to the heavens, as Paul heralds the mystery of the gospel, redemption through Christ for all. As a later hymn's chorus puts it, "Jesus paid it all," and Paul's voice might be the loudest in the choir. But he would continue to sing the second clause of that great hymn, "all to Him I owe."[2] Our debt to sin has been paid; with that we are free to become debtors to Christ and to his people, the church. This image of sin as a debt will be discussed in more detail below. At this point I will note that the NPP highlights what has been muted at times within the church, namely, the communal and transformational aspects of Paul's gospel message. The gospel brings good news of sins forgiven in Christ and of the creation of a new people holy to God through the working of the Holy Spirit. In other words, forgiveness of sins is not an end in itself but a doorway that leads to new life with Christ and his body (the church), built and sustained by the Holy Spirit.

---

1. Francis Watson, *Paul, Judaism, and the Gentiles: Beyond the New Perspective*, rev. and exp. ed. (Grand Rapids: Eerdmans, 2007), 124, notes that the influential Pauline interpreter Ernst Käsemann, while acknowledging that Paul specified the Jewish way of life in his phrase "works of the law," nevertheless believed that such a phrase signaled an abstraction, what Watson calls the "generic *homo religiosus*." Watson resists such a move, insisting that Paul intended simply and only that "distinctive way of life of the Jewish people."

2. "Jesus Paid It All," lyrics by Elvina Hall, written in 1865; music by John T. Grape. The entire refrain reads: "Jesus paid it all, / All to Him I owe; / Sin had left a crimson stain, / He washed it white as snow."

The New Perspective on Paul in Pauline Scholarship

The recent investigation into the Jewish world of the first century CE was made possible in no small part because of the discovery of the Dead Sea Scrolls and recent archaeological finds.[3] Moreover, theologians took to heart the sharp critique against anti-Semitism (and anti-Judaism) within twentieth-century Western Christianity.[4] The NPP is first and foremost a theory describing Judaism during the later Persian and Hellenistic periods, beginning with the rebuilding of the temple during the period of Ezra and Nehemiah, flourishing during the rise of Hellenism and the early Roman imperial period, and finishing with the advent of rabbinic Judaism. The NPP argues that characteristic of this period was a concern for upholding the law in the face of Hellenism's challenges, and thus there was increased attention on maintaining specific distinctive practices such as circumcision, food laws, and Sabbath rest.[5] We could express this in terms of social identity, that a Jew distinguished himself or herself as a member of God's people and lived into that reality by faithfully carrying out the teachings God had delivered to his people. And we could nuance the statement in theological terms: a Jew's faithfulness to God's law did not *earn* him or her salvation; rather this obedience represented the correct response to God's election or call.[6]

Jewish Identity in the New Perspective

Jews understood themselves to be members of God's family by birth and thus privileged to take up the requirements God established with Abraham's descendants. Within the literature of this time, Jews discussed God's election of Israel and debated who might be a member of the righteous elect, but all agreed that Israel was separated from the nations by God's actions.[7] For

3. James D. G. Dunn, *The New Perspective on Paul*, rev. ed. (Grand Rapids: Eerdmans, 2008), 4–16, notes that the hymn in 1QS 11.11–15 and its emphasis on grace, and 4QMMT with its phrase "works of the law," moved him to inquire more deeply into the nature of Second Temple Judaism and Paul's theology.

4. Gavin I. Langmuir, *Towards a Definition of Antisemitism* (Berkeley: University of California Press, 1990), and also David Nirenberg, *Anti-Judaism: The Western Tradition* (New York: W. W. Norton, 2013).

5. Watson, *Paul, Judaism, and the Gentiles*, 20–21, argues that "works of the law" does not refer to boundary markers but to the Jewish way of life broadly speaking over against the gentile community's way of life.

6. The ancient world would not have divided things in this way ("secular/social" versus "religious"), but it is helpful in our context to be clear.

7. Matthias Henze, "The Chosenness of Israel in the Apocrypha and Pseudepigrapha," in *The Call of Abraham: Essays on the Election of Israel in Honor of Jon D. Levenson*, ed. Gary A. Anderson and Joel S. Kaminsky (Notre Dame, IN: University of Notre Dame Press, 2013), 171.

example, *1 Enoch* distinguishes between Abraham and his offspring, chosen by God, and a second, smaller group chosen from that pool. These latter faithful are contemporary with the author and are identified as the "everlasting plant of righteousness" (*1 En.* 93:10). Again, the *Testament of Moses*, written at the end of the first century CE, explains that God created the world on behalf of his people (*T. Mos.* 1:12) but kept this secret. Paul speaks of the mystery of Christ—namely, that gentiles could be full members of the family of God through Christ (Eph. 3:6). The Wisdom of Ben Sira, written about 180 BCE, postulates Israel's election before creation (Sir. 24:1–12), whereas biblical texts tend to root the election of Israel in history with the call of Abraham and the exodus (see Exod. 19:3–8; Deut. 7:6–8).[8] Ben Sira's claims sound similar to Paul's declaration in Ephesians 1:4–5 that God established before the foundation of the world the election of his people, in this case the church, the body of Christ.[9] These brief examples show that Paul's narrative fits the wider conversation within Judaism, even as he sees all things now through the lens of Christ's work on the cross. In sum, the NPP argues that Second Temple Judaism did not present "works righteousness" or a position that encouraged "earning" one's salvation. Rather, Second Temple Judaism emphasized the importance of ethnic identity based on God's election and expressed in key ways, especially through circumcision, Sabbath rest, and food laws. These rites distinguished Jews as God's people who followed the one true God by his law and who worshiped in his one temple in Jerusalem.

Exploring the subject further, Shaye Cohen argues that Jewish identity in Second Temple Judaism was based on (a) religious, cultural, and political affiliation and on (b) ethnicity and geography.[10] The latter refers to one's status at birth, being born to Jewish parents who were from Judea. The former points to choices made in regard to Jewish expression and obedience to the law. This category, which develops in the late second century BCE, helps explain the Jewish sects (Pharisee, Sadducee, Essene, Zealot) and the popularity of charismatic figures such as John the Baptist. All Jews have an ethnic identity, and many choose to convey this through a religious or cultural identity. Paul expresses this well in 2 Corinthians 11:22 and Philippians 3:4–6, noting that

8. Greg Schmidt Goering, "Divine Sovereignty and the Election of Israel in the Wisdom of Ben Sira," in *The Call of Abraham: Essays on the Election of Israel in Honor of Jon D. Levenson*, ed. Gary A. Anderson and Joel S. Kaminsky (Notre Dame, IN: University of Notre Dame, 2013), 165–66.

9. Henze, "Chosenness of Israel," 179, notes that "the implied scope of the Mosaic statement is remarkable: the election of Israel effectively *precedes* creation." He adds on 195n37 the similarities with Eph. 1:4.

10. Shaye J. D. Cohen, *The Beginnings of Jewishness: Boundaries, Varieties, Uncertainties* (Berkeley: University of California Press, 1999), 70–92.

he was born a Jew and had chosen to follow the Pharisaic expression of Judaism. It is immediately obvious that this sort of identity shaping is dissimilar to typical sentiments among Christians today, as evidenced in the saying "there are no second-generation Christians." However, Jews described on the pages of Paul's letters seek to live into their ascribed or ethnic identity as members of God's people in particular religious and cultural manners.

Identity in the Greco-Roman World

In this, Jews resembled other ethnic groups around them that stressed group identity and faithfulness to tradition. For example, the Middle Platonists, a diverse group who represented a significant revival and reconsideration of Plato's thought, reflected on ethics and ethnicity in relation to universalism and unchanging truth. These Greco-Roman philosophers pondered the importance of each ethnic group following the ethics of its ancestors. A widespread conviction held that from the very beginning, various gods governed regions of the world, and the ethnic groups who dwelled in those regions were given customs and traditions that pleased these divine authorities. To deviate from ancient practices showed a lack of wisdom and virtue.[11] Celsus, a second-century antagonist of Christianity, used just such an argument to condemn Christians (Origen, *Against Celsus* 5.25).

In the early third century, the Christian scholar Bardaisan of Edessa wrote a treatise that in part discussed the effect of stars (or fate) on human culture. Cohen sums up the treatise's argument: "Astrological signs do not have any power over us, as is evident from the fact that the individual members of various countries follow their national customs, no matter what astrological sign or star was ascendant when they were born."[12] Bardaisan knows customs from numerous regional groups; for example, he notes that some Hindus eat meat, and others are vegetarians. This disparity, he argues, disproves the notion that a star governs a region, for if that were so, the inhabitants would follow similar practices. Again, he notes that some nationalities practice the same customs regardless of where they live, which proves false the idea of regional astral authorities. For evidence, he points to the Jews, noting that they circumcise their infant sons on the eighth day regardless of the stars' configuration in the heavens. Again, they do not worship idols, regardless

11. Philippa Lois Townsend, "Another Race? Ethnicity, Universalism, and the Emergence of Christianity" (PhD diss., Princeton University, 2009), 93–100.

12. Shaye J. D. Cohen, "Jewish Observance of the Sabbath in Bardaisan's *Book of the Laws of Countries*," *Near Eastern Languages and Civilizations*, Harvard University, preprint (2013): 2, http://nrs.harvard.edu/urn-3:HUL.InstRepos:10861157.

of the country in which they reside. Moreover, they follow specific practices on the Sabbath. Bardaisan reveals no anti-Jewish animus in this list, which is merely descriptive of a people who live within many different areas, and yet who maintain specific cultural or religious practices.[13]

In the mid-second century, the Christian apologist Justin Martyr defends Christianity against charges that it encouraged its followers to leave their ancient customs, a highly problematic teaching to many pagans. Justin Martyr does not challenge the criteria that values a custom's antiquity or God's changeless nature; rather, he stresses that both Adam and Noah had no law, yet God was pleased with them. Only later did God establish circumcision with Abraham or the law with Moses (*Dialogue with Trypho* 19). Therefore, the church was "returning" to the earliest customs of those who followed after the one true God, while the practices of Judaism can be seen as additional precepts given for specific reasons (*Dial.* 23).[14] My point in this brief history lesson of the second and third centuries is to highlight that Paul's discussion about Jews and gentiles is not an idiosyncratic preoccupation of his own, or simply an intra-Jewish discussion, or even an invention of the NPP, but a familiar way of interpreting communities and wrestling with concepts of identity within the ancient cities.

Jews and Gentiles in Ephesians

A careful reading of Ephesians suggests that Paul was aware he addressed two different groups, "we" Jews and "you" gentiles (Eph. 2:11–14). Their paths to Christ might overlap in places, but in others they were miles apart. Paul urges both these groups, now one in Christ, to live lives honoring to God. Readers must hold in careful tension the "we" and "you" with the "one in Christ," for several reasons. First, although Paul includes Jews and gentiles together as a single entity called "humanity," he understands Jews and Judaism of his day as superior to paganism on account of God's revelation to Abraham, Moses, and the prophets (Rom. 9:1–5). Paul himself is Jewish, a Jew who follows the Jewish Messiah, Jesus.

Following this, we must not imagine that Paul critiques Judaism as narrowly ethnocentric and gentiles/the church as abstractly universal and culturally neutral. I raise this concern in light of Caroline Johnson Hodge's statement

13. Ibid., 5. Cohen notes (9–10) that Philo of Alexandria (*De providentia* 1.84) also argues for the moral responsibility of humans over against the claim that humans are subject to their horoscopes, and highlights that Jews freely follow their ancestral customs of circumcision, Sabbath, and food laws regardless of where or when they were born.

14. Townsend, "Another Race?," 133–34.

that sums up a common reading of Paul: "*Ioudaioi* [Jews] are defined by their commitment to unnecessary practices. Thus Paul juxtaposes confident, spiritually mature Gentiles, which he designates as 'strong' and identifies with himself (Rom. 15:1), against inferior *Ioudaioi* who are still too attached to their ethnic practices and thus are 'weak.'"[15] While Johnson Hodge wisely calls into question a reading of Paul that suggests a high confidence in his gentile followers, she fails to give theological weight to Paul's understanding of the new community created in Christ, and thus empties "strong" and "weak" of their theological and eschatological power. Paul sees Jewish practices as unnecessary *for gentiles* within the body of Christ, and thus as unnecessary in the pursuit of holiness within the wider fellowship. However, Paul makes clear earlier in Romans that neither meat eaters nor vegetarians have the prerogative to enforce their views on the other (Rom. 14:3–4, 10, 13, 22). Again, those who mark one day (Sabbath) as special cannot mandate rest on that day for the whole body of Christ. Labeling as "weak" those who refrain from work on Sabbath or from meat most likely reflects Paul's general use of this term in reference to this present age and to the frailty of human existence. His sharply critical comments are reserved for the "strong" who fail to act in love, and thus by their arrogance nullify any supposed superior position. Johnson Hodge does not give full consideration to Paul's criticism of the "strong" in Romans 14:1–15:9, and does not mention Paul's refusal to side with the "strong" in Corinth (1 Cor. 9:19–22). But she is right to call out later interpreters of Paul who sneak into his argument an anti-Jewish assessment.

One might argue that we do not need the Jew/gentile categories to explain Paul's message, for the believer/unbeliever dichotomy works equally well, if not better. Yet problems arise if Paul's language is universalized and homogenized. First, we should be clear that if Paul wanted to use the believer/unbeliever category, he was able to do this easily—for example, in 1 Corinthians 14:22–25. But this is not what Paul says. Note that in Ephesians 2:11–12 Paul says, "Remember that formerly you who are Gentiles by birth and called 'uncircumcised' . . . , you were separate from Christ, excluded from citizenship in Israel and foreigners to the covenants of the promise, without hope and without God in the world."[16] The "we" includes Jews such as Paul who were born into the promises and covenants, who were born citizens of Israel. The "you" are the gentiles who respond positively to the gospel, a message of good news that the promised Messiah of Israel has come. I will say more about this below.

15. Caroline Johnson Hodge, *If Sons, Then Heirs: A Study of Kinship and Ethnicity in the Letters of Paul* (Oxford: Oxford University Press, 2007), 47.
16. Scripture quotations in this chapter are from the NIV.

Second, when we psychologize the language of Jew and gentile, treating the words as states of mind—"believer"/"unbeliever"—we open ourselves to abstraction. This can lead to seeing Scripture only or primarily as propositional and the *Ioudaios* or Jew as a type. This hermeneutical move has led to unforeseen and sometimes disastrous results as the church promoted anti-Jewish rhetoric. As Johnson Hodge points out, the irony here is that the believer/unbeliever dichotomy relies for its power on the historical (not abstract) fact that the majority of first-century Jews rejected the messianic claims of Jesus of Nazareth.[17] Then the historical reality is reshaped to serve as an abstract type, a "Jew" who represents the pride and arrogance that plague humanity. The NPP has shown that the Jews of the first century were no more arrogant than humanity in general, and thus cannot serve as a foil for the "humble" Christian.

While the NPP focuses on Second Temple Judaism and the particular practices that define the Jews' ethnicity over against idolaters/gentiles, we must also recognize that the gentiles of this day carried cultural baggage. From a sociological standpoint, both Jews and gentiles bring their ancestral customs into the believing community. It is not Jews who have traditions, while gentiles are a cultural blank slate. Even more, it is not that gentiles are embryonic Christians, awaiting the moment of birth when Paul speaks the gospel to them. Rather they are *ta ethnē*, a collection of Greeks, Romans, Egyptians, Syrians, and so on,[18] whose ancestral traditions include specific worship practices, and whose mother tongues and traditional diets served to separate them from one another. In other words, *gentile* is not a single group in the ancient world, nor are gentiles proto-Christians. Thus, from a sociological standpoint, a Jew and a gentile each have a culture, a heritage, an ethnicity. However, from a theological standpoint, the gospel condemns the gentile's idolatry, and it restricts aspects of the Jew's Torah obedience to an ethnic expression, not a set of practices to be shared by gentiles within the believers' fellowship. The gospel establishes its own religious rites, baptism and Eucharist, and insists that the entire community practice them.

Here is the nub of the question, are Jewish dietary practices religious or ethnic? The correct answer, I think, is "both." While gentiles had no analogue to the Torah and no parallel practices to the Sabbath and food laws that distinguish the Jewish people, that does not mean that gentiles had no religious

---

17. Johnson Hodge, *If Sons, Then Heirs*, 44.
18. Ibid., 47. Johnson Hodge lists these groups and notes that her American students at College of the Holy Cross tend to see the biblical gentiles as Christians and thus much like themselves.

sensibilities. What it means is that those sensibilities could be swept up into the category "idolatry" and sharply critiqued. Not so with the Torah, which the Jews (including Jesus and Paul) believed expressed God's revelation. Such ethnic practices as food laws, Sabbath, and circumcision were also religious commands and thus had to be examined socially and theologically by the gospel's message. I suggest that Paul *theologically* shifts the doing of the (ritual and cultic) law from a universal mandate for God's people to a *sociological* category representing a cultural display expressing Jewish heritage. The Jewish believers continue to practice their heritage but must refrain from insisting that gentile believers within the same community embrace Jewish cultural practices.

God's Story of Salvation in Ephesians

In Ephesians, God's story of redemption begins not with the ministry of Jesus but in the prehistoric past, at the time of creation. Before time, God the Father in and through Christ the Son established that believers would be adopted as sons/children of God, sealed with the Holy Spirit. Yet within this beautiful, mysterious story, we also find that something has gone amiss; Paul assumes God's need to reconcile the cosmos. God's reconciliation plan includes forgiveness of sins as well as the calling of Israel, the making of covenants, and the giving of God's law. This revelation created two groups of people: Jews, the people of God, and gentiles, those who were not the people of God. The latter are "darkness" (Eph. 5:8); the former have God's light to guide them.

But God is not finished. In his ultimate goal to reconcile the cosmos, we have Jesus the Son sent by the Father. Christ's incarnation, his ministry, his death—these all provide for the reconciliation of the cosmos. Christ's death and resurrection secure humanity's forgiveness. These historical events, however, are effective not only in the past; they also continue their effects in Paul's present. Christ's resurrection connects with his exaltation, which believers enjoy in a partial sense now as Christ is seated at God the Father's right hand, and which will be fully realized in the eschaton. Moreover, Christ's exaltation is in some sense also the believer's spiritual reality, as he or she is seated with Christ in the heavens, together with all the saints. Ephesians celebrates the church in all its fullness. As such, this epistle makes known the contours of our salvation from its birth in the mind of God the Trinity, to its execution in the cross and resurrection of Christ, and its current reality in the life of the people of God enlivened by the Holy Spirit.

Reading Ephesians with the New Perspective

Reading Ephesians with the benefit of the NPP invites us to a deeper examination of this believing community. Ephesians highlights key aspects of Paul's challenge to the church, specifically in terms of (1) racial and ethnic reconciliation within the church, (2) community identity among believers in both the local church and the global church, and (3) personal holiness as befits a member of God's people.

Jew and Gentile: One in Christ

Why begin the argument by speaking about Jews and gentiles reconciled in Christ? Why not begin with the global church, or even the local church as a believer's locus of identity? In my judgment, the NPP's most powerful insight is spotlighting the gentile question. For a first-century Jew such as Peter or Paul, the idea that God would send his *Holy* Spirit onto a gentile who believes in Christ broke all categories about holiness and community. The NPP rightly highlights that the "gentile question" shapes beliefs about the *ekklēsia*, the community of faith, both local and global. The "gentile situation" forced the fledgling church of Jewish believers to recalibrate their understanding of a holy people of God. This is made plain in Acts 10 with the conversion of Cornelius the God-fearer, an event that, I suggest, prompted the "conversion" of Peter's imagination that heretofore had not pictured the Holy Spirit filling a gentile (Acts 10:34). Equally important for Paul, the community gathered in Christ makes visible Christ's work on the cross. Just as the raised body of Christ confirms Christ's victory over death and thus assures believers of their own similar end (1 Cor. 15:49–53), so too the people of God that includes gentiles as full members of the community gives clear evidence to the power of the cross to make all believers new.

Forgiveness of one's sins is half of the equation; the other half is one's new self. The new self is one made new in Christ, sealed with the Holy Spirit, not just in the abstract, but visible in the here and now. To declare a person new in Christ but have no visible manifestation of that reality would fail to persuade. In a similar sense, a holy people of God that demonstrates holiness through faith empowered by the Holy Spirit, and not through practices that define Jewish communities, proves the mysterious power and wisdom of God to humans and to the spiritual forces of the universe.

Paul reflects this new gospel reality in several ways in Ephesians. First, he speaks directly to this in 2:11–18, in his declaration that Jew and gentile are joined together in Christ's body. Second, in 3:6 he declares that the inclusion of gentiles *as gentiles* into God's family is a mystery, a special act of God demonstrating his wisdom and love. Third, throughout Ephesians, Paul's language and argument reflects the categories of "we Jews" and "you gentiles." Paul inherited this schema of the world, and reworks it to explain believers' new unity reflected in the body of Christ.

Jew and Gentile: The Two Made One in Christ (Eph. 2:14)

Paul makes an astonishing statement in Ephesians 2:14, "For he himself is our peace, who has made the two groups one," and again in the following verse, "His [Christ's] purpose was to create in himself one new humanity [*anthrōpos*] out of the two, thus making peace." Verse 16 adds, "and in one body to reconcile both of them to God through the cross." The union of Jew and gentile in the body of Christ fulfills God's purposes in redemption. Paul foreshadows this astonishing reality early in the letter as he describes the promised unity of all things in Christ. In Ephesians 1:5–11, Paul announces that God grants believers an inheritance, predestining the redemption of humanity through the vehicle of *adoption* to sonship.[19] This inheritance includes participation in Christ through the unity he brings to all things.

As with any metaphor, the reader must ascertain the background or set of assumptions the author and audience shared that gives force and meaning to the metaphor. In the wider Greco-Roman world, adoption was common, at least among its elite members. The *paterfamilias* (leading male in the family) might adopt an heir, typically a young male, to ensure the family would continue to the next generation and to ensure the family estate was inherited by worthy heirs.

In the Hebrew Bible, we find a concern for inheritance, but based on a different pattern, one that centered on sonship. In the wider Mesopotamian world of the Assyrians and Babylonians, adoption was done to secure heirs, to protect and care for aged adults, and even to carry on a family business.[20] It is entirely plausible that Israelites were aware of these legal practices and

---

19. The term *adoption* used by Paul refers exclusively to adopting males. A separate term, *thygatrothesia*, refers to adoption of females (sometimes *teknothesia* is used). Thus Paul's metaphor would have drawn on the entailments and benefits a male gained when adopted. That Paul imagined these same benefits extended to female believers in God's family follows naturally, but it is a second step that relies for its power on the sonship honors bestowed in Paul's day. See Erin Heim, "Light through a Prism: New Avenues of Inquiry for the Pauline *Huiothesia* Metaphors" (PhD diss., University of Otago, Dunedin, New Zealand, 2014), 18–19.

20. For a discussion of ancient adoption practices in Assyria and Babylonia, see Elizabeth C. Stone and David I. Owen, *Adoption in Old Babylonian Nippur and the Archive of Mannum-mešu-liṣṣur* (Winona Lake, IN: Eisenbrauns, 1991), 1–33.

might even have shared them, but the biblical text is concerned to express God's provision for Israel through patrilineal descent. Israelites were concerned with patrilineal continuity, that is, that a father had a son related to him biologically to carry forward the tribal identity.[21] Levirate marriage provided that, should two brothers be dwelling together and one of them die without a son, his brother would marry the widow. An heir produced by that union would be counted as the dead man's heir (Deut. 25:5–10).

The idea of sonship surrounds Abraham's calling. In Genesis 12:1–3, God chose Abraham to be the father of a nation devoted to God. From this point, the story of Israel is of a people welcomed by *birth* into the family of God.[22] God provided biological heirs for the patriarchs, thereby fulfilling his promises. Thus even if the patriarchs were aware of adoption practices, as perhaps evidenced in Abraham making Eliezer his heir (Gen. 15:1–3), the hope was for God to bring forth a seed from Abraham to fulfill God's promises. Again, God identified David as his son and the Davidic line as that through which the Messiah would come (2 Sam. 7:12–16).

Interestingly, in Second Temple Jewish writings, the situation of Moses, raised by Pharaoh's daughter (Philo, *On the Life of Moses* 1.19; Josephus, *Jewish Antiquities* 2.232), or Abram accepting Lot as his son (*Jubilees* 47:5) is described with the language of adoption, indicating that Jews saw parallels between their ancient history and the convention of adoption in the Greco-Roman world. In the case of Moses, for example, his identity as a member of Israel is a key factor in the unfolding biblical story. Philo retains this concern, noting that Moses's own mother nursed him, as is natural for a mother to do. Philo notes that Moses valued his Israelite kinsmen and ancestors much more highly than he did the Egyptian culture and knowledge (*On the Life of Moses* 1.32), although he was grateful to his adoptive parents for their care.

Paul's use of the adoption metaphor in Ephesians 1:5 signals a rethinking of the mechanism for membership in God's family. Now in Christ, God the Father adopts both gentiles *and Jews* through faith in Christ.[23] Paul stresses

21. The terms (semantic domain) used for "adoption" are not found in the Septuagint, but an example of fictive sonship can be seen in Gen. 15:1–3, in which Abraham's servant, born in his house, is called Abraham's heir.
22. Heim, "Light through a Prism," discusses the Old Testament understanding of sonship and current scholarship on the relationship of that metaphor to Paul's use of *adoption*. She suggests that while sonship likely plays a role in understanding Paul's meaning, the conventional meaning current in the wider Greco-Roman context should be privileged in interpreting Paul (see pp. 108–26).
23. The phrase *pistis Christou* has been understood to mean both "faith in Christ" (objective genitive) and "the faithfulness of Christ" (subjective genitive). For our purposes, we can

that *all* believers inherit salvation, linking inheritance with adoption, not with birthright or paternity. The familial images (adoption, inheritance) not only establish the secure salvation enjoyed in Christ by Jew and gentile alike but also invite the new believers to understand their status as coheirs with others who had not been part of their "natural" family. Looking at the subject from another angle, Kevin Vanhoozer notes that Paul's language of "in Christ" is helpfully explored by the metaphor of adoption because the latter "pertains both to the question of covenant membership (i.e., who is in God's family) *and* of legal standing before God (i.e., rights of inheritance)."[24]

Paul likely hopes that these familial metaphors of adoption and inheritance create an emotional response of loving concern among the believers, Jew and gentile alike, who make up the Ephesian church. That is, the opening metaphor of adoption and the continuing use of language of inheritance stress both the vertical relationship every believer has with God the Trinity and the horizontal relationship they should pursue as members of a single family. Additionally, the entire family is made up of adopted children; all share equal footing before their Father. The power of the adoption metaphor comes from its implicit alternative, which is being born into the people of God. For the metaphor to carry this power, the reader today must recognize the historical situation (highlighted in the NPP) of the Jew, *born* a member of the people of God, and the gentile, *born outside* the family of God.

The Adoption Metaphor Today

The metaphor of adoption is a powerful one for understanding one aspect of our salvation, but it should not be used as the best or only window through which to view our right standing before God and with one another. Said another way, the adoption metaphor is not a synonym for salvation. Metaphors are not reducible to propositions. Moreover, metaphors function within a set of assumptions about the meaning and scope of the terms used. In this case, I suggest that the adoption metaphor takes its primary shape from the wider Greco-Roman practice of adopting young adult males to carry on the family heritage and to enjoy the father's inheritance. The metaphor also echoes with God's choosing Israel as "my son" to enjoy God's inheritance as God's people.

understand the phrase as carrying both meanings, for the redemptive plan centers on Christ's work, which believers respond to with faith.

24. Kevin Vanhoozer, "Wrighting the Wrongs of the Reformation? The State of the Union with Christ in St. Paul and Protestant Soteriology," in *Jesus, Paul and the People of God: A Theological Dialogue with N. T. Wright*, ed. Nicholas Perrin and Richard B. Hays (Downers Grove, IL: IVP Academic, 2011), 254.

As with any metaphor, there are limits to its intentions and applications. First, Paul does not use the metaphor when describing his own position as "father" to his congregations (1 Cor. 4:15). Paul the apostle has no power to create God's family; that is the work of the Trinity. In Ephesians 1:5, the metaphor of adoption occurs in Paul's prayer in acknowledgment of God's blessings that far and away exceed anything imagined by humanity. Adoption through the work of Christ allows the Holy Spirit to reside in the believer, creating a new self and a new inheritance, one that is shared by all other siblings, as all are adopted. There are no "natural" children in God's family; thus the familial emotional connections between believers occur through the Spirit.

A second caution follows from the first—namely, that Paul does not imply that gentiles are poor, impoverished people who are rescued by God through adoption into his family of natural children, the Jews.[25] Rather, Paul challenges ethnic and cultural hegemony and pride by insisting with this metaphor that God adopts humanity—Jew and gentile—to anticipate joyfully together the inheritance of the new heavens and new earth. In Paul's day, the lived reality of the body of Christ, God's adopted family, did not erase or judge as evil all past culture, language, and social particularities. For example, Paul fulfilled vows alongside nonbelieving Jews at the Jerusalem temple (Acts 21:26). Titus retained his gentile heritage and did not undergo circumcision (Gal. 2:3). Family members were enjoined to care for their biological kin as a matter of Christian virtue (1 Tim. 5:8). Marriage vows retained their force even after one or both spouses turned from idolatry to Christ (1 Cor. 7:12–16). Believers in Christ retained their birth family's language, diet, occupation, location, and many social practices that were determined to be *adiaphora* to the gospel (Rom. 14:2–6). The New Testament record, then, suggests that while we are all new in Christ, aspects of our "natural" life within human culture can be enjoyed, even celebrated.

Thus adoption as a metaphor in Paul does not invite an easy assimilation to the modern American evangelical (white, middle-class) movement of adopting young children from poor countries for purposes of evangelism.[26] The adoption

25. In Rom. 11:13–25, Paul cautions gentile believers against arrogance, explaining that they are as branches of a wild olive tree grafted onto the cultivated olive tree, namely, faithful Israel. Paul's point is to stress God's grace extended to gentiles, which leaves them no room for boasting. Thus although Paul uses the language of "natural" to describe Jews, his point is not that gentile believers must become Jewish to be full members of God's family, but rather that God's unsearchable mercy extends to Jew and gentile alike.

26. This topic is of personal relevance as my niece was adopted as an infant from a foreign country. Our family is immeasurably grateful to have her as a full member in our midst. We know the birth mother and the very difficult situation she faced surrounding the adoption of

metaphor in Paul is dissimilar to the new movement in at least two ways. First, Paul does not speak of evangelism in the context of the adoption metaphor; however, some adoption rhetoric used in the United States today suggests that the adopted child needs to be rescued, "saved," out of their situation and into a better situation. While that might be true from a medical or financial standpoint, we should not claim that the metaphor of adoption in Paul supports what is sometimes called "orphan care" theology in the West.[27] In Paul's world, many who were adopted chose to be adopted; today most overseas adoptions are of infants or young children, and families of the adoptees are not always aware of the entailments of their actions. Again, today most adopt out of a desire to have a family, while in Paul's day adoption was often done so that parents would have someone to care for them in their old age. I suggest that rather than lining up with the metaphor of adoption, the new movement has more in common with the call in Scripture to care for the most vulnerable in society. Understood in this way, the orphan-care movement should consider widening its perspective to consider widows *and* orphans (James 1:27)—that is, to help struggling families around the world stay together.[28]

Second, Paul's adoption metaphor insists that this mechanism diminishes ethnic differences and creates a brand-new family where *everyone* is adopted. The current movement sees the adoptive parents as welcoming into their existing family a new adoptee; thus only half of the family is adopted, and only the adopted child is expected to change language, culture, and perhaps religion. Russell Moore illustrates this in his description of his own family. His sons were adopted from Russia, and in speaking about their ethnic legacy Moore writes that they were taught the Moore family history, because that is their sons' heritage now.[29] I cannot comment on whether this represents best practices for adoption today, but I submit that this approach is dissimilar to Paul's message. Moore suggests that his actions are consistent with Paul's injunction that our old identities, based on race or class or life situation, no longer apply in our new life in Christ. However, his actions might be the exact opposite of

---

her daughter. Language of "rescue" and "saved" suggest a parochial, even arrogant, mentality that has no place in what is usually a complicated, complex, and heart-rending set of circumstances and decisions.

27. David M. Smolin, "Of Orphans and Adoption, Parents and the Poor, Exploitation and Rescue: A Scriptural and Theological Critique of the Evangelical Christian Adoption and Orphan Care Movement," *Regent Journal of International Law* 8, no. 2 (Spring 2012): 267–324.

28. Ibid., 309. Smolin notes that Scripture tightly links the care of the fatherless (orphan) to the desperate plight of widows, for whom family, especially children, are key to survival.

29. Russell D. Moore, *Adopted for Life: The Priorities of Adoption for Christian Families and Churches* (Wheaton: Crossway, 2009), 36. Interestingly, earlier in the chapter (p. 30) Moore notes that Israel was adopted (Rom. 9:4) even as Israel was also once part of the gentiles (Ezek. 16:3).

Paul's proposal, as though Paul asked gentiles to reject their lived history in Galatia or Macedonia, for example, and embrace their true heritage as members of Israel, including its language, culture, and religious practices. Moore conflates the spiritual reality of new birth and new self with the social reality of cultural difference. In so doing, he privileges American culture, history, language, and religious practices. Holly Taylor Coolman rightly complicates the reality of adoption today and notes that "parents who adopt transracially . . . discern that supporting the goods of their child's birth—and fully living out their family's new multi-racial reality—will require fundamentally new forms of living, working, and making social connections."[30] More attention must be given to the struggles and redemptive aspects of birth parents' actions, as well as to alleviating hardships faced by poverty-stricken widows.

In sum, the adoption metaphor in Paul highlights a way of thinking about the movement of God the Trinity with regard to our salvation. A human adult adopting a human child is a demonstration of love, a virtue that all believers are to demonstrate. But love shown through adoption is not of a different sort, a higher sort, or a more salvific sort; it does not mirror the Godhead in any unique sense. To imagine as much is to move beyond the meaning and intention of Paul's adoption metaphor, which takes its power from the new family created, a family of Jews and gentiles, brothers and sisters in the Lord by the power of Christ. No other force could create such a mysterious and holy union, as we will see in the next section.

Gentile Inclusion in the People of God: God's Great Mystery (Eph. 3:6)

Not only is adoption a key metaphor in Paul's explanation of God's rich redemptive blessings, but Paul also shapes redemptive language temporally and spatially. The working out of salvation cosmically on the world's stage is linked to the experience of Jews and gentiles being made one in Christ. This union of peoples is part of the wider project of God to bring all things in heaven and earth under Christ's lordship, which will culminate in life in the new heavens and new earth.

While adoption as sons was God's plan before the foundation of the world (Eph. 1:4–5), as we await our inheritance (1:13–14), Paul notes that the present age is one ruled by powers and authorities that undermine God's people and challenge Christ's authority. These powers work through their own "children," or as Paul describes them, "sons of disobedience." Their father is the ruler of the authority of the air (2:2). From a temporal perspective, then, Paul starts

---

30. Holly Taylor Coolman, "Adoption and the Goods of Birth," *Journal of Moral Theology* 1, no. 2 (2012): 111.

from before time began, where in the mind of God the plan of redemption was established. This plan was executed in Paul's day with the work of the promised Messiah, Jesus Christ, and the gift of the Holy Spirit to all believers (1:13). And this plan will be fully realized when, in the age to come, Christ's dominion will be evident, even as he is now ruler over all authorities (1:21).

From a spatial perspective, Christ's work is evident on earth among humanity by the mysterious wisdom of God that unites Jew and gentile into one holy people. Such union of seemingly antagonistic opposites not only speaks to the watching human population at large but shouts to the spiritual powers and authorities of God's superior wisdom and love (3:10). The gospel challenges the spiritual rulers and principalities[31] that keep their power in part because they separate and destroy; they "build" hatred between peoples rather than tear down dividing walls of hostility. The peace these rulers promote is pacification of the weak by the strong. This is not the peace of Christ, which brings together all members of his body in love.

We and You: Paul's Language of Jew and Gentile in Ephesians

The NPP explains well Paul's focus on Jew and gentile as one in Christ, the mystery of the gospel that gentiles *as gentiles* are members of God's family. Why would such a distinction matter to us now, as the church is overwhelmingly gentile? Its importance lies in the modeling of nonprivileging of status. Today's church should not be organized on the basis of who got here first, or who has been Christian the longest, or who has tradition on their side. Christ's character is not defined by the believing community; rather, the believing community takes its character from Christ's disposition.[32] For example, the church in its Western tradition stretches back to the patristic period and develops especially in the trajectory of the Latin fathers. The liturgies, the mystics, the Reformation and Counter-Reformation—this history and various experiences of God's people can be celebrated. But it should not be set up as the standard for the global church today.

Perhaps it is endemic to any group, the temptation to see one's own people as the "we" in Paul's letters. Nevertheless, "we" Americans must humbly acknowledge the historical reality that we were first of all the "you" in Paul's

---

31. Timothy G. Gombis, *The Drama of Ephesians: Participating in the Triumph of God* (Downers Grove, IL: IVP Academic, 2010), 21–31, notes that Paul's apocalyptic perspective stresses the real victory of God not yet fully apparent in the present age. He notes that sin's power is not limited to personal actions but includes the systemic evil within institutions and suprahuman beings and cosmic entities that play havoc with our world, including inciting racism, addictions, idolatry, etc.

32. My thanks to my Wheaton College colleague Sandra Richter for this insight.

letters, those graciously added to God's family through adoption. The "we" of the American churches needs the "you" of the global South and the Asian churches. The "we" of Paul and his Jewish compatriots is not a "we" of dominance, of paternalism, of superiority; it is a "we" of chronological experience of God's revealed truth. God spoke to Israel, "we Jews," first in creating a people unto himself. This chronological fact is a declaration not of spiritual worth but of God's infinite wisdom in drawing all people to himself. It provided Paul an opportunity to expand his understanding of what God's people looked like and to separate the unessential, if beautiful, expressions of ethnic identity from the bedrock distinctiveness of faith in Christ. He could both celebrate his own people's call by God and rejoice that this call is extended to those who now shared the perfect way to God—namely, through Christ.

In the context of differing histories and cultures, believers today can see not only the gospel but also their own selves and cultural presuppositions with new clarity. For example, years ago I spent some time praying with families in a children's ward in a Kenyan hospital. After several days, the Kenyan chaplain told me that the parents liked to have me pray for their child because my prayers were more effective—God gave the gospel to me (a white American) before it came to Kenya, and therefore God must love me more. I was horrified. What a tragic, unintended consequence of the gospel proclamation. As a more general example, most US citizens assume that representative democracy is the best (only!) form of good government, and also that new is always improved, and young is better than old. However, fellow believers in other cultures around the world often value more highly the wisdom and collaborative efforts of its senior members, and privilege consensus over personal rights and voting. An American's reading of Scripture might highlight the need for personal choice to follow Christ, whereas another culture's Scripture study underlines the necessity of group participation and identity. Paul's "we/you" language challenges any "we" group to look outward to see the "you." Perhaps even more important, Paul's language invites any "we" group to examine themselves so that they do not confuse their own rich traditions and history with the essential core of the gospel.

Community Life within the Church

A typical image of church community in the United States might be a potluck supper, or vacation Bible school, or a Christmas pageant. It might be a long-standing men's prayer group or women's Bible study, or the church choir. These events bring people together around a common purpose, and relationships are formed in the doing of the task. These everyday, commonplace practices reinforce the reality that the local community is "family." These activities put into practice and witness to the reality that believers grow in their faith as they grow with one another. The body of Christ, the church, is not just "family"; it is to be holy, a community that lives in peace.

The New Humanity

We return again to Paul's opening statement to the Ephesians, in which he stresses that in the mysterious, wonderful plan of redemption, God the Trinity sought to bring together under one head (Christ) all creation (Eph. 1:10). The term Paul uses to stress this unity (*anakephalaioō*) includes the root *kephalē*, "head," which Paul develops further as he expands the metaphor of the church as Christ's body (4:15). Paul speaks of a "new humanity" (*anthrōpos*) that is created by Christ's redemptive work (2:14–15), and he declares that the church is one "man" (*anēr*) growing to maturity (4:13). This new "man" is not Jewish, nor is it gentile, but a new thing. Paul reinforces this point in a most remarkable comment when he distinguishes the Ephesian believers from "the gentiles" (*ta ethnē*), even though these believers are not part of the other available category, namely, Jews (4:17). Paul declares a new category of identity, "in Christ," shared by Jew and gentile—each a member of God's household (2:19) and (to mix metaphors) part of the holy temple of the Lord (2:21).

The new body of Christ, like a human body, grows to maturity, and behaviors affect its growth. Paul cautions against human wisdom being the guide. Human wisdom is characterized in several ways in this epistle, including as infantile, as darkness, and as relying on the flesh. First, Paul describes human wisdom as immaturity or infantile thinking. Such thinking vacillates, is easily swayed by deceitful people who take advantage of others, and seemingly refuses to do the hard work of growing up (4:14). Such thinking is futile, empty, and leads to irreverence and frivolity. Paul indicates that God has made a way forward to maturity by gifting the body of Christ with leaders to educate and coach believers toward more faithful service (4:11–12).

Second, Paul likens human wisdom to darkness. Paul distinguishes the believers from gentiles who walk with a darkened mind that reveals itself in unrestrained desires, including greed and sexual impurity (4:18). This path moves away from God, as gentiles have turned their backs on God to follow their own desires. Even more, Paul describes gentiles *as* darkness (5:8). It is not simply that gentiles choose a dark path but that they are themselves darkness, a harsh assessment that Paul explains implicitly in the next statement. He calls believers *children* of the light, those who are light in the Lord. Again, we see Paul's use of kinship language, reinforcing for the gentiles their new identity as children of God, not children of darkness, and reminding Jewish believers of their new family ties.

Third, Paul explains human wisdom as driven by the flesh. In this, Paul lumps together both Jew and gentile as susceptible to the frailty of the flesh that is weak in the face of evil desires (2:3). Such evil desires come with the reality that our present age is evil (5:16), dominated by the ruler of the kingdom of the air who promotes disobedience (2:2). The remedy is not a stronger stance in the face of desire, or an eschewing of emotion. Rather than tame the flesh, we are to judge it defeated, retire it to the back of the closet, and put on our new self. If I may indulge in a nonserious analogy for a moment, may I say to the female reader of a certain age that the old self should be hung right next to the padded-shoulder suit jacket? And for the male reader of a certain age, that the old self be folded beside the 1970s basketball uniforms with their unflatteringly short-shorts? In other words, the old self is not destined for a fashion comeback. And when we are tempted by nostalgia to bring out these old clothes, we must rely on our fellow believers who remind us that we have put on a new self, one that represents what is truly fashionable, a heart and mind renewed in Christ.

Of course, Paul speaks not of frivolous fashion but of fellowship of the deepest kind. The community Paul has in mind is much more costly and much more permanent. He uses images of buildings and bodies, things that take up space, objects visible to all around (Eph. 2:19–22; 3:6). Once a brick is in place in a building's wall, it does not move from that spot. Again, an eye remains an eye, stuck in the face, looking and not listening, seeing and not singing. The brick is nothing without the wall, and the eye is nothing outside the person; their purpose and joy come from being part of the whole.

The New Perspective and Apocalyptic Thought in Ephesians

The NPP insists on the continuity of worldview, broadly speaking, between Jesus and his earliest followers and their Jewish neighbors in the context of salvation history. This position has led to some dissatisfaction among certain scholars who see Paul's message containing a strong apocalyptic viewpoint that stresses discontinuity with Israel's past covenants and history. Those who emphasize the apocalyptic Paul focus on the cosmic battle between God and the forces of evil described in Paul's letters. The powers of Sin and Death fight against the Lord and his followers, threatening to enslave them.[33] This

---

33. For a recent discussion, see Beverly Roberts Gaventa, ed., *Apocalyptic Paul: Cosmos and Anthropos in Romans 5–8* (Waco: Baylor University Press, 2013).

view stresses the new age that breaks in with Christ's death and resurrection, severely fracturing the present age.[34] The two approaches need not conflict, but debate centers on which aspect, NPP or apocalyptic, to privilege. As James Dunn reflects on Second Temple Jewish thought, "In short, an apocalyptic perspective was a way of affirming salvation-history continuity when the faithful were suffering persecution and could see no other way for the covenant and its promises to be sustained."[35]

Our discussion of Paul's apocalyptic posture offers a connection between the corporate experience of the church and that of the individual follower of Christ. Paul locates a believer's identity as new in Christ, together with all who embrace the gospel, Jew and gentile alike. In Ephesians 3:9–10, Paul, using the term *mystery*, indicates that the gentiles are now coheirs with believing Jews who embrace God's eternal wisdom in Christ. This inheritance showcases God's grace and wisdom to the powers and principalities (including evil forces) in the heavenly realms. Such wisdom is rejected by many of these spiritual forces, and thus Paul instructs the Ephesians to put on God's armor, for they are to join the spiritual battle (Eph. 6:11). Timothy Gombis focuses on apocalyptic as central to Ephesians, arguing that the letter is best read as a drama "portraying the victory of God in Christ over the dark powers that rule this present evil age, and the letter becomes a script for how God's people can continue, by the power of the Spirit, to perform the drama called the triumph of God in Christ."[36]

The clearest evidence of this victory is the body of Christ, a mystery now revealed wherein gentiles worship as coheirs with Jews as God's new people, as God's new temple. The members of God's people put on the armor of God; this image suggests a battle, but Gombis rightly notes that the apocalyptic warfare Paul imagines is not aggressive, triumphalist swaggering.[37] Instead the battle happens at the level of treating believers with respect, with generosity, extending forgiveness. Indeed, *battle* might be the wrong word to use; Paul asks believers to be a "community of resistance,"[38] as God the Father in Christ has already won the campaign against evil powers and principalities. Moreover, the church is to model Christ's life of faithful self-sacrifice (5:2),

---

34. Accompanying this argument, although not neatly mapped on top of it, is the theological question of whether Paul argues from plight to solution, or solution to plight. That is, does Paul start with the problem of sin (plight) and move to the solution (Christ's death and resurrection), or does he begin with Christ's new work (solution) and from there understand the problem of sin and the law (plight)?

35. Dunn, *New Perspective on Paul*, 260.

36. Gombis, *Drama of Ephesians*, 19.

37. Ibid., 119.

38. Ibid., 159–60.

which will include service rather than control, and vulnerability over against assertion of raw power.

Today in most US churches, it takes daily diligence to resist the siren call of consumerism, nationalism, and individualism and to embrace fewer material goods and more global church identity. Paul's kinship language would be a good place to start in renewing our minds and thus our practices and pocketbooks. A goal would be an ethnically and racially integrated local church experience, one that does not privilege one ethnic or racial approach over another. A baby step in this direction might be partnerships between currently homogeneous churches within a city. The danger here is that the wealthier church might call the shots or imagine itself as the "senior partner" of the pair. This same temptation exists when an American church partners with a church in the global South. Paul's call to be one body requires tremendous restraint of will in the relinquishing of control by the dominant group and the intentional empowering of the least of those in its midst.

The Place of Personal Piety in Ephesians

Christ's work provides the bridge that crosses over from darkness to light, accomplishing for all a safe passage to the new kingdom. However, while the power of darkness lies defeated, humanity nevertheless still exists with mortality, in a body of flesh. We might describe this reality as did Martin Luther, "*simul iustus et peccator*" (both justified and sinner), or as John Barclay puts it, "*simul mortuus et vivens*" (both mortal and eternally alive).[39] Even as the physical reality of Christ's church as composed of Jew and gentile proves the victory over the cosmic powers and principalities, so too the physical reality of faithful living in the Holy Spirit's power testifies to the reality of the new age brought in with Christ's death and resurrection.

It is only by God's gift made through Christ that humans move from the kingdom of darkness to that of light. As such, the gift began in the mind of God (Eph. 1:3–5) and was accomplished by God's power and wisdom alone. Barclay rightly notes that God's gift of grace is given "without *prior condition of fit or worth*" of the recipient.[40] Nevertheless, Barclay warns that the free gift brings with it an invitation to a relationship between the gift giver and the gift recipient. This subsequent fellowship will include demands as suits

39. John M. G. Barclay, "Under Grace: The Christ-Gift and the Construction of a Christian *Habitus*," in *Apocalyptic Paul: Cosmos and Anthropos in Romans 5–8*, ed. Beverly Roberts Gaventa (Waco: Baylor University Press, 2013), 66.
40. Barclay, "Under Grace," 61 (emphasis in original).

the new relationship. Barclay notes the gift "was, if you like, *unconditioned* (based on no prior conditions) but not *unconditional* (carrying no subsequent demands)."[41] This expectation fits the nature of the gift, which is a new self, holy and righteous (4:24). This gift is light, which invites the believer to rise up from sleep/death that Christ's light of salvation might shine on them (5:8, 14).

John Calvin draws in part on Ephesians as he explains that righteousness is found by being in Christ, which includes partaking in his sanctification.[42] Calvin points to Ephesians 4:23 and Romans 12:2 in his call to devoted service to God, for "we are God's,"[43] and as such we are consecrated and made holy to him. Thus our actions cannot be profane without dishonoring God. Kevin Vanhoozer summarizes Calvin's view on justification and sanctification in this way: "The two graces are like sunlight, in which 'the brightness cannot be separated from its heat.'"[44] Again, for Luther, God's love is that which reaches to the unlovable, and not with the condition that such a one might change and become lovely or lovable. This is God's loving grace, without condition and external to the believer.[45] And Luther, while interpreting the phrase *pistis Iēsou Christou* as faith *in* Jesus Christ (objective genitive), nevertheless represents this as inseparable from participation in Christ. That is because Christ is both the object of faith and the one who possesses the believer; Christ is present in the faith as God's gift.[46] Therefore, believers draw daily on Christ's righteousness and resist the self that has died with Christ and no longer lives. Luther explains that "a Christian lives not in himself, but in Christ and his neighbor. Otherwise he is not a Christian."[47] Thus for these key Reformers, the conviction of God's sufficient grace alone unto salvation is intimately connected with a Christian life of discipleship, much as the sun's light and heat cannot be separated.

The apostle to the gentiles was confident that the good works required by God would be accomplished "in Christ" by the empowering Holy Spirit (Eph. 2:10; 3:16; 5:18). A trinitarian conception of God is crucial to understand

41. Ibid., 64 (emphasis in original).
42. John Calvin, *Institutes* 3.16.1; see discussion in Vanhoozer, "Wrighting the Wrongs," 253.
43. John Calvin, *Institutes* 3.7.1.
44. Vanhoozer, "Wrighting the Wrongs," 254.
45. Stephen Chester, "It Is No Longer I Who Live: Justification by Faith and Participation in Christ in Martin Luther's Exegesis of Galatians," *New Testament Studies* 55, no. 3 (2009): 327. Chester writes, "Luther certainly provides explanations of justification that are both christological and participatory, but in these explanations grace and faith are defined in a manner incompatible with the view that grace is an infused habit and that justifying faith is formed by love."
46. Ibid., 321.
47. Martin Luther, *The Freedom of the Christian* (*Luther's Works* 31:371 = *Weimarer Ausgabe* 7:69, 12–13).

Paul's anthropology and his expectations for a believer's life of faithfulness. The instruction for believers to imitate God (5:1), however, suggests at first glance a naively robust view of human capacity. To further understand Paul's command in 5:1, we would do well to pause and examine Jesus's prayer, the Our Father. Here we note similarities between Paul's injunctions and Jesus's words in the Lord's Prayer as stated in Matthew's Gospel. Specifically, we will see how Paul connects ideas of forgiveness, sin, debt, and greed in ways similar to teachings in the Gospels.

Sin and Forgiveness in the Teachings of Jesus

In the Lord's Prayer in Matthew 6:9–13, we find the plea "forgive us our debts, as we also have forgiven our debtors." Typically, the Greek term translated "forgive" (*aphiēmi*) would have been understood as "remit" without any religious overtones. However, our English translation accurately reflects Matthew's Semitic idiom articulated in Greek that links sin and debt (*opheilēma*). Moreover, the Septuagint follows the Semitic practice of connecting sin and debt, and thus forgiveness and remittance. Interestingly, in Luke's presentation of the Lord's Prayer (Luke 11:2–4), we find the term "sins" (*hamartiai*). Gary Anderson explains that Matthew's version of the prayer preserves the Jewish concept of sin as related to debt, while Luke adjusts his wording because the Greek culture did not use the term *debt* as a synonym for *sin*.[48] Additionally, Anderson points to Jesus's encounter with the rich young man in Mark 10:17–31 (parallels Matt. 19:16–30; Luke 18:18–30) as further support for his claims. Jesus requires that this young man who desires eternal life should give all his money to the poor, thus gaining treasure in heaven, and then come with Jesus. This teaching shocks and scares Jesus's followers, as Jesus calls them to embrace a similar future (Mark 8:34–35). Giving all to the poor is as though one presented all one's belongings on the temple altar before God. Jesus asks this young man to give up everything for the sake of another, one who cannot repay. As Anderson explains, "Jesus's injunction to give alms was meant to turn the young man's earthly focus heavenward through the agency of the poor."[49] Jesus promises that God will repay with a hundredfold blessings now and eternal life in the age to come (Mark 10:29–31). The risk is great, to give up everything. The rewards are immense, beyond anything a human could achieve, inviting the question, do you believe?[50]

48. Gary A. Anderson, *Sin: A History* (New Haven: Yale University Press, 2009), 31–32.
49. Ibid., 177.
50. Anderson (ibid., 156–57) cites Ephrem, the fourth-century Syrian theologian: "For we have given him our alms on loan, in turn, let us demand their repayment" (*Hymns on Faith*

Anderson highlights this final point because otherwise it could seem as though the language of sin/debt and almsgiving suggests credit balance sheets that humans worked on to earn salvation points. He notes that neither rabbinic nor Christian thinkers saw God's economy as a zero-sum game when it came to almsgiving. This is in line with the NPP's contention that Second Temple Judaism did not practice works to earn salvation, but pursued faithfulness in obeying God's law as befitting those elected by God as his people. Anderson explains that the one who gave alms to the poor miraculously kept the capital and gained interest. Indeed, the more that was given, the more was gained, for giving to the poor is lending to the Lord (Prov. 19:17). Why is giving to the poor rewarded in this way? Because it is a moment of unmerited favor and grace. "Giving money to the poor was and still is an utterly gracious deed; nothing is required of the recipient."[51] God the Father decreed this "economy," and Jesus calls his disciples to express this generous spirit as a testimony to their own forgiveness before God.

Note that in Mark's Gospel, Jesus's conversation with the earnest young man comes between the second and third statements by Jesus that the Son of Man will suffer and die (Mark 9:31–32; 10:33–34, 45). Sandwiched between Jesus's predictions of his own death, the encounter becomes parabolic of the self-sacrifice required of all believers *and* the promise of God to repay a hundredfold all that was given. Nathan Eubank argues that we find this same logic in 1 Timothy 6:6–19, where the author "solemnly command[s] Timothy to give alms until the return of the Lord, perhaps implying that at that time he will be rewarded."[52] Eubank makes the case that "the commandment" would have been understood as an idiomatic reference to almsgiving, citing Second Temple and rabbinic literature. The second-century church father Irenaeus explains almsgiving as an act of worship: "For God, who stands in need of nothing, takes our good works to Himself for this purpose, that He may grant us a recompense of His own good things."[53]

Paul's Understanding of Sin and Forgiveness in Ephesians

Having looked at Jesus's teachings, we are now ready to look at the subject of forgiveness in Ephesians. Notice that in 4:32 Paul commands the believers

---

5.17). This confidence rests on God's promise of grace. Anderson suggests that Ephrem's insight is that "timidity about the reward for such a loan reveals nothing other than a lack of faith."

51. Anderson, *Sin*, 188.

52. Nathan Eubank, "Almsgiving Is 'the Commandment': A Note on 1 Timothy 6:6–19," *New Testament Studies* 58, no. 1 (2011): 149.

53. Irenaeus, *Against Heresies* 4.18, quoted in Anderson, *Sin*, 166.

to forgive (*charizomai*) one another even as God in Christ forgave each of them. He follows this with a second command to be imitators of God, as beloved children (5:1). How could a human ever imitate God the Father? Paul may be thinking of sin as a debt, and forgiving sin as forgiving debt, much as Jesus taught in the Lord's Prayer. Believers can imitate (though not replicate) God's undeserved grace as they forgive the sins against them and cancel the debts of fellow believers, even as their own debt of sin was paid by Christ. In so doing, they declare confidence in God that he has forgiven their sins and paid their debts.

For further evidence that Paul thinks of forgiveness within the metaphorical narrative of debt payment, we turn to Colossians 2:13–14. Paul writes that God forgave our trespasses and canceled the record of debt, setting it aside by nailing it to the cross. Paul uses language found in Jesus's parable of the gracious creditor (Luke 7:41–44). Jesus describes a compassionate figure who forgave or canceled the debts of two debtors, one who owed much and one who owed little. Jesus speaks this parable in answer to an implied question of Simon the Pharisee concerning Jesus's acceptance of a gift of anointing presented by a sinful woman. Jesus explains to Simon that the one who has been forgiven much loves much. Irenaeus picks up the image of the cross here in Colossians and explains that humanity became God's debtors in eating the forbidden fruit from the tree of knowledge of good and evil in the garden of Eden. And this debt was paid when the Lord hung from a tree, for "by means of a tree we were made debtors, [so also] by means of a tree we may obtain the remission of our debt."[54]

Additionally, in Ephesians 5:5, Paul warns against sexual immorality, impurity, and greed, stating that such practices constitute idolatry.[55] While Jews in Paul's day often connected impurity and sexual immorality with idolatry, the inclusion of greed in the list invites comment. At one level, labeling greed as indicative of idolatry is remarkable in that Paul knew overt idolatry; he saw idols in every city he visited, and shrines to the gods and goddesses along every thoroughfare he traveled. Yet in Second Temple Judaism, greed and the love of money was associated with idolatry. For example, Philo of Alexandria condemns both the wealthy and their love of money *and* the poor who want such money and who prostrate themselves before the wealthy.[56] Linking idolatry and greed makes sense, as both represent the inversion of God's grace

54. Irenaeus, *Against Heresies* 5.17, quoted in Anderson, *Sin*, 119.
55. See also Col. 3:5: "Put to death, therefore, whatever belongs to your earthly nature: sexual immorality, impurity, lust, evil desires and greed, which is idolatry."
56. Philo, *On the Special Laws* 1.23–25, speaking of Exod. 20:23. See also *Testament of Judah* 19:1. For a discussion, see Joel Marcus, "Idolatry in the New Testament," in *The Word*

and forgiveness. Greed is a tight fist in the presence of need, and almsgiving is an open hand extended to the poor. If (a) extending forgiveness is being like God, and (b) sin is understood as being in debt, then (a¹) alms is the perfect image of free giving beyond what is owed to those who can never repay, and (b¹) greed is the outward manifestation of a heart hardened to God. If idolatry is making a god after one's own image, or worshiping a false god, then greed may be the most accurate representation of the stone-hearted idolater.

In Paul's day, the canceled-debt image spoke volumes to the forgiven believer and was to guide his or her engagement with other believers. But this canceled debt achieved by means of Christ's cross also, ironically, made a mockery of the powers and principalities and their greed-filled, "me first" battle cry. Paul frames his injunctions to practice forgiveness with his conviction that spiritual evil forces rampage about the world, wreaking havoc and suffering. Humans are victims of such powerful evil. Paul asks the community to put on their "new self" that is fitted for godly behavior that imitates God and walks as Christ walked (Eph. 5:1–2). This new humanity, Jew and gentile, one in Christ, by its very existence declares ultimate victory over sin and death, and life eternal in the new heavens and new earth for all who call upon the name of the Lord.

Conclusion

The NPP offers a reconstruction of Second Temple Judaism that draws on new literary and archaeological evidence to suggest that Jews in this period practiced the law on the basis of their standing as God's chosen people. The keeping of the law did not save; instead, following the law demonstrated God's election of Israel. When Paul's epistles are read against this historical backdrop, new insights are illuminated. Most important, readers today appreciate Paul's theological conviction that Christ's work creates a new humanity, a singular fellowship that defies human social and cultural codes and challenges the cosmic forces. This redeemed body of Christ stands as a testimony to the world of God's unfathomable grace to all and his promise that all will be made right in the end.

Leaps the Gap: Essays on Scripture and Theology in Honor of Richard B. Hays, ed. J. Ross Wagner, C. Kavin Rowe, and A. Katherine Grieb (Grand Rapids: Eerdmans, 2008), 115–16.

3

Faith, Works, and Worship

Torah Observance in Paul's Theological Perspective

BRUCE W. LONGENECKER

W hat does Paul's engagement with first-century Jewish covenantalism have to do with Christian life in the twenty-first century?
Addressing this issue is best done in relation to the much larger
canvas of Paul's theological vision. That is, we need first to overview the broad
contours of Paul's theological landscape in order then to see how the issue at
hand plays a part within the broader complex of Paul's gospel.

Consequently, part 1 of this essay explores what I will call "faith works"
within the context of Paul's larger theological canvas; part 2 will then explore Paul's theological reasoning regarding Torah observance against that
backdrop. In the process, it will become evident that Paul's engagement with
first-century Jewish covenantalism operates as a case study in discerning Paul's
view of the moral ethos of Christian community—an ethos that itself helps
to foster legitimate forms of worship for those who "worship in the Spirit of
God and boast in Christ Jesus and have no confidence in the flesh" (Phil. 3:3).[1]

---

1. Scripture quotations in this chapter, unless otherwise noted, are from the NRSV.

Part 1: Faith Works in Paul's Theological Perspective

Faith Works?

When writing to Christians in Galatia, Paul sometimes employed irony to capture his audience's attention and immerse them in his complex world of theological wonders. By the time the audience gets to Paul's words in Galatians 5:13, they have already heard eight occasions in which he contrasts the Christian life with slavery—most recently in 5:1: "For freedom Christ has set us free. Stand firm, therefore, and *do not submit again to a yoke of slavery*." But twelve verses later in 5:13, he exhorts his audience in this way: "through love *become slaves to one another*." Presumably the audience is expected to sit up and take note. Paul is enticing them into the multifaceted textures of his gospel: do not submit again to a yoke of slavery, but instead become slaves to one another through love.

Something similar may be evident in Paul's use of the Greek *erg-* word group, traditionally translated by the English term *work*. Having heard six occasions in which "works of Torah" are differentiated from faith (2:16; 3:2, 5, 10), the audience next hears the word *work* in a completely different context (5:6): "For in Christ Jesus neither circumcision nor uncircumcision counts for anything; the only thing that counts is faith working practically through love" (AT). Aha—earlier in Galatians works of Torah are contrasted with faith, but here faith works!

If these features look like they are drenched in irony, they in fact open up some of the most important and complex vistas of Paul's theologizing. These complexities have sometimes gone undervalued. At times, Paul's contribution to Christian theology has been conceived simply in terms of establishing that Christians are free from having to do anything since they enjoy eternal salvation in the heavenly world of perfect glory by means of their faith in Christ. But Paul did not expect the Christian to live a life devoid of "good works." He did not think that Christian activity jeopardizes the eternal destiny of the "soul." Doing good is not, in fact, foreign to Paul's view of the Christian life. As we will see, Christian activity is an essential component of Paul's theologizing about God's engagement with the world.

Ephesians 2:8–10 captures the dynamics of this perfectly (regardless of whether Ephesians was written by Paul or by his most astute disciple). On the one hand, it affirms that salvation is "by grace . . . through faith . . . [and] the gift of God," and that it is "not your own doing" and is "not the result of works." On the other hand, it affirms that Christians have been "created in Christ Jesus for good works [*epi ergois agathois*], which God prepared beforehand to be our way of life." A host of other passages illustrate the same point, some of which will be noted later in this essay. For now, it is enough to note how, in his most embattled letter where he polemicizes against the need for gentiles to adopt "works of Torah" as part of their Christian practice, Paul nonetheless charges Christians to "do good to all" (Gal. 6:10 NIV; see also 1 Thess. 5:15).

This serves to raise the question with poignancy: What is the relationship between Christian freedom from "works of Torah" and Christian faith that "works"? Answering this question gets us into the deep folds of Pauline theology. Perhaps the best way into those depths initially is to ask the question, How does faith work, and what do "faith works" look like? I have cheated, perhaps, by slipping two questions into one, but this is precisely what happens when a question is asked of Paul's texts—a simple question merges into another, and perhaps another and another after that. This is because Paul's theology is so multifaceted, with a variety of components intermixing within his theological discourse. But we must start somewhere, so a simple question is sufficient, even if we should expect to receive a complex answer in return.

All the World's a Stage

If we ask, "How does faith work and what does it look like?," Paul might simply respond in the manner of Philippians 1:21: "For to me, to live is Christ." This brief claim answers our double question in a nutshell. Perhaps things are not so difficult after all. But if we ask what Paul means by this short sentence, it does not take long for things to get much more complicated, interesting, and intriguing.

Paul's claim that "to live is Christ" takes us right to the heart of his theologizing. The most extended articulation of this theological center is found in Romans 6. There Paul describes Christians as "we who died" (6:2). Christians have died because they have been "baptized into [Christ's] death" (6:3), being "united with him in a death like his" (6:5). In this form of theological discourse, it is not that Christ died so that Christians do not have to die; Christ died precisely so that his followers will die—with him.

Why do Christians die with Christ? There are at least two immediate answers to that question (and more that we will see further on). The first: so that they might come alive in him. There is a future orientation in this dimension of Paul's thought, as in the claim that those who die with Christ will be "united with him in a resurrection like his" (6:5), with the promise of "eternal life" (6:22–23).

The second reason Christians die with Christ is so that he might come alive in them. Paul makes the point in relation to his own biography in Galatians 2:19–20, where he depicts himself as a dead man who has become animated by the living Christ: "I have been crucified with Christ; it is no longer I who live, but it is Christ who lives in me." As we'll see, Paul does not imagine this happening only to him; his story is simply a crystal-clear example of what is to be happening within the stories of all Christians. And while "Christ in me" plays a role in a much larger future-oriented story, its immediate focus is toward the present—a present that moves organically into the future, just as the future moves organically into the present. The fact that Christians die with Christ serves not merely to give them eternal life beyond the grave; it serves to reconstruct their daily lives prior to the grave in ways that resonate with that future—or as Paul puts it in Romans 6:4, so that "we too might walk in newness of life."

This "newness of life" does not involve the absence of "good works." Taken independently, some of Paul's statements might be read in this way, as in the affirmation of Romans 10:9 (NIV): "If you declare with your mouth, 'Jesus is Lord,' and believe in your heart that God raised him from the dead, you will be saved." But Paul also held that such affirmations of faith had a life-changing DNA about them. To confess that Jesus is Lord is to participate in transformational power that flows from God and lies at the heart of what God is doing in Christ. This is probably how we are to understand the phrase "the obedience of faith" that Paul uses to begin and end his letter to the Romans (see Rom. 1:5; cf. 16:26)—a phrase that most likely connotes "the obedience that faith inspires," or "produces," or "awakens." Paul intended Christians in Rome to regard his ministry as inspiring obedience by means of faith. And he expected the same of Christians in Corinth, whom he lauds for what he calls "the obedience that accompanies your confession of the gospel of Christ" (2 Cor. 9:13 NIV). Such pronouncements are commentaries on the pronouncement of Galatians 5:6 that the only thing that matters is "faith working practically through love."

If we ask what faith looks like when it "works," the answer (which has already been hinted at) is quite simple: it looks like Jesus Christ. Jesus Christ comes alive in the lives of his followers. Paul articulates the point by using various images. For instance, he likens being "baptized into Christ" to being "clothed . . . with Christ" (Gal. 3:27)—almost thespian imagery of an actor consumed by the character being performed, to the extent that the role imprints itself onto the actor's own identity. Paul imagines that Christians can "act out" Jesus Christ within their daily lives, with the whole of life being the stage in which their Lord continues to be evidenced. Elsewhere Paul tells the Galatians of his desire that Christ would be "formed in you" (Gal. 4:19), or tells the Corinthians that they, as a community of Christians, are "being transformed into [Christ's] image" (2 Cor. 3:18 NIV). For Paul, in a sense, when others look at a follower of Jesus Christ, they are to see nothing other than Jesus Christ himself. Jesus is, in essence, what faith looks like when it works.

Mathematics Gone Awry

But this throws us back onto the question of how this transpires. Can Christians simply pull themselves up by their spiritual bootstraps to look like Jesus and perform him in character?

Paul takes a different route. Performing Jesus Christ requires the transformation of moral character, which itself flows from the character-forming influence of the Spirit. This is what Paul calls "the new life of the Spirit" (Rom. 7:6; cf. 2 Cor. 3:6: "the Spirit gives life"), which he unpacks in a complex double-image in Romans 8:9 and 8:11. There he depicts Christians as those who are "in the Spirit" and in whom "the Spirit of God dwells"—they are in the Spirit, and the Spirit is in them. Notably, between these two verses Paul can speak not simply of the Spirit dwelling in Christians but of Christ dwelling in them (Rom. 8:10), as if to say the same thing on each occasion. Paul can do this not because he has an unrefined sense of what distinguished Christ and the Spirit of God, but because he envisions that the Spirit of God brings Jesus Christ alive prominently in followers of Jesus (see esp. 2 Cor. 3:17–18). To have the Spirit active in one's life is (in the imagery of Gal. 4:19) to give formation to Jesus Christ within one's life.

This "we in him and he in us" phenomenon is difficult to label. In 1930 Albert Schweitzer tried to pin it down with the term "Christ mysticism."[2] In 1977 Ed Sanders preferred "participationistic eschatology."[3] In 2005 Douglas Campbell tried out "pneumatically participatory martyrological eschatology," although he later abandoned that term.[4] But whatever we try to call it, this dramatic both-and (the Spirit in us and we in the Spirit) lies at the heart of Paul's vision of the Christian life.

Notice, though, that Paul's conception of the Christian life is foreign to the way we tend to think about cause-and-effect relationships. In particular, Paul's view of causality is strange to our normal way of thinking. We are used to dividing causality into parts that, when placed together, equal 100 percent, as in the old saying "Genius is 1 percent inspiration and 99 percent perspiration." A person's success in life might be attributed to her family upbringing (at, say, 35 percent), her character (25 percent), her choice of partner (20 percent), her education (15 percent), and her good fortune to be at the right place at the right time (5 percent). This is obviously a very simplistic example, without any scientific foundation or considered reflection; it is simply intended to

2. Albert Schweitzer, *Die Mystik des Apostels Paulus* (Tübingen: J. C. B. Mohr, 1930); translated by W. Montgomery as *The Mysticism of Paul the Apostle* (London: A&C Black, 1931).

3. E. P. Sanders, *Paul and Palestinian Judaism* (Minneapolis: Fortress, 1977).

4. Douglas A. Campbell, *The Quest for Paul's Gospel* (New York: T&T Clark, 2005).

articulate the manner that we are accustomed to think about causal factors in life, with various parts all contributing to something totaling 100 percent.

Paul, however, seems to have thought about "success" in the Christian life in a completely different fashion. In Galatians 5:25, for instance, Paul says with poignancy, "If we live by the Spirit, let us also walk in step with the Spirit" (AT). Do Christians live by the Spirit 50 percent of the time and walk in step with the Spirit 50 percent of the time? Or is it 60/40? Or 85/15? These very questions demonstrate the futility of applying ordinary perceptions of causality to Paul's conception of the Christian life. Paul imagines causality along wholly different lines when it comes to the moral configuration of the Christian life.[5]

Other passages make the same point. Compare, for instance, Paul's elegant articulation of causality and initiative in Philippians 2:12–13. After reciting the glorious "Christ hymn" (Phil. 2:6–11), Paul does not proceed to delve deeply into the mysteries of the incarnation, or tease out trinitarian niceties, or retell the story of salvation history—although he might have obliged if he had been asked to elaborate on them. Instead, he simply urges Christians to "work out your own salvation with fear and trembling," adding immediately the ironic phrase "for it is God who is at work in you, enabling you both to will and to work for his good pleasure." Or again, when describing his own apostleship, Paul writes the following in 1 Corinthians 15:10: "By the grace of God I am what I am, and his grace toward me has not been in vain. On the contrary, I worked harder than any of them—though it was not I, but the grace of God that is with me." In Paul's theologizing about the Christian life, textbook mathematics and commonsense causality are thrown out the window.

The Look of Love

Paul is convinced that the Spirit is powerful (e.g., Rom. 15:13, 19; Gal. 3:5) and lives within Christians to empower them in Christian living (Eph. 3:16; 2 Tim. 1:14) as they become instruments for enacting Christ within a broken world.[6] This seems to be what he means by "faith working practically through love."

---

5. A fuller exploration of Paul's perception of the Christian life would include highlighting other necessary factors, such as (1) a healthy Christian community in which the individual is formed in relation to (2) the story of Jesus and (3) the reading of Scripture in a fashion that promotes relationships of care and support in conformity with the gospel.

6. See also Rom. 5:5, where Paul claims that divine love has been poured out into our hearts by the Spirit—a verse that probably references God's love for us, our love for God, and our love for others through the Spirit. On this, see Bruce W. Longenecker, "The Love of God (Rom. 5:5):

This leads us to reflect on what Paul meant by *love*—not least since popular notions of the word barely touch upon Paul's understanding of it. If an emotional component has a foothold within Paul's understanding of the word, that is far outstripped by the eschatological and moral components that lie deeply embedded within Paul's conception of this term.

Again, the Spirit is central here. It is the Spirit that produces "fruit" within the lives of Christians, and Paul's list of the fruit of the Spirit is headed by "love" (Gal. 5:22–23). Paul has provided a christological underpinning to the notion of love earlier in Galatians, where he speaks of "the Son of God, who loved me and gave himself for me" (2:20). In this instance, loving and giving one's self for the benefit of others are virtually synonymous concepts. It is as if Paul has redefined the word *love* in light of the story of the self-giving Son of God. It is not surprising, then, that Paul begins his letter to Galatian Christians referring to Jesus as the one who "gave himself" (1:4). Nor is it surprising that Paul exhorts the Galatians to "become slaves to one another" through love (5:13)—a verse that we noted at the start of this essay, and one amplified a few verses later in the instruction to "bear one another's burdens" (6:2). Burden bearing among Christians and others is, in essence, a reflection of the saving event of Jesus's self-giving in death and his resurrection to life and lordship by God the Father.

For Paul, then, the self-giving of Christians flows from the cruciform self-giving of the Son of God, who gave himself for others.[7] In fact, Paul understands self-giving love to be the embodiment and advertisement of the power of God, who, through Christ, is overcoming the chaos that lurks in the crevasses of creation and who is restoring right relationships at every level of the created order. This is what C. K. Barrett meant when he wrote that, for Paul, God in Christ is "putting his world to rights" and doing it through the Spirit, "who begins to bring the future into the present"—a future in which all things are reconstituted in relationships of rightness.[8]

That process of bringing the future into the present has not happened completely, of course—as Paul notes in Galatians, where he speaks of the Christian "hope for [the culmination of] righteousness, through the Spirit" (Gal. 5:5 AT; cf. 6:8, where the hope is spoken of in terms of "eternal life").

Expansive Syntax and Theological Polyvalence," in *Interpretation and the Claim of the Text*, ed. Jason Whitlark et al. (Waco: Baylor University Press, 2014), 145–58.

7. See also Eph. 5:2, 25 for the explicit coupling of Jesus's love and self-giving; Phil. 2:5–11, where self-giving is the focus of the identity of the one in "the image of God"; 1 Cor. 9, where Paul's own self-giving is done through imitation of his Lord; and so forth.

8. C. K. Barrett, *Freedom and Obligation: A Study of the Epistle to the Galatians* (London: SPCK, 1985), 66.

But the process is happening nonetheless, and it is happening in the lives of Christians who, animated by the Spirit, live out the future triumph of God within their lives of service. If we could ask Paul what the future triumph of God will look like, his response might foreground a realm in which the needs or "burdens" of all are met. Participating in that future realm, Christian communities instantiate the future even within the present.

There is a radical dimension to this, precisely since "burdens" are often (but not exclusively) economically configured. Just as Jesus's message of "good news to the poor" threatened configurations of ill-practiced power in Galilee and Judea, so too Paul's gospel held a special place for those whose burdens were usually neglected by ancient configurations of power throughout the Mediterranean basin—that is, the economically poor. This dimension of Paul's thinking has been neglected in much of Pauline studies, but it is increasingly being recognized as an essential aspect of his theologizing. It explains, for instance, why Paul fills his discourse about the collection for "the poor among the saints at Jerusalem" (as he calls it in Rom. 15:26) in markedly theological terms in 2 Corinthians 8–9. There he speaks of caring for others as a demonstration of Christian "obedience to the confession of the gospel of Christ" (2 Cor. 9:13), enhancing the point with reference to divine "grace" (8:1, 6–7, 9, 19; 9:8, 14), Christian "service" (8:4; 9:1, 12, 13), and "righteousness" (9:9–10)—the righteousness of both God himself and those who would be obedient to him. For Paul, Christian self-giving in the form of the financial collection was intricately associated with the gospel that he proclaimed. This was because the gospel—itself "the power of God for salvation" in which "the righteousness of God" is revealed (Rom. 1:16–17)—shows God to be setting the world right and to be doing so in the first instance in communities of self-giving love, animated by the Spirit who replicates Jesus Christ in the eschatological living of Christians.[9]

No wonder "faith working practically through love" is the only thing that matters to Paul; it encapsulates the gospel in a nutshell. But there is even more in the nutshell to be considered.

Weapons of Mass Destruction

If aspects of Paul's theologizing look foreign to modern ways of thinking, there is one aspect of it that is perfectly at home in a twenty-first-century view of reality and "how things work." In order to understand why Spirit-inspired, Christ-appearing love is so important to Paul, it is helpful to understand what

---

9. For much more on this issue, see especially Bruce W. Longenecker, *Remember the Poor: Paul, Power, and the Greco-Roman World* (Grand Rapids: Eerdmans, 2010).

he places it against, what he contrasts it with, what its opposite or negative counterpart looks like. This is easily done but is no less significant for that.

Romans 7 provides a strong foothold for teasing out what Paul sees as the opposite of Christlike burden bearing. Regardless of how the "I" of Romans 7 is to be interpreted, it is clear that the speaker of that chapter experiences his struggle with sin in the form of covetousness. When the "I" of Romans 7 cries out that he is infected with "every kind of coveting" (7:8 NIV), he is confessing that covetousness has invaded the whole of his moral character. Paul must have imagined this moral cancer to pervade the human condition; if even the admirable "I" of Romans 7 who so desperately wishes his situation were different cannot escape this configuration of his character, that same condition must be a universal within the human heart.

The term *covet*, not popularly used in contemporary theological discourse, can be unpacked with terms virtually synonymous to it, such as brute self-interestedness, sordid self-centeredness, and unabashed self-promotion. In all of its forms, covetousness is the theological equivalent to social Darwinism, the notion of "the survival of the fittest" played out within human relationships, in which regard for "the other" is vacuous.

There is, then, a fairly straightforward distinction within Paul's moral compass: Christlike burden bearing is the antithesis to competitive covetousness. For this reason, when Paul urges Galatian Christians to "form" Christ within their community by enslaving themselves to one another through love (Gal. 4:19; 5:13), he presents the opposite to be a situation of "bit[ing] and devour[ing] each other" to the extent that "you will be destroyed by each other" (5:15 NIV).

This might sound extreme, but it is a natural outworking of Paul's view of what's on offer beyond the burden bearing that lies at the heart of his conceptualization of Christian community. The precariousness of interpersonal relationships beyond Christian community is reflected a few verses later in Galatians where Paul outlines the kind of acts that derive from human enslavement to the power of Sin (more on this below). In his list of "works of the flesh," Paul (in good Jewish fashion) includes not only acts of sexual immorality, drunkenness, and idolatry but also various entries that seem to target violent attitudes and activities between people and between groups. Here are eight entries from Galatians 5:20–21 that demonstrate the point, with six of them being listed in the plural, as if to speak not simply of attitudes (for example, hatred) but of actions undergirded by those attitudes (that is, acts of hatred):

1. Acts that induce hatred between people
2. Competitive strife between people

3. Envious jealousy between people

4. Acts that are motivated by and incite anger between people

5. Acts that promote rivalry between people

6. Acts that promote division between people

7. Acts that induce schisms between people

8. Acts of selfish envy[10]

These are variations on what Paul will later call "covetousness" in Romans 7, not unlike what he says in Galatians 5:26 (NIV), where human "conceit" is amplified in terms of "provoking and envying each other." For Paul, social destruction is the end result of this moral world beyond the Christian community. Evidently Paul knew this destructive moral world well, or so he suggests in one of his autobiographical reflections (Gal. 1–2), in which he depicts himself as having been a man of violence prior to the coming alive of the self-giving Jesus Christ within him (Gal. 1:13).

Paul imagined covetousness, in its various forms, to be like weapons of mass destruction. They are not hidden away in underground silos, invisible to ordinary human perception. They are more like chemical viruses released into the atmosphere, having the potential to infiltrate the whole of life in all of its aspects. For those beyond the boundaries of Christian community, Paul imagines a world permeated by a destructive moral ethos.

The Cosmos Grabbers

We have seen that the problem of covetousness resides within the human heart. But we also need to recognize that the problem encapsulates a much greater complex than the human heart. If the individual is culpable for his or her covetousness, culpability also far outstrips the individual. In Paul's worldview, God created a good creation that came under the threat of being hijacked by suprahuman cosmic forces that oppose the ways of the creator God. In particular, these forces include the powers of Sin and Death—forces with intentionality that roam within God's good creation and have conscripted the human race in their efforts to denude God of his creation. The power of Sin (written here with the capital S to distinguish it from human acts of sin) has found the human heart to be its spawning ground for perpetuating chaos within God's good creation.

This is why Paul can claim in Romans 3:9 that what he has already written in the first two chapters of that letter proves that all humanity is "under the

---

10. These entries are translated in a way that diverges from common translations in order to bring out the sense of the plurals that Paul uses, which correspond to the word "acts" in this translation.

[cosmic] power of [S]in," even though it is only human transgression or "sin" that he has spoken about prior to that point. In Paul's view, human sinfulness advertises the fact that malign powers are at work in God's creation, twisting the created order into their perverse, chaotic, destructive image. In Romans 5, Paul speaks of the powers of Sin and Death as powers that "reign" like cosmic overlords (5:14, 17, 21 NIV; see also 6:12), as testified to by the fact that humans sin and die. The power of Sin is also in full view in two passages that we have already mentioned briefly above—Romans 6 and 7. In Romans 6, Paul speaks of the Christian as having died to the power of Sin. (No wonder Christians are to die with Christ; death is the way they escape from the clutches of the power of Sin!) And in Romans 7, the "I" who decries his covetousness analyzes his failures in relation to the suprahuman power of Sin, to which he is enslaved (7:14, but obviously the whole of 7:7–25 is relevant here).[11]

If "Jesus is the answer," we need to know what the problem is. Although human covetousness is the front-and-center showcase of the problem, the problem itself goes much deeper than that. The problem includes cosmically ingrained powers that embed themselves within the insatiable drive for self-advancement at the cost of others—something Paul imagines to run rampant throughout humanity. For Paul, repairing humanity through divine self-giving love is an essential component of the gospel, *but* there is more to be done than the reparation of the human heart. Jesus did not die simply to take care of human sins, but also to eradicate the cosmic forces that capture human hearts within their grasp and manipulate them like puppets in a program of turning God's created order into chaos.[12]

This is what the letter to the Ephesians seems to be capturing when it speaks of God ultimately reclaiming his creation from the "cosmos grabbers" (*tous kosmokratoras*, 6:12, AT), who seek to wrestle creation away from God. This is why the same verse can portray Christians as having been drafted into a battle that is "not against flesh and blood" (NIV) but against spiritual conglomeration of malevolent spiritual power—which Paul discusses in the same verse (together with "cosmos grabbers") under the terms "rulers," "[spiritual]

11. On Rom. 7:25a as the Christian voice of Paul, with the rest of 7:7–25 being the voice of "the non-Christian Jew" (articulated in ventriloquist fashion by the Christian Paul in terms derived from his gospel), see Bruce W. Longenecker, *Rhetoric at the Boundaries: The Art and Theology of New Testament Chain-Link Transitions* (Waco: Baylor University Press, 2005), 88–93.

12. The infectious influence of the powers can be found even today, Paul would think, on street corners, websites, TV programs, magazines, comic strips, children's sitcoms, employment policies—you name it. Regardless of whether cultures are Western, non-Western, developed, developing, Christian, non-Christian, or anything else, Paul would probably examine the various levels of life in the twenty-first century as testifying to the continuing influence of these cosmic powers.

authorities," and "the spiritual forces of evil in the heavenly realms" (NIV). If the struggle is not yet complete, the victory is nonetheless assured, as Paul notes simply in 1 Corinthians 15:24 (NIV): "Then the end will come, when he hands over the kingdom to God the Father after he has destroyed all dominion, authority and power." These passages encapsulate the main focus of Paul's understanding of the problem, a problem whose solution includes the "faith works" of Christians, enlivened by the Spirit of the loving and (therefore) self-giving Son.

Hostile Environments

We have already seen that Paul imagines an epidemic of self-interestedness to have engulfed humanity and brought destruction in its wake. And we have seen that this problem is not restricted simply to the individual in his or her relationship to God but involves the influence of cosmic powers that lie hidden from human view (apart from the destruction that they induce). But the problem does not reside simply with the individual as a puppet of these malignant cosmic forces; the cancer of unbridled self-interest has spread into every sector of human life—whether individual, corporate, cultural, societal, national, or international.

This infiltration of covetousness into intergroup relationships, for instance, is a demonstrable facet of the lordship of Sin. To take one example, Ephesians 2:14 identifies the barrier separating groups of people as "the dividing wall of hostility" between them. For Paul, hostility that divides distinct identities testifies to the lordship of the cosmic power of Sin, as it instills chaotic, dysfunctional relationships between people.

It is little wonder, then, that toward the very end of Romans, Paul urges his readers to "watch out for those who cause divisions . . . contrary to the teaching you have learned" (Rom. 16:17 NIV). Little wonder, as well, that he adds, a few verses later, "The God of peace will shortly crush [the] Satan under your feet" (16:20). Aha, there it is—the Satan. Long before the first century, the Satan had become known as the embodiment of all that runs contrary to God's ways. It is not surprising that the Satan appears in this mix of cosmic forces—perhaps as their perpetrator, although Paul never quite says as much.[13] It is almost as if the Satan stands behind the creation of divisions, that "dividing wall of hostility," where God intends to bring relationships of peace.

This is probably how we are to interpret the infamous phrase of Galatians 4:3, "the *stoicheia* of the world" (cf. 4:9). In Paul's day, the *stoicheia* were

13. The closest we get to that is the claim about the "lawless one" in 2 Thess. 2:8–10, if Paul authored that text.

commonly understood as the elements of matter out of which the world was constructed—that is, earth, wind, fire, and water. But Paul uses the term in a different way. Evidently, as others have rightly argued, somewhere along the way the Galatian Christians have been introduced to a new understanding of what the *stoicheia* were, and Paul seems to be building on those localized perceptions.[14]

The identity of the *stoicheia* has been and will continue to be an issue highly debated by Paul's interpreters. My own take on the matter is this. Powerful yet strangely indeterminate forces, the *stoicheia* play a role in creating precisely the opposite of what we see in the loving unification of distinct groups of people "in Christ" (Gal. 3:26–29); that is, the *stoicheia* are those forces that make use of differentiation and distinction in order to promote relationships of discord within (what Paul calls) "this present evil age" (1:4).

In Paul's view, identity differentiation between individuals and between groups is not problematic in and of itself. Paul thought that certain forms of differentiation have been created by God, such as gender differentiation ("male and female he created them") and ethnic differentiation (the Jewish people and the gentiles, and presumably also differentiation within the gentile nations). Contrary to popular opinion, Paul did not want to destroy Jewish identity within Christian communities. Romans 14–15 demonstrates the steps Paul took to affirm the legitimacy of Jewish identity among Christ followers.[15] In fact, it is essential for Paul's ethic that differences be preserved "in Christ" in order to testify to the transforming power of God; in Paul's view, caring for those of difference is attributable only to the Spirit of God, since actions of self-giving toward those who are notably different is not an attribute of the human condition.[16]

But in contrast to the healthy unification of distinct groups that Paul perceived in Christian communities, the *stoicheia* of the world bastardize God-ordained diversities, transforming those diversities into relationships of destructive disharmony, rather than offering creative possibilities of self-giving.[17] The *stoicheia*

---

14. See, for instance, Martinus C. de Boer, *Galatians* (Louisville: Westminster John Knox, 2011), 252–56. More needs to be said about the *stoicheia* than the constraints of this essay permit.

15. The best reconstruction of the situation behind Rom. 14–15 is John Barclay's "'Do We Undermine the Law?' A Study of Romans 14:1–15:6," in *Paul and the Mosaic Law*, ed. J. D. G. Dunn (Tübingen: Mohr Siebeck, 1996), 287–308. My take on what Paul is doing in that passage is somewhat different from Barclay's, however.

16. It is sometimes relatively easy to offer practical, involved assistance to those who share one's own demographic profile. The more others look like you, the more they share your skin color, your economic level, your racial heritage, your political views, your educational background, and the like, the easier it is to extend assistance. But the more those similarities disappear, the less likely that embodied forms of "other regard" will be exercised.

17. We might imagine the *stoicheia* even creating their own forms of unhealthy relationships along the way—such as slave and free. Attributing that contrast to the influence of the

enslave by taking the good things that God has created and perverting them so that relationships between the differentiated parties become riddled with injustice and discord. Regardless of whether the focus is on the individual or on larger group configurations, the same problem emerges, since the *stoicheia* have established a matrix whereby self-identity promotes discordant differentiation from others.

For Paul, as Christians die with Christ so that he might live in them, so they find themselves alive "in Christ"—in a corporate realm where diversity of identity is welcomed and is (to be) free from the self-centered discord that testifies to the overlordship of suprahuman forces attempting to dethrone the God of creation. All those "in Christ" are "children of God" (Gal. 3:26), and all of God's diverse children are unified as one body in service to one another and to others (e.g., Rom. 12; Gal. 3:28; 5:13–14; 6:10; 1 Thess. 5:14–15; etc.). Or in the words of Ephesians 2:16, the triumph of God includes the reconciliation of hostile groups "in one body through the cross, thus putting to death that hostility through it [the cross]."

To the Glory of God the Father

Having noted how strongly the current of cruciform self-giving flows through Paul's worldview, we need now to track the way in which that current ultimately flows into the ocean of worship.

Notice, for instance, how the main theological discourse of Romans concludes in such a way as to link cruciformity to worship. In 15:2, 5–6, Paul concludes with these admonitions: "Each of us must please our neighbor for the good purpose of building up the neighbor. . . . Live in harmony with one another, in accordance with Christ Jesus, so that together you may with one voice glorify the God and Father of our Lord Jesus Christ." As the high point in Paul's discourse from 14:1–15:6, Romans 15:1–6 envisages diverse identities being housed within groups whose "other-regard" is a central ingredient in their corporate glorification of God.

This should not be surprising. For Paul, the body of Christ, necessarily engorged by diverse identities as a reflection of the rich diversity of God's good creation, is not the end in itself but the means to at least one other end—that is, the universal praise of the Creator. Paul cannot fathom the Creator's praise being restricted to one distinct group; instead, the chorus of praise deserved by the Creator must reflect the multiplicity of identities legitimated by the Creator within God's remarkable creation. This is reflected in the second half of the "Christ hymn" of Philippians 2:6–11:

---

stoicheia has no real foothold in Paul's own day, or even in Paul's own theologizing, although his discourse offers resources for ultimately seeing things in that light.

Therefore God also highly exalted him
  and gave him the name
  that is above every name,
so that at the name of Jesus
  every knee should bend,
  in heaven and on earth and under the earth,
and every tongue should confess
  that Jesus Christ is Lord,
  to the glory of God the Father. (2:9–11)

The motley communities that Paul established in urban centers of the Greco-Roman world were to be reflections of the diversity of humanity on bended knee, united in faith works, raising their voices in joyous praise to God the Father.

It is little wonder, then, that Paul's vision of diverse yet harmonious worship of God should morph from its moorings in Romans 15:5–6 to become something of a triumphant symphony of scriptural citations in 15:7–13. The importance of the theme of worship in that passage is underlined by the passage's placement within the flow of Paul's thought in Romans. As is frequently noted by commentators, this paragraph is in certain respects the theological capstone of Romans; it serves "to round off the body of the letter, both the theological treatise and the resulting parenesis," by "[tying] together central themes in the whole discussion" of Romans.[18] What is significant here is that worship is the thread that weaves together some central themes of the letter.

In this light, we can see that Paul's concerns for corporate unity and healthy relationships among disparate identities arise not so much from matters of "social ethics" or "corporate identity" or "ecclesiology" but primarily from matters of theocentric worship. That is, Paul is driven by an interest in promoting a chorus of praise for the Creator from within communities where healthy relationships arise between their constituent parts, in relation to the full diversity of created identities. For Paul, communities of Jesus-devotion should be microcosms reflecting the universal devotion that is deserved by the Creator. This is the Creator who fashioned identities of all kinds, who is deserving of praise from all those identities, and who, according to Philippians 2:9–11, will one day be worshiped by all of them. In the meantime, relationships of love expressed in the self-giving of Christians are

18. James D. G. Dunn, *Romans* (Dallas: Word, 1988), 2:844–45. This view, shared by others as well, is sometimes criticized by those who think that 15:7–13 is a climax only to Rom. 12–15. But this overlooks the fact that the theme of worship is raised already in Rom. 1:21, 25; on this, see the section "Centrism and the Worshiping Community of the Self-Giving Lord" below.

an essential prerequisite to the unified expression of praise for God among diverse peoples. In their diversity these peoples reflect the diversity created by God the Father, and in their regard for others they reflect the self-giving of the resurrected Lord Jesus Christ, from which transformation flows.

Destroying Strongholds

To us, the word *love* might sound like emotional sentimentality; *bearing burdens* might sound like a pastoral nicety; *becoming slaves to one another* might sound like a metaphorical platitude. For Paul, however, these were part of the arsenal in a cosmic battle against dysfunctional forces that collude to corrupt and corrode a world that God is reclaiming through Christ, to his praise and glory.

This is why cruciform "faith works" are important for Paul. As manifestations of God's transforming power in the character of God's Son, faith works both advertise and play a role in God's ultimate victory—his rectification of the cosmos as a result of the faithfulness of his character (Rom. 15:8). If support for those in need makes Christians vulnerable and exposes them to insecurities and potential disadvantage, Paul believes that their faith works are playing a part in a larger narrative of the triumph of God in which they themselves "are more than conquerors through him who loved" them (Rom. 8:37). "For I am convinced," says Paul, "that neither death, nor life, nor angels, nor rulers, nor things present, nor things to come, nor powers, nor height, nor depth, nor anything else in all creation, will be able to separate us from the love of God in Christ Jesus our Lord" (Rom. 8:38–39).

This is an inspiring vision, but it is also a challenging one, since it places Christian lifestyle and corporate practice front and center on the eschatological battlefield. In corporate unity nurtured by mutual support, Christian community is the place where the future triumph of God is manifest already, by the power of the Spirit, who fosters the character of the self-giving Christ among Christians, whose similar Christlike profiles are not monochrome but reflect the glorious richness of God's creative ingenuity. Worship of the Creator comes to its richest expression when all those ingredients are present in Christian communities.[19]

19. Paul might well have imagined that, in comparison to the ideal Jesus group, all other groups and associations were relatively monochrome in their corporate constituency; consequently, any forms of care for the other within those collections of people were not much more than expressions of care for one's own—being little more than a slightly complex form of self-interestedness or a corporately shared survival instinct. The transforming power of God can be attributed to the corporate life of a community only when care for others is expressed among groups of fully diverse members.

It is not surprising, then, that the church, embodying unity while embracing diversity in the worship of the God of creation, is said to be the means whereby "the wisdom of God in its rich variety [is now being] made known to the rulers and authorities in the heavenly places" (Eph. 3:10). And it is little wonder that Christians are said to "wage war" in ways that, contrary to human standards, "have divine power to destroy strongholds" (2 Cor. 10:3–4). And it is little wonder that Paul can say that, to him, "the only thing that counts is faith working practically through love" (Gal. 5:6), which he elsewhere calls "the harvest of righteousness that comes through Jesus Christ for the glory and praise of God" (Phil. 1:11).

Part 2: Torah Observance, Worship, and the Moral Ethos of Centrism

Having overviewed the primary contours of Paul's theological vision, we now have the resources to recognize two things about Paul's engagement with first-century Jewish covenantalism. First, we can recognize more clearly what it was about "works of Torah" that Paul resisted, and second, we can capture a better sense of how Paul's resistance to Torah observance by gentile Christians might be instructive for the Christian life more generally. The following paragraphs explore these issues against the backdrop of what we have already seen in part 1 above.

Centrism and the Worshiping Community of the Self-Giving Lord

Why did Paul resist making "works of Torah" an essential part of Christian identity? We may not be able to address that question from the point of Paul's early mission efforts in the 30s and 40s, a period about which we know relatively little. There may well be issues of development in Paul's thinking that we cannot address here. But by the year 50 or so, letters began to emerge from Paul's quill (in a sense), and from them we can trace out several forms of conviction that help us to address the issues at hand.

One reason for Paul's resistance to the necessity of Torah observance by gentile Christians has to do with the Spirit of God. Paul had witnessed the Spirit working powerfully among Jesus groups composed predominantly of gentiles who had not been observing "works of Torah"; on what basis, then, were "works of Torah" to be added to the mix?

Paul asks a form of this question in Galatians 3, where he expects the answer "no" in reply: "Does God supply you with the Spirit and work powerfully [*energōn dynameis*] among you on the basis of your observance of the Torah?" (Gal. 3:5 AT). Paul had already written the positive form of this question toward the very start of his earliest letter, 1 Thessalonians. There he notes, "Our message of the gospel came to you not in word only, but also in power [*dynamei*] and in the Holy Spirit" (1 Thess. 1:5). Paul reiterates much the same thing in a later letter to the Corinthians: "My speech and my proclamation were not with plausible words of wisdom, but with a demonstration of the Spirit and of power [*dynameōs*]" (1 Cor. 2:4). And at the very close of the main body of his letter to Christians in Rome, Paul includes a paragraph that, as we have already seen, houses the main terminal for most of the theological lines running throughout that letter—Romans 15:7–13, a section that culminates with Paul's blessing "that you may abound in hope by the power [*dynamei*] of the Holy Spirit" (15:13).

In these and other places, the Pauline corpus testifies to a fundamental conviction that the Spirit of God is active among groups of Christians and, moreover, is a powerful force animating their corporate and individual lives (see, for instance, Rom. 15:19; Eph. 3:16; 2 Tim. 1:7; and other passages already surveyed above).

Those who encouraged gentiles to observe "works of Torah" may not have disagreed, but may have imagined that experiences of the Spirit needed to be coupled with a disciplined lifestyle in conformity with the commands stipulated by God for observance by the ethnic people of Israel, whom God had chosen as his own. Paul saw things differently. Having encountered the risen Lord, who had commanded him to go to the gentiles, Paul differentiated (1) the identity of those "in Christ" and (2) the covenantal practices stipulated for ethnic Israel. Clearly these two phenomena could overlap legitimately— something Paul advocates in Romans 14–15 (where, as we have seen, he defends Jewish Christians for whom observance of the Torah continued to be an essential component of their identity before God). But if they could overlap, these two phenomena were not a necessarily interlocked pair.

Why did Paul see things differently from those early Christians who saw the two as essentially interlocked? One reason pertains to what the jazz-rock group Steely Dan calls "the architecture of your soul."[20] In Galatians 6:12–13, Paul is only too happy to oblige his readers in unmasking what lies at the heart of the moral configuration of the "agitators" in the Galatian situation. If the Spirit is working powerfully among Christian communities, Paul imagined the agitators to be seeking to tap into that power for their own advantage, hoping to employ what God has given in order to enhance their own reputation by coercing gentiles to be circumcised. So he depicts the agitators as "those who want to make a good showing in the flesh"; they are not concerned to tease out

---

20. From Steely Dan, "Cousin Dupree," on the album *Two against Nature* (Warner Bros. Records, 2000).

how God has been working and continues to work in history but, at least as Paul depicts them, are ultimately concerned to bolster their own reputations among others "so that they may boast in your flesh" (Gal. 6:12–13). This is precisely the character that he had already attributed to them in Galatians 4:17. "They make much of you, but for no good purpose," he said there, adding that their efforts among the Galatians are ultimately driven by the hope "that you may make much of them."

A similar depiction of people such as the agitators of Galatians emerges from Paul's letter to the Philippians, where he charges them in this way: "their god is the belly" (Phil. 3:19)—that is, behind it all lies a self-serving moral ethos. Much the same appears at the end of Romans, where Paul says that those who cause divisions are simply serving "their own appetites" (Rom. 16:18). As in Galatians, so too in Philippians and Romans, Paul places the moral character of the agitators in direct opposition to the character of self-giving love that is generated by the Christian gospel. Accordingly, it comes as little surprise that the agitators are depicted as wanting to avoid being "persecuted for the cross of Christ" (Gal. 6:12); by contrast, Paul carries "the marks of Jesus branded on my body" (Gal. 6:17; cf. 5:11).

If Paul consistently likens the agitators to deceptive charlatans who are ultimately motivated by self-interest and personal gain, are these accusations simply attributable to tit-for-tat polemic between factions within the early Jesus movement? Might they simply be standard forms of denunciation, without any real theological traction?

There might be something to that line of thinking, but in the end this approach is not able to offer a full explanation of wider phenomena within Paul's letters. This is because Paul often brings issues of moral configuration into his discussions about observance of the Torah, even when the agitators are not in his sights. That is, Paul's discussions of nomistic observance frequently converge with discourse about the moral identity of Christians, with issues of self-interest being central to the mix—bringing us right back to where we were in earlier sections of this essay. So, for instance, it is when Paul is discussing circumcision in Galatians 5 that his discourse spills over into talk of "works of the flesh," with their pronounced bent toward self-interestedness at the expense of the other (as we have seen). And it is when Paul discusses the Torah in Romans 7 that his discourse focuses on "covetousness," with self-interest at its center (as we have seen).[21]

---

21. Romans 7:7–25 outlines how the power of Sin hijacks even the God-given law, so that the law itself serves the chaotic purposes of the power of Sin. That allows Paul to designate the Torah in Rom. 8:2 as "the Torah of sin and death"—connoting that the Torah itself has become unwillingly engulfed within the program of the powers of Sin and Death.

What is going on here? Why does Paul continue to shift an issue that looks like a matter of salvation history so that it is seen in relation to moral configuration? Why does the question "Do Christians need to observe the commandments given to the ethnic people of Israel?" morph into the question "What kind of moral ethos is to animate the communities of Christians?"

The answer must be somewhere along the following lines: because Paul perceived the moral configuration of the gospel to lie at the christological axis of self-giving, he saw the attempt to force gentiles to be circumcised as a form of opposition to the moral configuration at the heart of the Christian gospel *precisely because he saw it as an unhealthy form of "centrism."* It represented the attempt by certain Christians to promote their own cherished identity over other forms of legitimate identity.

Certain passages stand out in this regard. First and foremost is Galatians 2:15, where Paul characterizes the world as being divided into two groups: "we who are Jews by birth" (NIV) on the one hand and "Gentile sinners" on the other hand. Here Paul momentarily adopts a point of view that differentiates groups from each other: just as east is east and west is west, so too there are "Gentile sinners" and there are "Jews." This point of view had currency in certain sectors of the Jewish world, where the term *sinners* was applicable to those beyond the boundaries of the covenant—either (1) Jews whose lives were seen as moral atrocities or (2) gentiles en masse. The first-century BCE work *Psalms of Solomon* combines both possibilities, first applying the term "sinners" to gentile oppressors (1:1; 2:1) and then to Jewish reprobates (17:5). A second-century BCE text explicitly describes the gentile nations as "sinners" carte blanche (*Jubilees* 23:24). Whereas other texts could depict gentiles as being as significant to God as "spittle" or as a single drop of water (Ps.-Philo *Liber antiquitatum biblicarum* 7.3; 12.4; *2 Baruch* 82:5; *4 Ezra* 6:56), the author of *Jubilees* makes the point plainly: "Separate yourselves from the gentiles, and do not eat with them, and do not perform deeds like theirs. And do not become associates of theirs. Because their deeds are defiled, and all of their ways are contaminated, and despicable, and abominable" (*Jub.* 22:16).[22]

To be clear, this attitude need not be seen as pervasive throughout every sector of the first-century Jewish world, but it is also clear that it did have a foothold within certain of those sectors.[23] Paul himself seems to have been cognizant of its foothold within certain sectors of the early Christian move-

---

22. Translation by O. S. Wintermute in *The Old Testament Pseudepigrapha*, ed. James H. Charlesworth (New York: Doubleday, 1985), 2:98.

23. It needs to be noted, of course, that this attitude of separation was given added impetus by the Hellenistic pogroms against the Jews in the second century BCE, as testified to in the martyrologies of 2 Maccabees and 4 Maccabees in particular.

ment. In his view, it was to have no place within that movement. In his theological worldview, this attitude represented a form of "centrism," with Jewish identity prioritized and other forms of identity considered ancillary at best. This form of centrism was simply a distraction from theocentrism—the only legitimate form of centrism in Paul's playbook. Whether the centrism of the individual engulfed in the trap of sinful "covetousness" or the centrism of a people engulfed in preserving a righteousness of "their own" (Rom. 10:3), Paul saw these two things as related aspects of the same underlying phenomenon—that is, a moral ethos running against the grain of the self-giving that undergirds Christian community.

This is where the "traditional perspective" (emphasizing the problem of the sinfulness of the human heart) and the so-called new perspective (emphasizing the problem of negotiating Jewish identity in Christian community) are to join hands, with both emphasizing different aspects of the centrism that Paul attributed to the cosmic powers. These two "perspectives on Paul" rightly focus on two different but related dimensions of Paul's vision of a world in the grip of the powers of Sin and Death. The "lordship" of those powers is manifest in and perpetuated by self-centeredness, which embeds itself in lifestyles of individuals and groups, lifestyles that compromise the other regard that lies at the heart of the gospel. Like layers of an onion, Paul saw cosmic powers to be at work in individual and corporate manifestations of "centripetal" living at the expense of others, in contrast to the "centrifugal" lifestyle that Paul attributed solely to the Spirit of the self-giving Lord.

Moreover, behind both so-called perspectives is something even more fundamental—worship. The importance of this theme has already been noted above. Here we can simply foreground one passage that takes on added significance in light of what we have seen. Speaking of God's activity in Christ for those who believe, Paul asks readers of Romans this poignant question: "Is God the God of Jews only? Is he not the God of Gentiles also? Yes, of Gentiles also, since God is one; and he will justify the circumcised on the ground of faith and the uncircumcised through that same faith" (Rom. 3:29–30).

The issue behind these verses, at least in the larger discursive flow of Romans, is not simply about inclusion into the people of God; it is ultimately about worship, and the worship of the one God by the multitude of diverse groups.[24] This theme does not merely come into play in the climax

24. Here I would differ from N. T. Wright when he says that "Paul does not want his addressees to see themselves as basically 'Jews' and 'gentiles' at all, but as Messiah-people" (*Paul and the Faithfulness of God* [Minneapolis: Fortress, 2013], 397). If we keep Wright's term "Messiah-people" in play, I would prefer to rework this sentence in the following way: "Paul does not want his addressees to see themselves primarily as 'Jews' and 'gentiles' per se, but

of Romans 15:7–13 (as seen above); instead, Paul registers the theme of worship toward the start of his letter, where he highlights worship gone wrong: "They did not honor him as God or give thanks to him, but they became futile in their thinking, and their senseless minds were darkened. . . . They exchanged the truth about God for a lie and worshiped and served the creature rather than the Creator, who is blessed forever! Amen" (Rom. 1:21, 25). When Paul asks in Romans 3:29 whether God is the God of the Jews only, he is ultimately asking about how worship is to be configured within Christian communities.

And we are back once more to the point made earlier, only with renewed vigor: for Paul, a spirit of other-regard was to permeate Christian community; only with that spirit in place could a community be characterized both by diversity in its membership and by unity in its worship of the one true God. Without legitimate diversity, worship of the God of creation was compromised; and without proper worship, diversity of membership was theologically meaningless. Holding both of these components together, in Paul's view, is the self-giving love of the Lord Jesus Christ, replicated by the Spirit in the communities and lives of his followers, who are freed from the powers that induce self-interestedness at the expense of others.

As a final pièce de résistance, Paul brings all this back around to his consideration of the Torah. In the light of God's redemption in Christ, Paul came to see that human beings could never adequately observe the Torah, due to the inadequacies of the human heart (e.g., Rom. 8:3) and the mastery of the all-encompassing power of Sin over even God's "holy" Torah (e.g., Rom. 7). Nonetheless, the Torah has a foothold even in Paul's vision of properly functioning Christian community. For it is there, says Paul, that the Torah ultimately finds its fulfillment (Rom. 8:4; 13:9–10; Gal. 5:14) as Christians shun "self-indulgence" (*sarx*) and adopt the attitude noted at the beginning of this essay: "through love become slaves to one another" (Gal. 5:13). There is, of course, much more to be said than we can say here about the role of Torah within the formation of Christian community. The only thing to note for our present purposes is how the story of the self-giving Jesus absorbs the potentially damaging centrism of some forms of Torah

as Messiah-people who worship the Lord as Jews and gentiles together." A similar hesitation applies to statements that the fellowship of faith results in "previous differences [being] transcended" (ibid., 833)—they are not really transcended so much as managed in health and wholeness. In particular, the fact that Paul's communities consisted predominantly of gentiles forced him to emphasize the relatedness of those communities to other communities in which a Jewish contingent was to the fore; see, for instance, 1 Cor. 1:2 in relation to 1 Cor. 16:1–4, where Paul outlines his initiative for the Jesus groups in Jerusalem (so too 2 Cor. 8–9; Rom. 15:22–29).

observance and metamorphoses it into healthy self-giving, in which the Torah ironically finds its true fulfillment.

Appreciating Paul's Vision

There is obviously much more that could and should be said about Paul's engagement with first-century Jewish covenantalism, but enough has been done to lay out the primary features of that engagement. In conclusion, how might all this be appropriated today?

We might do well, in the first instance, to consider this question in relation to the views of some Jewish scholars who have expressed appreciation for Paul's theological vision, despite their disagreement with its christological commitment. Occasionally, Jewish scholars have found Paul to be a laudable representative of the essential spirit of Judaism, precisely in breaking away from unhealthy fundamentalisms and undertaking a reform project analogous to reform movements elsewhere within Jewish history. For instance, Claude Montefiore commended Paul for finding a way to introduce an alternative (albeit flawed) form of universalism into the first-century Jewish discourse.[25] For Hans Joachim Schoeps, modern Judaism was to be reformed in the spirit of Paul himself, even if Paul's own solution is unacceptable.[26] Richard Rubenstein commended "Paul's dream of a united mankind in which tribal and creedal differences would finally be obliterated," finding Paul's gospel to be "consistent with a compelling strain in Jewish thought that has persisted from the days of the prophets to our own time."[27] Nancy Fuchs-Kreimer has applauded Paul's attempt to overcome the domestication of God within Second Temple Judaism by postulating a God who acted in surprisingly fresh ways, even in relation to the Torah.[28] And Daniel Boyarin has considered Paul to be "a Jewish cultural critic" whose "critique is important and valid for Jews today" and whose questions "about culture are important and valid for everyone today."[29]

25. See Claude Montefiore, *Judaism and St. Paul* (New York: Dutton, 1915).

26. See Hans Joachim Schoeps, *Paul: The Theology of the Apostle in the Light of Jewish Religious History* (Philadelphia: Westminster, 1961).

27. Richard Rubenstein, *My Brother Paul* (New York: Harper & Row, 1972), 128. He continues: "Nowhere is Paul more prototypically Jewish than in his strenuous pursuit of this universalist vision. . . . When carried to an extreme, Jewish particularism flies in the face of a profound yearning for union and community that has frequently moved men. . . . The more particularistic a group becomes, the more likely it is to generate a universalistic ideology as a way out of its own isolation."

28. See discussion of Nancy Fuchs-Kreimer in Daniel R. Langton, *The Apostle Paul in the Jewish Imagination: A Study in Modern Jewish-Christian Relations* (Cambridge: Cambridge University Press, 2010), 165–69.

29. Daniel Boyarin, *A Radical Jew: Paul and the Politics of Identity* (Berkeley: University of California Press, 1994), 2.

For Christians today, an appreciation of Paul's vision might lie along similar lines, although for them a full appreciation of Paul would include the recognition that his vision still mounts a considerable challenge for "working out" the Christian life today. This is because no matter where we turn in this complex of issues, we inevitably encounter self-giving love as the ethos in which God's power is manifest, in contrast to the cosmic powers that seek to destroy God's creation through the chaos of centrisms of all kinds. That challenging vision lies at the very heart of Paul's view of the diverse Christian community in its posture of humble, theocentric worship.

Stripped to its core, then, what Paul was ultimately fighting for when he wrote "not by works of Torah" was nothing other than cruciform self-giving as the overturning of self-interestedness, itself the product and foothold of cosmic powers opposed to God's program for the world. And where Paul would fight against the imposition of Jewish centrism in one context (e.g., Gal. 2:11–14), so he would fight against the imposition of what might be deemed "gentile centrism" in another context (Rom. 11:13–32; 15:27). Behind these different moments of engagement, Paul maintained a vision of those in Christ as a collection of diverse people, united in worship of the One who created distinctly varied identities, whose challenging corporate life can be sustained only through the power of the Spirit, who enlivens other-regard in transformational patterns replicating the self-giving of the Son of God. Judging by the extent to which he put his life and work on the line in defense of this vision of Christian community, Paul would no doubt present the same challenge to secure Christian churches of the twenty-first century that he presented to the fledgling Jesus groups of the mid-first century.

4

The New Perspective
and the Christian Life

Solus Spiritus

Patrick Mitchel

This book's main questions are, how did Paul understand the Christian life? What distinct contribution does the new perspective (NP) bring, if anything, to answering this question? These are important and practical questions. Unlike other contributors to this volume, I have not written a book related to the apostle Paul. I write as a theology lecturer with particular interests in Christology and pneumatology, familiar with the issues raised by the NP and passionate about teaching and preparing students for ministry in a post-Christendom culture on the western edge of Europe. I also write as a church person: an elder in a developing church-plant; a teacher and preacher who—since the Pauline corpus makes up most of the New Testament—faces regularly the task of bridging the hermeneutical gap between Paul's world and ours. Therefore, the aim of this chapter is constructive: to try to "earth" the discussion by focusing on the significance of the NP for understanding and living the Christian life. Part 1 will set the scene by reviewing various concerns underlying the debate,[1] and then part 2 will explore Paul's theological framework and inspiring vision for the Christian life as "life in the Spirit."

Part 1: Concerns New and Old

A useful tool when approaching a contentious debate is to step back for a moment from the presenting issues of disagreement to ask, what are the *concerns* that lie behind the disagreement? This can facilitate a fresh understanding of the motivations of the "other," distinct from technical argumentation. What follows then is a thematic sketch of concerns on both sides of the debate as I perceive them, not a tightly argued critical analysis of whether those motivations are justified or not.

Major Concerns of the New Perspective

When the new perspective was first articulated, one primary concern was that the old perspective (OP) *misrepresented Judaism*. One of Sanders's objectives in *Paul and Palestinian Judaism* was to overcome entrenched caricatures of Judaism within much New Testament scholarship (and Christianity in general).[2] The caricature was of a legalistic works-religion from which Paul is dramatically liberated. Jewish soteriology was, wrongly, portrayed as a system of merits in which good works had to outweigh the bad. The key, for Sanders, was that Israel had been elected as God's covenant people by God's saving grace. Since they were already "in," it made no sense that they would be trying to earn what they already possessed. Atonement and forgiveness was provided for within the covenant. Thus, seeing Judaism as a system of works righteousness not only misrepresented rabbinic Judaism but also had deeply damaging consequences for Jewish-Christian relations. Of particular

---

1. Some works assessing the debate include Francis Watson's revised edition of *Paul, Judaism, and the Gentiles: Beyond the New Perspective* (Grand Rapids: Eerdmans, 2007); Michael F. Bird, *The Saving Righteousness of God: Studies on Paul, Justification and the New Perspective* (Milton Keynes: Paternoster, 2007); James K. Beilby and Paul R. Eddy, *Justification: Five Views* (London: SPCK, 2012); and Michael F. Bird, ed., *Four Views on the Apostle Paul* (Grand Rapids: Zondervan, 2012). Neither of the latter two downplays the significant points of disagreement, but there is more willingness to recognize and affirm considerable points of overlap. In a substantial chapter in a revised edition of *The New Perspective on Paul*, James Dunn addresses four common criticisms and misunderstandings and also offers proposals on taking the debate forward. See James D. G. Dunn, "The New Perspective: Whence, What and Whither?" in *The New Perspective on Paul*, rev. ed. (Grand Rapids: Eerdmans, 2008), 1–97.

2. E. P. Sanders, *Paul and Palestinian Judaism: A Comparison of Patterns of Religion* (Philadelphia: Fortress, 1977).

concern was the negative Jewish stereotype within post–World War II German New Testament scholarship, in the work, for example, of Rudolf Bultmann and Ernst Käsemann.[3]

A corollary of the first concern was that the OP *led to a gospel of "bad news" prior to the announcement of "good news."* The NP built on Krister Stendahl's seminal essay "The Apostle Paul and the Introspective Conscience of the West" (1963), which argued that much Protestant scholarship tended to read Paul through Luther's guilt-ridden conscience and battles with medieval Roman Catholicism. This misreading of Paul had negative implications for the way in which the gospel was framed. Justification by faith, all agree, is the answer, but what is the problem? In the OP, the problem was not only Judaism's legalism but also how it served as a pattern for *humanity's* inherent tendency to works righteousness. One important purpose of the law, therefore, was to expose the "legalistic Jew" in all of us. The gospel *form* which emerged from this OP framework was shaped by a strong antithesis between law and grace combined with a highly negative anthropology. The implications for preaching, teaching, and evangelism within Protestantism were immense. But if Sanders was even partly right that Palestinian Judaism was a "religion of grace," then Paul's "problem" with Judaism cannot be reduced to works righteousness as assumed by the OP all the way back to Luther.[4]

The second concern links to a third: that the OP *tended to forge weak connections between justification and sanctification, between faith and works.* Paul's statement in Galatians 2:16 that we are "justified by faith in Christ and not by the works of the law" had long been read as the apostle wrestling against a Pelagian or semi-Pelagian earning of salvation.[5] Justification by faith, then, is Paul's response to legalism and takes the form of Christ's righteousness imputed to the believer, declaring a "not guilty" verdict through her faith in Christ. The NP concern is that this tends, whether intentionally or not, to locate the believer's initial acceptance by God as the *climactic resolution* of the problem of human inability to please God. Such a move can be seen in Bultmann's *Theology of the New Testament*, which coupled a very negative view of Judaism with a two-part structure: "Man Prior to the Revelation of Faith" and "Man under Faith."[6] It also connects to a deep, built-in Protestant fear of "works" ever taking an inappropriate place within justification. Yet

3. For further discussion, see Watson, *Paul, Judaism, and the Gentiles*, 31–40.
4. The potential for caricature of Luther is real here. However, Watson has a thorough discussion of how Luther sees misuse of the law occurring where sinful and deluded human beings seek to attain salvation by their own efforts. See Watson, *Paul, Judaism, and the Gentiles*, 28–31.
5. Scripture quotations in this chapter, unless otherwise noted, are from the NIV.
6. Rudolf Bultmann, *Theology of the New Testament* (London: SCM, 1952).

such an emphasis on the secondary status of works sits very uneasily with Paul's eschatological vision of personal and communal transformation empowered by the Spirit. This is a theme I will unpack in more detail in part 2.

A fourth concern followed: not only was the OP gospel framed negatively, but *it was inherently individualistic* in a manner foreign to Paul. The OP's historic focus was on the soteriological question of how one is put right with God. The concern of much NP writing has not been to deny the importance of this question but to locate individual justification within a wider social, ecclesiological, and eschatological framework since this is how Paul himself develops the doctrine.[7] While departing sharply from aspects of the NP, Francis Watson has been one of the strongest voices articulating the importance of the social reality behind Paul's theology of Judaism, gentiles, and the law. He writes:

> Attention to the social context and function of Paul's arguments produces an interpretation of Paul in some respects very different from one stemming from the Lutheran tradition. For example, it has been shown that the fundamental antithesis between faith and works is not to be understood as an abstract theological contrast between receiving salvation as a free gift and earning it by one's own efforts, but as an attempt to demarcate two different modes of communal practice.[8]

The NP concern is that an individualistic reading of Paul marginalizes the need for what Richard Hays has called an "ecclesiotelic" hermeneutic—that the purpose of the gospel of Jesus Christ is the formation of a people.[9] Historically, it is undeniable that evangelical Protestantism has tended to be weak on ecclesiology while being strong on individualism.[10]

A fifth concern was that the OP *tended to flatten Paul's imaginative and complex narrative theology under the weight of Protestant systematics dominated by justification.* In a sense, the aim of unpacking a unified narrative structure of Paul's theology summarizes much of N. T. Wright's,[11] Richard

---

7. This concern is expressed by N. T. Wright: "The gospel creates, not a bunch of individual Christians, but a community. If you take the old route of putting justification, in its traditional meaning, at the centre of your theology, you will always be in danger of sustaining some sort of individualism" (Wright, *What St Paul Really Said* [Oxford: Lion Books, 2003], 157–58).

8. Watson, *Paul, Judaism, and the Gentiles*, 245–46.

9. Richard B. Hays, *The Conversion of the Imagination: Paul as Interpreter of Israel's Scripture* (Grand Rapids: Eerdmans, 2005), 171.

10. For example, Michael F. Bird, *Evangelical Theology: A Biblical and Systematic Introduction* (Grand Rapids: Zondervan, 2013), 699–707.

11. N. T. Wright, *Paul and the Faithfulness of God*, Christian Origins and the Question of God 4 (London: SPCK, 2013); Wright, *Justification: God's Plan and Paul's Vision* (Downers

Hays's,[12] and others'[13] writings on Paul. There may be multiple subplots, but there is one "grand story," as Morna Hooker puts it.[14]

Now, not everyone who sees Paul's gospel as narratable is necessarily explicitly supportive of the NP (or vice versa).[15] Neither do all agree that there is one story being unpacked,[16] nor is there unanimity on the shape and content of the narrative.[17] The broader point is how the NP tends to emphasize the value in understanding the narrative dynamics of Paul, value that has tended to be overlooked within the OP's focus on systematic categories of sin, guilt, justification, and personal salvation.

Major Concerns of the Old Perspective

The OP literature is vast, and there is little value in replaying it here. What follows is a synthesis of what I see as *the* ultimate concern *behind* recurring criticisms of the NP—that of soteriology—and how it finds particular expression in two areas, justification and divine and human agency.

Justification

The response to the NP has, at heart, not simply revolved around technical debates about the precise meaning of the "works of the law" or whether "covenantal nomism" accurately describes Palestinian Judaism, but can be subsumed under one overriding concern: *the soteriological question of how sinners are put right with God.* To illustrate this point, it is worth briefly considering three objections to Wright's theology of justification.

First, there is an objection that the NP's reframing of Paul's relationship with Judaism—from one of humanity's innate self-righteousness to (primarily) one of how gentiles can be embraced within the covenant without having to

Grove, IL: IVP Academic, 2009); Wright, *The Climax of the Covenant: Christ and the Law in Pauline Theology* (Minneapolis: Fortress, 1993); Wright, *What St Paul Really Said.*

12. Hays, *Conversion of the Imagination*; Hays, "Is Paul's Gospel Narratable?," *Journal for the Study of the New Testament* 27, no. 2 (2004): 217–39; Hays, *The Faith of Jesus Christ: The Narrative Substructure of Galatians 3:1–4:11* (Grand Rapids: Eerdmans, 2002); Hays, *Echoes of Scripture in the Letters of Paul* (New Haven: Yale University Press, 1993).

13. For example, Bruce W. Longenecker, ed., *Narrative Dynamics in Paul: A Critical Assessment* (Louisville: Westminster John Knox, 2002).

14. Morna Hooker, "'Heirs of Abraham': The Gentiles' Role in Israel's Story; A Response to Bruce W. Longenecker," in Longenecker, *Narrative Dynamics*, 85–96.

15. Neither Dunn nor Sanders has made narrative a major part of their interpretation of Paul. Ben Witherington is a strong advocate of narrative but is critical of aspects of the NP (see *The Indelible Image: The Theological and Ethical Thought World of the New Testament*, vol. 1, *The Individual Witnesses* [Downers Grove, IL: IVP Academic, 2009]).

16. This is probably the main area in which Watson departs from Wright.

17. There is a good discussion of different views in Hays, "Is Paul's Gospel Narratable?"

follow the Torah—has inevitably *decentered* and *redefined* justification by faith alone. This realignment has negatively shifted focus from the vertical (how can sinners come before a holy God?) to the horizontal (how can Jews and gentiles be incorporated into the new covenant community?). Wright's articulation of justification in terms of God's covenant faithfulness and a believer's covenant membership does certainly represent a shift of emphasis from a traditional soteriological understanding of justification to an ecclesiological one. For some this threatens to undermine the heart of Reformation doctrine.[18] Less alarmist critics do not question Wright's orthodox or evangelical credentials but find that "he emphasizes the horizontal much more than he stresses the vertical. Both themes are certainly present. Nevertheless, Wright doesn't give us an in-depth and profound discussion on the nature of sin in Paul."[19]

A second OP objection revolves around the basis of justification. Wright is insistent that there is an absolute necessity and (Pauline) expectation of a transformed life, set within a broad concept of "righteousness" framed by his reconstruction of the eschatological, forensic, participatory, and covenantal elements of justification.[20] He also argues that justification is "pronounced as an act of utter grace on the basis of the Messiah's death."[21] Assurance is based on the declarative nature of justification in the present, which is permanent and anticipates the future verdict at the last day.[22] In between initial justification and final judgment, "Paul envisages a spirit-led life which does not in any way contribute to initial justification, *or to the consequent assurance of final justification which that initial justification brings.*"[23] Despite such explicit statements, Thomas Schreiner and many others question Wright's attempt to tie together initial justification, a Spirit-led life, assurance, and future justification. A comment from Wright like "Present justification declares, on the basis of faith, what future justification will affirm publicly on the basis of the entire life"[24] is read as making justification, in effect, a process and "works" constituent of saving faith. Schreiner asks, "If justification is based on works, then how can believers have assurance that they will be justified on the final day?"[25] But for

18. See John Piper, *The Future of Justification: A Response to N. T. Wright* (Wheaton: Crossway, 2007).

19. Thomas Schreiner, "N. T. Wright under Review: Revisiting the Apostle Paul and His Doctrine of Justification," *Credo*, January 2014, 53.

20. Wright, *Paul and the Faithfulness of God*, 925–1037.

21. Ibid., 957.

22. Ibid., 948–49.

23. Ibid., 1030 (emphasis original).

24. Wright, *What St Paul Really Said*, 129.

25. Schreiner, "N. T. Wright under Review," 54. Tim Chester argues similarly: "If justification in the future is our vindication at the final judgement, based on the work of Christ plus the life

Wright, it is not so much a question of "adding a 'horizontal' dimension to a 'vertical one.' This is to miss the point entirely, which is that the creator God called Abraham to be the means of rescuing humans and the world: a doubly 'vertical' theme if you like."[26] This is a complex debate revolving around detailed exegesis of the relevant texts and quite distinct understandings of justification.[27]

A third objection is that Wright rejects the classic Reformed view of imputation.[28] For Schreiner, in texts such as Romans 5:12–19 and 2 Corinthians 5:21, "what is at stake is whether Christ is our righteousness, whether our righteousness finally lies outside of ourselves and is found in Jesus Christ,"[29] whereas Wright argues that the concept of alien righteousness is a category mistake. For Schreiner, this sort of horizontal/vertical imbalance is also reflected in Wright's continuing broad acceptance of Sanders's covenantal nomism and a generally positive portrait of ancient Judaism.[30] Schreiner concludes that "here is another place where Wright focuses on the horizontal (boundary markers) and fails to see the vertical (one's relationship to God)."[31] The underlying issue is again soteriological, a criticism of which Wright is well aware.[32]

DIVINE AND HUMAN AGENCY

All of this is to say that a critical historical question then becomes whether ancient Judaism did exhibit forms of merit theology—the belief that at the eschaton one's ultimate status will be determined by one's obedience to the Torah. Was this the "problem" against which Paul developed the "solution"

---

we live in the power of the Spirit, then we cannot have assurance." See Chester, "Justification, Ecclesiology and the New Perspective," *Themelios* 30, no. 2 (Winter 2005): 16.

26. Wright, *Paul and the Faithfulness of God*, 928.

27. For one of the best critiques of Wright on justification, see David Wenham, "Tom Wright, *Justification: God's Plan and Paul's Vision*," *Evangelical Quarterly* 83, no. 3 (2010): 258–66.

28. Wright, *Paul and the Faithfulness of God*, 881–85.

29. Schreiner, "N. T. Wright under Review," 55.

30. Wright, *Paul and the Faithfulness of God*, 1322. "No doubt [Sanders] has oversimplified, as we all do, but his basic perception of Jewish practice as a response to the grace implicitly embodied in the covenant is substantially correct."

31. Schreiner, "N. T. Wright under Review," 56. It is baffling how he can say Wright "fails to see" the vertical dimension, given his extended discussion of the forensic nature of justification.

32. Wright describes the OP concern this way: if Judaism was, after all, a "religion of grace," this has the unintended effect of "sneakily transforming Christianity into a religion of works" by making "Christianity much more like Judaism, or at least Judaism of standard protestant polemic"; see Wright, *Paul and the Faithfulness of God*, 1323. In this context, Dunn's comments here probably confirm OP concerns: "The Judaism of what Sanders christened as 'covenantal nomism' can now be seen to preach good Protestant doctrine: that grace is always prior; that human effort is ever the response to divine initiative; that good works are the fruit and not the root of salvation." See Dunn, "The Justice of God: A Renewed Perspective on Justification by Faith," in *New Perspective on Paul*, 199.

of justification?[33] Thus, significant energy has been invested in researching this question in the post-Sanders era.[34] The results have been mixed. On the one hand is evidence that appears supportive of the NP, such as the publication in 1994 of 4QMMT, in which "works of the law" are spoken of in ways supportive of Dunn's "boundary markers."[35] Or take this delightful Jewish parable, most likely from Palestine in the Second Temple period:[36]

> A certain pious man [*hasid*] forgot a sheaf in the middle of his field. He said to his son, "Go and offer two bullocks on my behalf, for a burnt offering and a peace offering." His son said to him, "Father, why are you more joyful at fulfilling this one commandment than all the other commandments in Torah?" He said to him, "The Lord gave us all the commands in Torah to obey intentionally, but he only gave us this one to obey accidentally."

Deuteronomy 24:19 was the only law that could be fulfilled only accidentally; obedient action could only follow forgetfulness. The Jewish man is therefore overjoyed that his bad memory has given him an unexpected opportunity to keep the law. As with many of Jesus's parables, there is hyperbole present—in this case in the wildly expensive offering of two bullocks for sacrifice. The sense of exaggeration is making a serious point to the listeners. The parable does not talk about fear or an attempt to "attain salvation" as a motive for obedience. It is celebrating an unplanned and unexpected opportunity to obey another law out of the sheer joy of pleasing God and doing his will. Such findings endorse the NP's correction of popular caricatures of Judaism[37] and therefore support the argument that Paul was combating issues of nationalistic

33. For Bird, this is the "jugular of the issue." See Bird, *Saving Righteousness of God*, 89.
34. For example, D. A. Carson, Peter T. O'Brien, and Mark A. Seifrid, eds., *Justification and Variegated Nomism*, 2 vols. (Grand Rapids: Baker Academic, 2001); also Simon Gathercole, "After the New Perspective: Works, Justification and Boasting in Early Judaism and Romans 1–5," *Tyndale Bulletin* 52 (2001): 303–6. Thomas Schreiner has a useful summary of research in "An Old Perspective on the New Perspective," *Concordia Journal* 35, no. 2 (Spring 2009): 140–55. Also see Andrew Das, "Paul and Works of Obedience in Second Temple Judaism: Romans 4:4–5 as a 'New Perspective' Case Study," *Catholic Biblical Quarterly* 71 (2009): 795–812.
35. Dunn is most associated with the notion of "works of the law" as merely being "boundary markers" of Jewish identity. He subsequently clarified that he accepts that "works of the law" refers to all that the Torah requires. See Dunn, *New Perspective on Paul*, 23–28.
36. I thank David Instone-Brewer for pointing me to this parable from Tosefta *Peah* 3.8. I have omitted a second paragraph (likely a later addition) that explicates the first. See David Instone-Brewer, "Rabbinic Writings in New Testament Research," in *The Handbook of the Study of the Historical Jesus*, ed. Tom Holmén and Stanley E. Porter (Leiden: Brill, 2011), 2:1687–721.
37. Some, like Stephen Westerholm, agree that Paul is responding not to Jewish legalism but to the law's inability to produce righteousness in sinful human beings. See Westerholm, *Justification Reconsidered: Rethinking a Pauline Theme* (Grand Rapids: Eerdmans, 2013), 97.

exclusiveness in resisting the imposition of Jewish "boundary markers" on gentile believers. This indicates that the best way to think about the issue is not so much "legalism"[38] or some crass form of works righteousness, but that the Jews considered observance of the law's works to be a privilege and joy in response to God's gracious election.

On the other hand, research suggests that *also* in view is Paul's critique of *trust* in "works of the law" in attaining righteousness. Francis Watson comments that "distinctively Jewish practices do not and cannot serve *only* as boundary markers, and neither Paul nor his Jewish opponents understand them merely as such."[39] Andrew Das argues that "an adequate 'newer perspective' must account for the Apostle's critique of works considered apart from God's grace in Christ."[40] Bird concludes, "Paul's entire conception of Christ, the law, and salvation is mystifying apart from the assumption that he also attacked a form of grace-works synergism that was implicit in the attempt to force Gentiles to adopt a Jewish lifestyle."[41] In a recent work comparing Paul's soteriology with other Jewish sources of his day (particularly Qumran), Preston Sprinkle concludes that the overall picture is one of neither clear continuity nor wholesale discontinuity. However, it is in the area of divine-human agency in salvation that Paul exhibits the most discontinuity. His zealous passion to purify Israel in order to honor God was confronted on the Damascus Road by God's own agency in transforming him. "Paul's Pharisaic view of God as the one who will justify the righteous on the final day was not simply adjusted—it was *substantially transformed*. The Jewish God is now understood as the one who justifies the ungodly."[42]

Again, my aim here is not to enter into a debate that has been exhaustively replayed, save to make three brief observations. First, it is worth noting that both Dunn and Wright reject the charge that they are denying that justification is through faith alone by grace alone.[43] Second, exclusively "new"

38. It is surprising that Schreiner, in "N. T. Wright under Review" and "An Old Perspective," continues to insist on this unhelpful and misleading term.

39. Francis Watson, "Not the New Perspective" (unpublished paper delivered at the British New Testament Conference, September 2001).

40. Das, "Paul and Works," 812.

41. Bird, *Saving Righteousness of God*, 112.

42. Preston Sprinkle, *Paul and Judaism Revisited: A Study of Human and Divine Agency in Salvation* (Downers Grove, IL: IVP Academic, 2013), 249 (emphasis mine). The "ungodly" here are gentiles without the law.

43. Dunn writes, "From the first, my concern has been not to attack or deny the classic Christian doctrine of justification by faith. . . . I affirm as a central point of Christian faith that God's acceptance of any and every person is by his grace alone and through faith alone" (Dunn, *New Perspective on Paul*, 18–23). He has continued to seek common ground in arguing that the NP is not hostile or antithetical to the OP; the latter does not have to be "wrong" for the former to

or "old" perspectives are inadequate; each "side" has insights to offer the other. But my main point is that the consistent underlying concern of the OP is narrowly soteriological: to maintain the centrality of justification; to defend imputation; to reject any implication that final justification is based on works; and to affirm that Paul was, at least in part, rejecting the law as a means of attaining righteousness. The historical and theological dominance of justification within evangelical identity helps to explain why some Lutheran and Reformed evangelicals in particular[44] have reacted so vehemently to the NP, for when identity is threatened, battle lines get drawn.[45]

Pause and Reflection

The essence of the entire NP/OP debate revolves around questions of *how and where* Paul's theology reflects themes of both continuity and discontinuity with Judaism.[46] I'm generalizing here, but I think it is fair to say that within the OP, too sharp a sense of Paul's discontinuity with Judaism has, apart from sometimes fostering semi-Marcionite tendencies, left little room (or reason) to look for one unfolding narrative framework within his theology. This is not to say that the OP has ignored broader Pauline themes—Reformed theology especially is, of course, nothing if not strongly covenantal. However, the OP's persistently narrow focus on soteriology, and the virtual equation of justification with the gospel, has tended to *distort* the overall picture.

---

be "right" (see Beilby and Eddy, *Justification*, 176–77). Wright brusquely rejects "the attempt by some 'Old Perspective' writers to suggest that some of us who have been labelled as 'new perspective' thinkers have given up on ideas such as sin, salvation, atonement and so on" (Wright, *Paul and the Faithfulness of God*, 1038). See also his response to John Piper in Wright, *Justification*.

44. To be fair, not all critics of the NP are Lutheran or Reformed. Methodist scholars like Ben Witherington and Howard Marshall have expressed reservations on particular details. See Witherington, *Indelible Image*, 1:231–37; and I. Howard Marshall, *New Testament Theology: Many Witnesses, One Gospel* (Downers Grove, IL: InterVarsity, 2004), 446.

45. It is striking that two endorsements on the back of Stephen Westerholm's *Justification Reconsidered* contain military imagery. Simon Gathercole concludes that the book "throws down the gauntlet to the New Perspectivists. How will they respond?" Similarly, John Barclay comments, "Here is ready ammunition for an important ongoing debate."

46. This overarching point can be lost among the multiple views of scholars on different "sides" across a range of peripheral (if still important) issues. For example, imputation is rejected by Wright but also by Seifrid (Mark A. Seifrid, *Christ, Our Righteousness: Paul's Theology of Justification* [Downers Grove, IL: Apollos/InterVarsity, 2000], 171–77) and cautiously by Bird, who sees it as a legacy of medieval merit theology (Bird, *Saving Righteousness of God*, 61–87). Wright and Dunn disagree on the meaning of *pistis Christou*; whether it is best translated "faithfulness of Christ" or "faith in Christ" is not a definitive issue within the NP. The contested idea that Israel was in "exile" is distinctive to Wright but not to the NP per se. While the question of assurance takes a particular form within the NP ("getting in and staying in"), the issue has, of course, long been debated between Calvinists and Arminians.

This has been especially evident in Protestantism's historic marginalization of Pauline pneumatology and its struggles to develop a robust ecclesiology that matches that of the apostle. The "anxious Protestant principle" of not importing works into salvation has tended to marginalize what Paul has to say on the Christian life. In other words, the priority of how to "get in" has tended to make secondary the importance of the life lived once "in." This is despite moral formation being the *goal* of Paul's missionary work among his churches, as James Thompson has shown wonderfully well.[47]

In general, the NP has more emphasis on Paul's deep continuity with his Jewish thought world—while also having to explain the fact of discontinuity embodied in his mission to the gentiles. Sanders famously concluded that Paul's only real problem with Judaism was that "it was not Christianity."[48] Part of the challenge facing NP scholars since Sanders has been to articulate a more convincing explanation of Paul's theology and how he stands in both continuity and discontinuity with the faith of his fathers. The result, while certainly imperfect and open to criticism in places, has in my view forged fresh ways of appreciating the integration of the apostle's theology with *how it shapes his vision for the Christian life*. Once we step back from the detailed arguments, I suggest that it is easier to see that *the most significant contribution of the new perspective has been how it has acted as a catalyst for a renewed appreciation for the narrative coherence of Paul's thought.* This wider angle, in turn, helps to foster a renewed integration of Pauline theology and ethics and helps to focus attention on the *purpose* of justification within Paul's ecclesiology, eschatology, and pneumatology. There is no need to play one part of the narrative off against another. Therefore, this wider perspective helps to capture both the Jewishness of Paul's theology and Paul's radical discontinuity with Judaism created, primarily I believe, by his exalted Christology after his Damascus Road experience. Part 2 will attempt to unpack these proposals via a diagram that I use as a teaching tool.

Part 2: Paul's Storied Theology and the Christian Life

The diagram below (fig. 4.1), based mainly on Galatians, offers a broad sketch of Paul's theological framework and is admittedly therefore open to all sorts of potential criticisms. It is simplistic; Paul's thought world is too complex and multilayered to be captured in a picture. It idealizes a singular and neat

---

47. James W. Thompson, *Moral Formation according to Paul: The Context and Coherence of Pauline Ethics* (Grand Rapids: Baker Academic, 2011), and *Pastoral Ministry according to Paul: A Biblical Vision* (Grand Rapids: Baker Academic, 2006).

48. Sanders, *Paul and Palestinian Judaism*, 552.

Pauline theological vision and leaves little room for the messy contextual development of Paul's theology within a life of mission. It implies that there is a clearly identifiable and logically unfolding narrative substructure to Paul's thought; however, some reject the idea that Paul's gospel is narratable at all,[49] others think Paul is simply contradictory,[50] and yet others argue that there is no linear story in view but rather an eclectic potpourri of images, texts, and traditions that Paul is using as imaginative resources to explain the significance of Jesus Christ.[51] Despite such possible objections, the argument that Paul has a coherent and narratable theological vision has been persuasively made[52] and is assumed in what follows. Following brief discussion of Paul and the process of theological reflection, the figure will be unpacked as three interrelated themes, the first two (restructured monotheism and restructured Torah) setting up a concluding discussion of Paul's restructured eschatology (the Christian life *within the new age of the Spirit*).[53]

Figure 4.1
A Sketch of Paul's Storied Theology

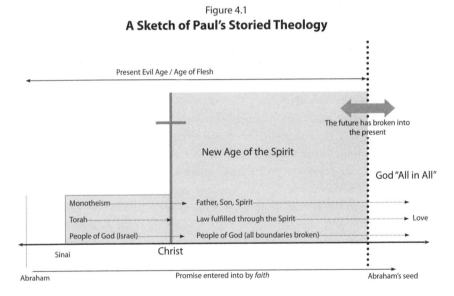

49. Francis Watson, "Is There a Story in These Texts?," in Longenecker, *Narrative Dynamics*, 231–40.

50. Heikki Räisänen, *Paul and the Law* (Eugene, OR: Wipf & Stock, 2010).

51. R. B. Matlock, "The Arrow and the Web: Critical Reflections on a Narrative Approach to Paul," in Longenecker, *Narrative Dynamics*, 44–57.

52. For example, see Witherington, "Paul the Paradigm Setter," in *Indelible Image*, 171–275, and much of Wright's work on Paul. For detailed discussion of the latter, see *Paul and the Faithfulness of God*, 456–537.

53. If there are obvious parallels here to the tripartite structure of Wright's colossal scheme in *Paul and the Faithfulness of God*, it is because these themes emerge clearly from Paul's narrative theology.

Paul the Inspired Reflective Practitioner

I like to think of Paul (and indeed all the writers of the New Testament) as an *inspired reflective practitioner*. I use the word *inspired* deliberately, to resist a reductionistic reconstruction of Paul that leaves little or no room for divine revelation to explain his transformation from persecutor to persecuted. Paul, of course, would not recognize a purely sociological or psychological explanation for his radical change of thinking and practice. Theological reflection has been described as "active, persistent, prayerful examination of personal experience and beliefs in light of Scripture and Christian tradition in order to learn about oneself and about God and so make plans for greater faithfulness."[54]

If the word *Christian* is replaced by the word *Jewish*, this definition becomes enormously helpful as a tool for thinking about the development of Paul's distinctive postresurrection theology. Through a process of theological reflection on his own experience of the risen Christ there emerges a profound restructuring[55] of his preexisting theological framework.[56] While Paul does not unpack the mechanics of this process, he alludes to it in Galatians 1:11–17, where he says he retreated alone to Arabia after receiving the gospel "by revelation from Jesus Christ." His main concern in these verses is to emphasize the divine origin of his call and subsequent mission to the gentiles (vv. 15–16); no one else was involved. Subsequent contact with the Jerusalem apostles is downplayed and only confirms the legitimacy of Paul's gospel to the gentiles (1:18–2:10). The strong implication is that the "new" apostle spent considerable time reassessing and reimagining his faith in light of the "brute fact" of the crucified Christ who is now revealed to be the living, risen Lord.[57] When Paul emerges, there is no sense of uncertainty about his gospel, mission, or new identity in Christ (Phil. 3:4–11). While Francis Watson explains Paul's gospel in terms of a nonnarratable "divine incursion" into the world,[58] there is no need to hold the shocking and completely unexpected idea of a crucified Messiah over against an imaginative restructuring of Israel's story in

54. I am grateful to Dr. Paul Coulter for permission to use this definition developed by him and the team at Belfast Bible College.

55. Different words can be and have been used here—*reconfiguring, reinterpreting, reimagining*, or *reformulating*, for example. I'm highlighting *restructuring* because it is useful to emphasize that Paul is *building* on his Jewish faith, not rejecting it.

56. One of the best resources here is Richard N. Longenecker, ed., *The Road from Damascus: The Impact of Paul's Conversion on His Life, Thought, and Ministry* (Grand Rapids: Eerdmans, 1997).

57. Longenecker says the Arabian sojourn could have been "principally for solitude to rethink his life and learning from the perspective of Christ's revelatory encounter" (Richard N. Longenecker, *Galatians* [Dallas: Word, 1990], 34).

58. Watson, "Is There a Story in These Texts?," 231–40. See a reply by Hays in "Is Paul's Gospel Narratable?," 236–39.

light of Jesus. Put differently, it is the astonishing implications of Paul's high *Christology* that determine how Paul reframes his understanding of God's saving purposes through his people Israel. This point brings us to how Paul chooses to communicate the meaning of justification by faith in the social and religious context of how both Jews and gentiles are incorporated within the redeemed people of God. Christology and soteriology are two sides of the same coin.

Monotheism Restructured

From his personal experience of Jesus, Paul not only learns radically new things about himself but also is shown previously hidden *mysteries* about God's identity and salvific purposes.[59] Thus, the story of justification begins for Paul, not at creation, nor even with Abraham, but at the climax of the narrative—the death and resurrection of the Messiah. Discussing Galatians, Gordon Fee contends that this focus on the work of Christ "is always kept within the larger framework of Paul's undiminished Jewish monotheism." God the Father is "ultimately responsible for everything."[60] Yet, consistent with what is more explicit elsewhere in Paul, there is evidence of an assumed high Christology where Jesus shares divine prerogatives. Thus, Galatians begins with a typically Pauline emphasis on the inseparable mission of Father and Son: "Paul, an apostle—sent . . . by Jesus Christ and God the Father, who raised him from the dead." He wishes them grace and peace from "God our Father and the Lord Jesus Christ." Jesus's self-giving atoning death "for our sins" was "according to the will of our God and Father" (Gal. 1:1–4).

Larry Hurtado has comprehensively demonstrated the unparalleled nature of what he terms this early Christian "binitarian devotional pattern," in which "Jesus figures prominently and uniquely along with God as the cause, content, and even co-recipient of devotion, including corporate worship."[61] Richard Bauckham prefers to interpret Paul's exalted Christology in terms of the inclusion of Jesus within the unique identity of the one God of Jewish

59. The idea of the gospel as a mystery now revealed by God is extraordinarily important in Paul. For example, see Rom. 16:25; 1 Cor. 2:7; Eph. 1:9; 3:3, 4, 6, 9; 6:19; Col. 1:26–27; 2:2; 4:3; 1 Tim. 3:16.

60. Gordon D. Fee, *Pauline Christology: An Exegetical-Theological Study* (Grand Rapids: Baker Academic, 2007), 207.

61. Larry W. Hurtado, *God in New Testament Theology* (Nashville: Abingdon, 2010), 52. For his fuller works, see *One God and One Lord: Early Christian Devotion and Ancient Jewish Monotheism* (Edinburgh: T&T Clark, 1998), and *How on Earth Did Jesus Become a God? Historical Questions about Earliest Devotion to Jesus* (Grand Rapids: Eerdmans, 2005).

monotheism.[62] While queried by Dunn,[63] the general thrust of Hurtado's and Bauckham's conclusions, while having distinct emphases, is persuasive. So much could be said here, but the relevant point for our discussion is that *Paul's restructured monotheism is fundamental to his new understanding of God and his saving purposes.* As Daniel Kirk puts it, "Paul is 'converted' neither to a non-Christian missional Judaism nor to a Torah-embracing missional Christianity."[64] Rather, it is the astonishing way that "God" is redefined with reference to Jesus that is crucial in explaining Paul's Torah-free mission to the gentiles.[65] In other words, it is precisely because of the unique identity of the crucified Messiah that his death is universally significant for *all* who have faith in him—whether Jew or Greek, male or female, slave or free (Gal. 3:28)—as they are all one *in* Christ Jesus. Christians are "baptized into Christ" and "have clothed [themselves] with Christ" and "belong to Christ" (Gal. 3:27, 29). This is "participationist soteriology," or union with the resurrected Christ, and results in Christ being "formed" in believers in a relationship of mutual indwelling (Gal. 4:19).[66] For this reason Paul can say, speaking generically of all believers, "It is no longer I who live, but it is Christ who lives in me" (Gal. 2:20a NRSV).

Paul's restructured monotheism (high Christology) and restructured soteriology lead inevitably to a restructured understanding of a life pleasing to God. The last line of our definition of theological reflection above talks about developing revised plans for greater faithfulness. This is exactly what Paul is doing in light of a revolution of his understanding of the Messiah. Faithful obedience to God is framed not in terms of Torah obedience but in terms of faith in, and becoming a servant of, Christ, the one true Lord who sits at God's right hand.[67] The "shape" the Christian life takes is cruciform: "The life I now live in the body, I live by faith in the Son of God, who loved me and gave himself for me" (Gal. 2:20b). The cross is not only the source of salvation; it defines Christian spirituality. Michael Gorman argues that

---

62. Richard Bauckham, *Jesus and the God of Israel: God Crucified and Other Studies on the New Testament's Christology of Divine Identity* (Grand Rapids: Eerdmans, 2009), 181.

63. James D. G. Dunn, *Did the First Christians Worship Jesus? The New Testament Evidence* (London: SPCK, 2010).

64. J. R. D. Kirk, review of *The New Perspective on Paul*, by J. D. G. Dunn, *Review of Biblical Literature* (2008): 416–22.

65. For an excellent discussion of God and Jesus in the New Testament, see Hurtado, *God in New Testament Theology*, 49–71.

66. Michael Gorman makes the case for seeing justification and participation as "two sides of the same coin" (*Reading Paul* [Eugene, OR: Cascade, 2008], 111–31). For his more extensive study, see Gorman, *Apostle of the Crucified Lord: A Theological Introduction to Paul and His Letters* (Grand Rapids: Eerdmans, 2004).

67. Rom. 10:9–10; 1 Cor. 12:3; Phil. 2:9–11.

"cruciformity is Paul's all-encompassing spirituality. It is the *modus operandi* of life in Christ."[68] It includes themes like self-giving, suffering (Phil. 3:10), co-crucifixion (Gal. 2:20a), and power in weakness (2 Cor. 12:10). Justification, understood in this way, establishes a new covenant relationship with God that is *inseparably linked to spiritual and ethical transformation.* This new life is lived within the radically redrawn covenant community, the body of Christ, in which he dwells, and is *patterned on the character and example of Jesus*, whom Paul regularly exhorts believers to follow (e.g., Phil. 2:4–11; Rom. 15:1–13).[69]

It is Pauline Christology, therefore, that displays significant *discontinuity* with Judaism—there is no Second Temple Jewish precedent that provides a parallel.[70] Yet, even here, there is not total discontinuity. Paul's high Christology is developed *from* his encounter with the risen Lord. It works backward, via theological reflection, to *explain from Scripture* how Jesus is identified with God—particularly in his divine sovereignty over all things.[71] This is why, in figure 4.1 above, Pauline monotheism reflects theological development rather than complete innovation.

Torah Restructured

It is *from* the vantage point of his restructured monotheism that Paul rethinks and reenvisions his previous understanding of the story of Israel. The writing on this topic is immense, but while much ink has been spilled about "the works of the law" and the "mechanics" of justification, Paul's overall narrative is clear. Our purpose here is simply to offer a sketch of the story in Galatians and to consider the place of the law in the Christian life. This will set up a concluding discussion of Paul, the Spirit, and the Christian life.

The foolishness of the Galatian gentile Christians was to believe the false gospel of Paul's opponents and to think that they were under obligation to observe the Torah (Gal. 3:1). Their reception of the Spirit through faith in Christ visibly and powerfully demonstrated (3:4) that they had nevertheless *already* been incorporated into God's redemptive purposes. Through inspired theological reflection, Paul looks back to Abraham as scriptural proof (3:8) that incorporation of the gentiles into the people of God was *always* God's

68. Gorman, *Reading Paul*, 147. See pp. 145–66 for wider discussion.
69. For further discussion of Jesus as the source of ethics in Paul, see Ben Witherington III, *The Indelible Image: The Theological and Ethical Thought World of the New Testament*, vol. 2, *The Collective Witness* (Downers Grove, IL: IVP Academic, 2010), 610–16.
70. Bauckham, *Jesus and the God of Israel*, 178–79.
71. For fuller discussion, see ibid., 152–81.

intent and that the purpose of the law was *never* to effect justification. Brian Rosner makes a useful point here that most quotations of Scripture in Paul's letters (over 80 percent) revolve around topics in which Paul's theology "departs most dramatically from previous exegetical traditions within Judaism. . . . It is when Paul is pressed to defend the new community's legitimacy and continuity with Scripture that we find him quoting Scripture most often."[72] This certainly seems to be the case with Abraham in Romans and Galatians.

Paul is telling a restructured historical-redemptive story. "Faith" was always the key to justification/righteousness, long before the law existed. It is not, therefore, that Paul is setting earlier Jewish "legalism" over against later Christian libertarian faith. Nor, emphatically, is the law opposed to the promises of God (Gal. 3:21). Through Christ and the Spirit believers become children of Abraham and heirs to the promise that God made with Abraham (3:9). Since Christ is the seed of Abraham (3:16), those in Christ are descendants of Abraham. Since the law could never justify (3:11) and had only a temporary guardian-type role (3:23–25), those who rely on observing it are under a curse (3:10). This is where Christ enters Israel's story; sent by God, "born of a woman, born under the law" (4:4), he eradicates the curse. Therefore, for the Galatians to choose to go under the law is to reject the path of blessing and promise for life under the curse—which explains the deep passion and worried frustration of Paul's appeal in the epistle.[73]

To link this discussion to figure 4.1, we can make use of a threefold framework proposed by Rosner for thinking about Paul and the law.[74] First, the law is uncompromisingly *repudiated* as a means of justification (Gal. 5:4). The Mosaic covenant has come to an end; the Abrahamic covenant is fulfilled. The law has no soteriological function (Gal. 3:21)—this is why the arrow after "Torah" in figure 4.1 comes to an end at the cross. This negative conclusion is strongly emphasized by Paul in the particular context of debates about admission of gentiles into the new covenant community. All have sinned (Rom. 3:28); Jew and gentile alike are lost, enemies before God (Rom. 5:10). Justification,

72. Brian S. Rosner, *Paul, Scripture and Ethics: A Study of 1 Corinthians 5–7* (Leiden: Brill, 1994), 190–91.

73. Todd A. Wilson argues that Paul's focus is the cessation of the law's curse for those who participate in redemption in Christ rather than the superfluity of the law per se. See Wilson, *The Curse of the Law and the Crisis in Galatia: Reassessing the Purpose of Galatians* (Tübingen: Mohr Siebeck, 2007).

74. Brian S. Rosner, *Paul and the Law: Keeping the Commandments of God* (Downers Grove, IL: IVP Academic, 2013), 45–205. Where he uses *replacement*, I'm using *fulfillment*, which I think better captures the unfolding narrative sense of Paul's thought. There is "one story" here, neither an ending and new beginning (supersessionism) nor two subsequent stories running in parallel to each other (*Sonderweg*).

forgiveness, new creation, and adoption into God's new covenant community is possible, not through the law, which could not impart life (Gal. 3:21), but only through God's grace in Christ. However, *taken on its own* (as in some forms of the OP), repudiation is an inadequate and potentially misleading description. Paul's view of the law is more subtle than simple rejection, as the next two points demonstrate.

Second, the Mosaic law is *fulfilled* by life in the Spirit (Gal. 5:5–6); the "entire law is fulfilled," not through Torah obedience, but in love of neighbor (Gal. 5:14). Paul tells the Galatians that "if you are led by the Spirit, you are not under the law" (Gal. 5:18). The fruit of the Spirit is held up in contrast to what the law could not accomplish ("against such things there is no law," Gal. 5:23). Galatian believers are to carry one another's burdens and so fulfill the law of Christ (Gal. 6:2).

Third, the law is *reappropriated* by Paul in at least two ways: (1) as prophecy, witnessing to the gospel of Jesus Christ, and (2) as a source for ethics. The former happens in multiple ways as Paul reflects theologically on the Scriptures in light of Christ. Rosner cites examples from 1 Corinthians, but dozens of others could be listed as Paul mines Scripture to explain the significance of Jesus's life, death, and resurrection. In Galatians, the Hagar/Sarah analogy fulfills this function as does Abraham himself. It is in this sense that Richard Hays argues that Paul's use of Abraham *confirms* rather than negates the law. Paul is doing Jewish theological interpretation to argue that the *Torah itself* points to the universally inclusive theology that affirms that God is the God of Jews and of gentiles.[75] Paul's gospel is actually a consummation of the Torah's promises (hence the arrow showing continuity between the people of God [Israel] and Jew and gentile believers in the new age of the Spirit, whom Paul calls the "Israel of God" [Gal. 6:16]). The latter form of reappropriation can also be seen in numerous places where the law is used as a source of moral guidance and wisdom. The "love command" for new Christian communities is developed from the Torah, where it applied to ethnic Israel (Gal. 5:14; Lev. 19:18). As James Thompson has elegantly demonstrated, the law has a positive place in Paul's ethics, but that place deliberately does not include the regulations on circumcision, Sabbath, food laws, and festivals. Paul "does not require the three boundary markers of the Torah that have become badges of Jewish identity"[76] because his focus is on the place of gentiles within the family of God. Contrary to some older perspectives, the apostle is not summarily dismissing the law. Rather, just as Israel is redefined in light of

---

75. Hays, *Conversion of the Imagination*, 61–84. Hays is discussing Abraham in Rom. 4, but the point stands.

76. Thompson, *Moral Formation*, 113. See pp. 111–34 and especially the discussion of the Old Testament background to Rom. 12–15.

the gospel (Gal. 3:28; Col. 3:11), so too the Torah has been restructured, or filtered, in light of Christ. The apostle's attitude to the law is well summed up in 1 Corinthians 7:19: "Circumcision is nothing and uncircumcision is nothing. Keeping God's commands is what counts." The law continues to frame Paul's moral teaching in a multitude of ways. As Richard Hays comments in his classic text on New Testament ethics, "The Old Testament suffuses the whole enterprise."[77] Where Paul does not explicitly appeal to Scripture as a basis for instruction (1 Thessalonians, Philippians, Philemon), he still thinks within Israel's symbolic world and Jewish moral tradition. In other writings, he often appeals to Scripture and assumes its narrative thought world to instruct on specific behavior.[78] Thompson puts it succinctly: "Paul shapes the moral consciousness of his gentile converts by instructing them with the vocabulary of ancient Israel."[79] Developing this point, Rosner makes a convincing case for how, when Paul faces issues such as tithing, stealing, idolatry, murder, incest, homosexual conduct, sexual immorality, marriage, and divorce, the law provides a critical and formative basis for his moral teaching. However, crucially, Paul does not use the law *as law* since his readers are not under the law. Rather, the law is developed as a source of wisdom for Christian living.[80]

Eschatology Restructured: Life in the Spirit in the Overlap of the Ages

This leads us, finally, to the third part of figure 4.1, where Paul now turns to look *forward* to articulate an eschatological vision for a life pleasing to God and "worthy of the gospel" (Phil. 1:27)[81]—the astonishing news of a crucified Messiah who "died for our sins according to the Scriptures" (1 Cor. 15:3) but whose resurrection means that "in Christ all will be made alive" before "God may be all in all" (1 Cor. 15:22, 28).[82] I'm proposing that Paul continues to practice "active, persistent, prayerful examination of personal experience and beliefs in light of Scripture and Jewish tradition" as he has to develop practical and ethical responses for "greater faithfulness" amid all the unpredictability, contingencies, and localized questions that arise within

77. Richard B. Hays, *The Moral Vision of the New Testament: Community, Cross, New Creation; A Contemporary Introduction to New Testament Ethics* (San Francisco: Harper-SanFrancisco, 1996), 309.
78. Thompson, *Moral Formation*, 115.
79. Ibid., 62.
80. Rosner, *Paul and the Law*, 159–205.
81. The idea of a worthy response to God's redemptive grace is a consistent theme in Paul: 1 Thess. 2:12, "worthy of God"; 2 Thess. 1:5, "worthy of the kingdom of God"; 2 Thess. 1:11, "worthy of his calling"; Eph. 4:1, "worthy of the calling"; Col. 1:10, "worthy of the Lord."
82. While it's obviously not from Galatians, I've inserted 1 Cor. 15:28 in the diagram as a pithy summary of Paul's eschatological vision.

his life of mission to the gentiles. He does this in light of his restructured monotheism/soteriology and restructured understanding of Israel/Torah; but to these we must add a third, and quite possibly the most radically innovative, theme within his theological framework—that of the Spirit. John Levison remarks that "antiquity has given us no writer more enamored of the spirit than the Apostle Paul."[83] Yet it is this aspect of Paul's theology, I suggest, that historically has tended to play second fiddle to the first two. However, setting the first two in tension to the work of the Spirit in the Christian life would be incomprehensible to Paul, whose breadth of vision needs to be understood in an integrated way *if due weight is to be given to his overwhelming concern for the moral transformation of new believers under his care.* This section, then, will attempt to outline the empowering and transformative role of the Spirit in the Christian life.

PAUL, THE SPIRIT, AND THE PEOPLE OF GOD

As we stay with Galatians for the moment, Paul begins the letter stating that the purpose of the atoning work of Jesus Christ was to "rescue us from the present evil age" (Gal. 1:4). Immediately it is evident that his pastoral response to the crisis is framed within a wider eschatological narrative. Galatians is typically Pauline in this respect; Hays summarizes it this way: "Paul sees the community of faith being caught up into the story of God's remaking of the world through Jesus Christ. Thus, to make ethical judgements is, for Paul, simply to recognize our place in the epic story of redemption."[84]

Figure 4.1 illustrates how the fulfillment of God's promise to Abraham has inaugurated a new age in his redemptive purposes for the world. This new age currently overlaps with the present one, which not only is "evil," but life under the law is associated with enslaving "basic principles of the world" (Gal. 4:3).[85] Paul prays that he may "never boast except in the cross of our Lord Jesus Christ, through which the world has been crucified to me, and I to the world. Neither circumcision nor uncircumcision means anything; what counts is the new creation" (Gal. 6:14–15; cf. 2 Cor. 5:17). While we don't have space for detailed exegesis, the overall picture is clear and reaffirmed repeatedly elsewhere. The new creation has broken into the present. This world "in its present form is passing away" (1 Cor. 7:31) and tends to be seen by Paul in a distinctly negative light. Regardless of previous religious identity, those marked by faith in Christ have "died" to their old

83. John R. Levison, *Filled with the Spirit* (Grand Rapids: Eerdmans, 2009), 253.
84. Hays, *Moral Vision*, 45–46.
85. Longenecker, *Galatians*, 166.

life. They now belong within the new creation and are to live accordingly (Gal. 6:9) as they "eagerly await by faith the righteousness for which we hope" (Gal. 5:5). The Christian life, therefore, is thoroughly eschatological. In this sense Moltmann is absolutely right: "From first to last, and not merely in the epilogue, Christianity is eschatology, is hope, forward looking and forward moving, and therefore also revolutionizing and transforming the present."[86]

But, while important, appreciating Paul's eschatological framework is, on its own, an inadequate basis from which to unlock the "heartbeat" of the apostle's theology of the Christian life. Paul is no Enlightenment rationalist. He forcefully reminds the Galatians that their Christian lives began through faith in the crucified Christ *and the intimately linked gift of the Spirit* (Gal. 3:1–3). Similarly, it is by the Spirit *alone*, not through the Torah, that they can attain their goal. While the goal is not specified, Paul later expresses his heartfelt (motherly!) concern that "Christ is formed" in his "dear children" (Gal. 4:19). In this sense, *the goal of the Christian life is profoundly relational*—to be conformed to the image of the Son (Rom. 8:29; 2 Cor. 3:18). This process of transformation happens through "the Spirit of his Son," whom God sent into believers' hearts and who enables them to call God *Abba* (Gal. 4:6). Paul's Christology and pneumatology are inseparable and are located within the breathtaking scope of his reframed eschatology.[87]

Therefore, justification is not an end in itself, nor is it primarily individualistic. Too often the promised blessing has been limited to soteriology/justification and Abraham portrayed as an individual, to be imitated today, who "discovered" justification by faith alone over against works. Rather, Paul's concern is to show that the patriarch is the "father" of *both* Jewish and gentile believers. His focus is more on Abraham as an inclusive representative character through whom God's blessing flows to all nations, not through physical descent but through faith in Jesus (Rom. 4:23–25). God's promised blessing results in a reconstituted *people* of God, both Jew and gentile, led and empowered by the Spirit (not by the law, Gal. 5:18), who *alone* enables believers to fulfill the law (Gal. 5:14, 22; cf. Rom. 8:4). Nowhere else does the apostle expound more explicitly how the coming of the Spirit fulfills and transcends the old covenant than in 2 Corinthians 3:3–18. There, through

86. Jürgen Moltmann, *Theology of Hope: On the Ground and the Implications of a Christian Eschatology* (Minneapolis: Fortress, 1993), 16.
87. Elsewhere in Paul, the Spirit is the "deposit" or "seal" (Eph. 1:12–14; 2 Cor. 1:21–22) or "firstfruits" (Rom. 8:23) indicating that God's new age has invaded the present and will be consummated in the future.

allusion to Jeremiah 31, Ezekiel 36, and Exodus 34, Paul argues that it is in the covenant of the Spirit that believers are freed from the bondage of the law, which had a temporary, fading glory and actually prevented Israel from truly understanding the law and seeing the Lord (2 Cor. 3:14–15).[88] Given such a strong contrast, it is not surprising that Preston Sprinkle concludes that, in comparison to Qumran and other Jewish sources, Paul exhibits marked *discontinuity* in the way he "locates the transformation of the human heart in the eschatological work of the Spirit."[89]

The Galatians' reception of the Spirit by faith, *just as much as their justification by faith*, is a fulfillment of the blessing promised by God to Abraham (Gal. 3:14). John Bertone makes the valid point that whenever Paul reminds believers of the decisive moment of their conversion, he consistently points them to the role played by the Spirit and includes *himself* along with his readers (e.g., Rom. 5:5, "God's love has been poured out into *our* hearts through the Holy Spirit, who has been given to *us*").[90] Bertone argues that pneumatology is the interpretative key to Paul's new perspective on the law and is likely rooted in the apostle's own transformative experience. As a result, Paul's pneumatology "should not be absorbed by his Christology."[91] One does not have to follow all of Bertone's complex argument to acknowledge his point. Coming at the same issue from another direction, David Beck has argued that "pneumatology has taken a subordinationistic tone" within the institutional churches of the Reformation. In a significant study, he reflects on how the Reformers located the work of the Spirit in the sacraments and the Word and identified the Spirit as the agent through whom Christ's atonement is applied to all believers. A consequence has been that the Spirit's work has "become a function of the church and Christ."[92] This subordinationistic tendency is reflected, for example, in Barth's treatment of the Spirit as a mode through whom Christ is present and active in the world. This sort of "institutional pneumatology" has strengths but fails to do justice to Paul's rich, deep, and

88. M. Turner, *The Holy Spirit and Spiritual Gifts: Then and Now* (Carlisle: Paternoster, 1996), 114–15.

89. Sprinkle, *Paul and Judaism Revisited*, 241. For Levison, Ezek. 36–37 is paradigmatic for Paul and Qumran in how the corporate gift of the Spirit is also deeply personal. The more important point of contrast with Qumran is how Paul associates the Spirit with death, new creation, and resurrection life. See Levison, *Filled with the Spirit*, 253–316.

90. See also Rom. 8:15–16: "The Spirit you received brought about your adoption to sonship. And by him *we* cry, 'Abba, Father.' The Spirit himself testifies with *our* spirit that *we* are God's children."

91. John A. Bertone, *The Law of the Spirit: Experience of the Spirit and Displacement of the Law in Romans 8:1–16* (New York: Peter Lang, 2005), 315.

92. T. David Beck, *The Holy Spirit and the Renewal of All Things: Pneumatology in Paul and Jürgen Moltmann* (Cambridge, UK: James Clarke & Co., 2010), 1.

pervasive pneumatology that shapes his thought and experience. Importantly for our discussion, Beck argues that it is the complex, all-embracing vision of Paul's eschatology that is critical to countering a reductionism that isolates one figure or event as the key to the story of salvation at the expense of others. Whenever this happens, the "impact on theology is deleterious," and in regard to the Spirit, an anemic pneumatology usually results.[93] While evidently it is correct to see Paul's theology as Christocentric, even Christ "takes his place within a greater narrative," and rather than see "Christ as the hub of eschatology, with all other events and figures connected to him like spokes on a wheel," Beck proposes that in Paul's theology, if there is a hub, it is God the Father, who sends Christ and the Spirit to redeem all of creation for the sake of his own glory.[94] The relevance of Beck's argument in terms of the distorting effects of an overly dominant theology of justification is clearly apparent.

No one has demonstrated the absolutely crucial role of the Spirit for Paul in *every aspect* of Christian life and experience more than Gordon Fee in his magisterial, and still unsurpassed, *God's Empowering Presence: The Holy Spirit in the Letters of Paul*. Through detailed exegesis, Fee demonstrates that the visible reality of the eschatological Spirit meant for Paul "the return of God's own personal presence to dwell in and among his people." For this reason Paul can describe them corporately as God's temple (1 Cor. 3:16–17) and even their bodies as "temples of the Holy Spirit" (1 Cor. 6:19). This corresponds to how Paul elsewhere describes the new communities of Christians in the language of Israel. They are *laos* (a people, 2 Cor. 6:16; Titus 2:14; also used in the Septuagint to refer to Israel); *hagioi* (saints), a common Pauline term that echoes Israel's identity in Exodus 19:5–6; *elect* (linking to Israel, God's chosen people, 1 Thess. 1:4; 2 Thess. 2:13; Col. 3:12; Eph. 1:4, 11); the *Israel of God* (a unique phrase in Gal. 6:16 explicitly locating believing Jews and gentiles corporately within Israel); and *ekklēsia* (the church, used in the Septuagint as a translation of the Hebrew *qāhāl*—the congregation of Israel). Fee concludes that "this abundant use of Old Testament 'people' language makes it clear that Paul saw the church not only as in continuity with the old covenant people of God, but as in the true succession of that people."[95] Figure 4.1 attempts to capture this sense of both continuity and

93. Ibid., 233–36. Beck gives an example of Moltmann's pneumatology in *Theology of Hope*.
94. Ibid., 236.
95. Gordon Fee, *God's Empowering Presence: The Holy Spirit in the Letters of Paul* (Grand Rapids: Baker Academic, 1994), 871. This is not to deny that the apostle also holds that God's promises to Israel are irrevocable (Rom. 9–11), but how to interpret Paul's argument continues to be an issue of lively debate.

discontinuity; the *one story* of the people of God continues to unfold,[96] yet now, through Christ and the Spirit, believing gentiles have been included in that story on equal terms within a reconstituted "family" of God in which all members are *adelphoi*.[97]

LIFE "ACCORDING TO THE SPIRIT" VERSUS LIFE "ACCORDING TO THE FLESH"

This brings us to Paul's antithesis between the Spirit and the flesh (*sarx*) in Galatians 5 and elsewhere (Rom. 8:3–17; Phil. 3:3). The historically dominant paradigm has been to assume an internal spiritual conflict *within* the believer—her "sinful nature" battling against her new "spiritual nature."[98] This has been tied to an interpretation of Romans 7 as describing the rather desperate (and pessimistic) inner struggle of the Christian life. It is not difficult to see how closely such a view has often been tied to the OP with its focus on individual soteriology and its duality between law and grace. In a significant work on the Spirit/flesh contrast in Galatians, Walter Russell traces how Luther's remark on Galatians 5:16 that "there be two contrary captains in you, the Spirit and the flesh," has been "repeated in some fashion by almost every commentator since."[99] This sort of belief continues to be massively popular within contemporary Christian spirituality. *Flesh*, in this perspective, is seen as an anthropological term: Paul viewing humanity in a vertical and metaphysical sense, with *sarx* and *pneuma* becoming two capacities or "natures" within the individual. The Christian life becomes, in this view, an ongoing battle of the will between two natures. It is in this context that Luther's dictum *simul iustus et peccator* is best interpreted.

However, as we have seen, Paul's framing of Abraham, Christ, justification, the law, Israel, and the place of believing gentiles has been within an unfolding historical/theological narrative (Gal. 1–4). It is more consistent, and exegetically persuasive, that Paul, rather than jumping to a highly introspective analysis of a Christian's inner struggles, continues to develop his argument in Galatians 5–6 within this broader framework. The erroneousness of the

96. Contra Mark Nanos, who appears to propose a sort of "tripartite covenant" *Sonderweg* scenario, in which Paul's fellow Jews who did not believe in Christ were nevertheless still in the covenant, while Jews and gentiles who did believe continued to be distinguished by Torah observance. See Nanos, "A Jewish View," in Bird, *Four Views on the Apostle Paul*, 159–93.

97. Paul uses this term over 120 times in his seven undisputed letters. The church is ultimately a fellowship of siblings in which all are equal.

98. Such a paradigm has been reflected and bolstered by translations rendering *sarx* as "sinful nature" (NIV 1984), "lower nature" (NEB), and "human nature" (GNT).

99. Walter Russell, *The Flesh/Spirit Conflict in Galatians* (Oxford: University Press of America, 1997), 7.

"inner conflict" interpretation is highlighted in how Paul talks about the acts of the flesh in *overwhelmingly* negative terms that are *utterly incompatible* with the kingdom of God (Gal. 5:19–21) and that lead to destruction (Gal. 6:8; cf. Rom. 8:13). Romans 8:5–8 describes not an inner conflict but two distinct groups of people, one which lives *kata sarka* (according to the flesh) and the other which lives *kata pneuma* (according to the Spirit). It is *impossible* for the former to please God (Rom. 8:8). It thus becomes inconceivable that the flesh could be part of a Christian's inner identity. Rather, Paul is contrasting life within the overlap of the ages: life according to the flesh versus new life according to the Spirit. Max Turner, one of the foremost theologians of the Spirit around today, puts it this way: "Life 'according to the flesh' is not life according to some anthropological part of me that the Spirit opposes, but the totality of the old human order of existence. For believers, 'the flesh' in the latter sense has been decisively put away, 'crucified' as Galatians 5:24 puts it (like 'the world' of Gal. 6:14)."[100]

Life *kata sarka* is life without Christ and without the Spirit (Rom. 8:9); it is life still under condemnation, sin, and death (8:1–2); it is life hostile to God (8:6). The law could not overcome sin because it was "weakened by the flesh" (8:3). Note how the law itself is not equated with sin; its problem is essentially that it *does not have the power to produce life* because it belongs to the old age. Only the Spirit can give life (8:11). "The alternative to the Spirit and life is the flesh and death."[101] Only in Christ are sin and death overcome. Only those in Christ who live by the Spirit can fulfill the law (8:3–4). Life *kata pneuma* leads to life and peace with God. It is at this point that one could wish that another *sola* had been articulated at the Reformation—*solus Spiritus*[102]—for the Christian life is life in the Spirit from beginning to end.

LIVING THE CHRISTIAN LIFE

All of this is not to deny that the Christian life involves spiritual conflict, tough moral choices, temptation, sinful failure, repentance, and personal transformation. The enduring popularity of the view that the Christian life is an inner conflict of two competing "natures" is due to how well it corresponds to the realities of personal experience. Nevertheless, the fact remains

---

100. Turner, *Holy Spirit*, 125.

101. J. D. G. Dunn, "'The Lord, the Giver of Life': The Gift of the Spirit as Both Life-Giving and Empowering," in *The Spirit and Christ in the New Testament and Christian Theology: Essays in Honor of Max Turner*, ed. I. H. Marshall, V. Rabens, and C. Bennema (Grand Rapids: Eerdmans, 2012), 12.

102. By this I do not mean that there is no place for human cooperation with the Spirit in the Christian life. As with other *solas*, the idea is not isolation but primacy.

that this is simply not what Paul has in mind. His concern is to affirm that God's promises have been fulfilled and that the Spirit *alone* is sufficient for life in the new age where Torah no longer applies (see fig. 4.1).

What then does the all-too-real struggle of the Christian life consist of? To sketch it briefly, beginning with Romans 8:9–11, the Spirit *alone* identifies those who belong to Christ (v. 9). Each believer is indwelt by the Spirit—the empowering personal presence of God. The presence of the Spirit indicates that the believer has life *now* because of the righteousness effected for her by Christ.[103] Yet the reality is that her physical body will die because sin and death still reign (v. 10; cf. Rom. 5:12). Her present experience of the Spirit, however, gives a sure and certain hope that her mortal body will be resurrected through the Spirit as Christ has been (8:11). This idea is paralleled in 1 Corinthians 15:44, in which Paul contrasts the natural body (*sōma psychikos*) with the resurrected spiritual body (*sōma pneumatikos*). The Christian life for Paul consists of a paradox—of outer decline, suffering, and death coinciding with inner empowering, transformation, and hope that will culminate in a glorious resurrected body (Rom. 8:29; 1 Cor. 15:49; Phil. 3:21) within a renewed creation (Rom. 8:18–25; 1 Cor. 15:24–28). So both the "natural" and "spiritual" body "belong" to the Spirit, and everything done in the body should honor the Spirit. Fee comments, "If that is too somatic for those whose deepest roots are in the basically dualistic Western philosophical tradition, it is not so for Paul."[104] Paul's vision for the Christian life consistently embraces this tension between the external/now/physical weakness and the internal/not-yet/spiritual renewal.[105]

"Externally," the Christian life inevitably involves suffering—usually in the form of persecution and opposition (e.g., Gal. 5:11; Rom. 8:18). There is therefore no contradiction at all in the apostle's mind between a dynamic individual and corporate life in the Spirit and the experience of weakness. The apostle can "*delight* in weaknesses, in insults, in hardships, in persecutions, in difficulties" (2 Cor. 12:10)[106] precisely because these things point to how Christ was "crucified in weakness, yet he lives by God's power" (2 Cor. 13:4), and thus to how his followers, while presently weak, look forward to a similar destiny.[107] Suffering is interpreted eschatologically: it produces perseverance, character,

103. Fee, *God's Empowering Presence*, 549.

104. Ibid., 268.

105. For useful discussion on this theme, see Wojciech Szypuła, *The Holy Spirit in the Eschatological Tension of Christian Life: An Exegetico-Theological Study of 2 Corinthians 5:1–5 and Romans 8:18–27* (Rome: Gregorian Press, 2008).

106. See 2 Cor. 11–13 and Rom. 8:26; 1 Cor. 2:3; 15:43.

107. In discussion of the Spirit and suffering in Acts, Keith Warrington concludes that suffering is to be incorporated into the Christian life with fortitude and joy as it was by Old

and hope in the here and now (Rom. 5:2–4); it is radically relativized to such a degree that it can be described as "light and momentary troubles" (2 Cor. 4:17; cf. Rom. 8:18); it paradoxically reveals Christ's life (2 Cor. 4:10–12); it is even a way to know Christ, the crucified Messiah (Phil. 3:9–10). In light of this, Turner comments that the "Christian life is no smooth transformation. It is the jagged process of the destruction of the 'outer man' and renewal of the inner." Paul's account of life in the Spirit is dominated by the cross as well as the resurrection.[108]

To speculate for a moment, it is likely that such an understanding of the Christian life is counterintuitive for much of contemporary Western Christianity. The church exists within a relentlessly this-worldly, hypercapitalist culture dedicated to an endless process of generating and meeting (if temporarily) restless desires for comfort, pleasure, and happiness.[109] In such a context, to embrace and rejoice in suffering becomes both incoherent and incomprehensible. Suffering is not something to be enjoyed or sought, but for Paul it was a welcome opportunity to follow Christ. If the church loses Paul's razor-sharp awareness of the eschatological shape to the Christian life, the motive for mission and discipleship inevitably drains away.

"Internally" or "spiritually," as we have seen, the goal of the Christian life is eschatological: to be conformed to the image of the Son. Paul prays that believers would be "blameless for the day of Christ" (Phil. 1:10; cf. 1 Thess. 3:13). But how does this work? Paul's revolutionary answer is, again, by the Spirit *alone*. Thompson contrasts this response with the Greco-Roman and Jewish answers to moral advancement.[110] In the Greco-Roman world, lack of control of the passions (*pathēmata*—things like desire, pleasure, love, and grief) hindered a moral life. Because the passions were linked to false beliefs, there was optimism that human flourishing would develop if one was educated to be in harmony with a proper view of existence. For the Stoics, since the passions had destructive force, the goal was not so much their control as their elimination through reason, a cure for the diseased soul and the path to virtue. In the Jewish world, the Torah was the path to life and blessing and a means of overcoming evil desires and injustice.

Paul eschews both reason and Torah as means of overcoming the *desires* of the flesh (Gal. 5:16, 24), which result in destructive and enslaving "acts

Testament prophets, Peter, Paul, and Jesus himself. See Warrington, "Suffering and the Spirit in Luke-Acts," *Journal of Biblical and Pneumatological Research* 1 (2009): 15–32.

108. Turner, *Holy Spirit*, 127.

109. For an excellent analysis of these themes, see William T. Cavanaugh, *Being Consumed: Economics and Christian Desire* (Grand Rapids: Eerdmans, 2009).

110. Thompson, *Moral Formation*, 135–56.

of the flesh" (5:19–21). He is at once more negative and more positive than either Greek or Jewish options. His anthropology is negative in that, while the law is good and holy, it cannot be kept, and reason is not the path to virtue. The *only way* of overcoming such desires is to "walk by the Spirit" (5:16), be "led by the Spirit" (v. 18), and "keep in step with the Spirit" (v. 25). Paul is positive in that he is supremely confident that if someone lives by the Spirit, they "will not gratify the desires of the flesh" (v. 16). Such a life will result in moral flourishing that fulfills the purpose of the law, made visible in community marked by the fruit of the Spirit: love, joy, peace, patience, kindness, goodness, faithfulness, gentleness, and self-control. The basis for Paul's confidence is Christ's death and resurrection: those "who belong to Christ Jesus have *crucified* the flesh with its passions and desires" (v. 24). The subsequent life-giving work of the Spirit has ushered believers into the new creation, leaving behind the age of the flesh. This represents an astonishingly assured vision of the Christian life as one of freedom from sin, death, and the flesh (5:1, 13).

Yet Paul is not claiming that life in the Spirit is one of triumphant progress beyond the possibility of going back to the old life of the flesh; his exhortations not to return to the flesh are clearly not hypothetical (Rom. 8:12–13; Gal. 5:13; 6:8). It is this tension, or ambiguity, in Paul between the empowering experience of the Spirit and the continuing reality of the flesh that leads to differing interpretations of how exactly moral transformation "works." Dunn, while in substantial agreement with the eschatological framework described here and on the transforming experience of the Spirit, has a more negative emphasis on the Christian life as one of inner conflict and frustration, driven largely by exegesis of Romans 7:14–8:25 as describing the simultaneous Christian struggle of life in the overlapping ages of flesh and Spirit.[111] Turner puts it this way: "The believer is not 'free' simply to drift as she wishes. She is caught up in a cosmic war, and so she must actively take her side either with the Spirit (leading to life) or with the flesh (leading to destruction)."[112] While Fee is the most positive, he says little about the reality of the internal struggle of the Christian life, arguing that Paul simply presupposes believers have a dynamic experience of the Spirit.[113] It is this lacuna in Fee's work that Volker Rabens has sought to fill in an outstanding recent work on the theological and practical

---

111. James D. G. Dunn, *Jesus and the Spirit: A Study of the Religious and Charismatic Experience of Jesus and the First Christians as Reflected in the New Testament* (London: SCM, 1975), 308–18. See also Dunn, *The Theology of Paul's Letter to the Galatians* (Cambridge: Cambridge University Press, 1993), 101–20.

112. Turner, *Holy Spirit*, 126.

113. Fee, *God's Empowering Presence*, 433.

aspects of how the Spirit transforms and empowers believers for religious-ethical living.[114] In brief, and at the risk of oversimplifying a rich and detailed thesis, he proposes a relational approach to the work of the Spirit whereby the Spirit effects ethical life through "*intimate relationships* created by the Spirit *with God [Abba], Jesus and fellow believers.*"[115] A believer is brought into the sphere of influence of the Spirit. One consequence is a more remote relation to the flesh and a new set of Spirit-created relationships. It is the dynamic interplay of these relationships that leads to gradual *transformation* as well as empowerment for living the Christian life.

Rabens's study is a forceful reminder of how, for Paul, individual discipleship is always imagined within a corporate context. But more than simply stating this truism, it is when believers are *together*, as a *fellowship* of the Spirit that experiences the *love* of God through the *grace* of the Lord Jesus Christ (2 Cor. 13:14), that spiritual transformation and empowering occurs. Paul is in no doubt that churches, which are eschatological communities of the Spirit,[116] will be attractive places where the presence of God is manifest even while the flesh remains a powerful force in the world. Paul's frequent "one another" language describes the radical commitment that believers show one another. They are members of one another (Rom. 12:5; Eph. 4:25) and are to build up one another (1 Thess. 5:11; Rom. 14:19); to care for one another (1 Thess. 3:12; 4:19; 2 Thess. 1:3; Rom. 13:8); to pursue one another's good (1 Thess. 5:15); to bear with one another in love (Eph. 4:2); to bear one another's burdens (Gal. 6:2); to be kind and compassionate to one another, forgiving one another (Eph. 4:32; Col. 3:13); to submit to one another (Eph. 5:21); to consider one another better than oneself (Phil. 2:3); to be devoted to one another in love (Rom. 12:10); and to live in harmony with one another (Rom. 12:16). While not always stated explicitly, it is the vital role of the Spirit that enables this process both to begin and to be sustained.

The corporate context for the Christian life also leads us to our final point: the central place of love in the apostle's ethics. His churches (like many today) were mixed communities across boundaries of race, religious background, personality, gender, socioeconomic status, education, intelligence, age, theology, language, culture, and spiritual experience. Holding together such diversity in unity was one of Paul's continual challenges—and is why most of his

---

114. Volker Rabens, *The Holy Spirit and Ethics in Paul: Transformation and Empowering for Religious-Ethical Life* (Minneapolis: Fortress, 2013).

115. Ibid., 126 (emphasis original).

116. Richard N. Longenecker, "Paul's Vision of the Church and Community Formation in His Major Missionary Letters," in *Studies in Paul, Exegetical and Theological* (Sheffield: Sheffield Phoenix, 2004), 73–88.

letters are written in the first place. While Thompson cautions that love was not Paul's only criterion for behavior, it is without doubt *the* indispensable core attitude for every aspect of the Christian life within the newly formed family of God.[117] This is a big topic, which we can only touch on here.[118] As an illustration, we can return to our sample text of Galatians. Paul states (remarkably) that "the *only thing* that counts is faith expressing itself through love"—neither circumcision nor uncircumcision has any continuing relevance (Gal. 5:6). Love is the first characteristic of the fruit of the Spirit, a primacy of place typical for Paul (Gal. 5:22).[119] The Christian life is not antinomian; rather the *purpose* of Christian freedom from the flesh is to "serve one another humbly in love" (Gal. 5:13). Echoing Jesus and Leviticus 19:18, Paul says that "the whole law is summed up in a single commandment, 'You shall love your neighbor as yourself'" (Gal. 5:14 NRSV; cf. Rom. 13:8–10). Even this quick survey demonstrates how love is understood as *a climax of Paul's narrative theology and is inseparable from the new covenant ministry of the Spirit.* As believers actively "keep in step" with the Spirit, it "produces" love in their lives.[120] It is through the Spirit that believers experience God's love (Rom. 5:5). The love of God has been most supremely demonstrated in Christ's death on the cross (Rom. 5:8). Indeed, it is fair to say that Paul's letters are saturated in love. God's people are loved by God (1 Thess. 1:4; 2 Thess. 2:13, 16; Rom. 1:7; 2 Cor. 13:11, 14; Eph. 1:4–5; 2:4; 3:17–19; 5:1–2; Col. 3:12). Nothing in all creation will be able to separate them from his love expressed in Jesus (Rom. 8:37–39). Believers are to act in love for one another (1 Thess. 4:9; Rom. 14:15; 1 Cor. 8:1; Eph. 4:2, 15–16; Phil. 2:1–2; Col. 2:2). Famously, in 1 Corinthians 13:1–3 Paul teaches that all Christian life and ministry is of no value at all if it is not done in love. At the close of the letter he simply commands, "Do everything in love" (1 Cor. 16:14). This all-embracing command is echoed in Ephesians 5:2 ("walk in the way of love"), in Colossians 3:14 ("put on love," which is at the top of a list of virtues), and in 1 Thessalonians 5:8, in which Paul includes himself in the exhortation to "put on faith and love." The apostle often expresses his deep love for his communities (e.g., 1 Thess. 2:8; 1 Cor. 16:24; 2 Cor. 2:4; 11:11; Phil. 4:1). Husbands are to love their wives (Eph. 5:25; Col. 3:19). Paul prays that believers' love would grow (1 Thess. 3:12; Phil. 1:9) and is glad to hear of a church's love (e.g., 1 Thess. 3:6; 2 Thess. 1:3). He is thankful when Christ is preached "out of love" (Phil. 1:16). He rejoices when he hears of believers' love for God's people (Col. 1:4; Philem. 5, 7) and

117. Thompson, *Moral Formation*, 12.
118. For discussion of "putting love into practice," see ibid., 157–80.
119. Fee, *God's Empowering Presence*, 446.
120. See Col. 1:8, in which Epaphras tells Paul of the Colossians' "love in the Spirit."

prays that the Lord would direct their "hearts into God's love" (2 Thess. 3:5). Rather than use apostolic authority, he prefers to appeal to Philemon about Onesimus "on the basis of love" (Philem. 9).

By any measure, this is an extraordinary picture of Paul the man, his theology, and his vision of the Christian life. It is also remarkable, and telling for how Paul's theology has been so often atomized, how relatively marginalized a Pauline theology of love has been within Protestantism given that love is a much more pervasive theme in his writings than, for example, justification.[121] Consistent with all that we have discussed, love is to be understood eschatologically. Out of the triumvirate of faith, hope, and love, it is love alone that continues in the new creation to come (see fig. 4.1) and is therefore the greatest (1 Cor. 13:13).

Conclusion

If we have covered a lot of ground—from Christology and soteriology, to multifaceted use of the Torah, to a life of love within the new age of the Spirit that overlaps with the flesh—it is only because we've been trying to sketch (literally) something of the theological depth, breathtaking scope, and consistently pastoral focus of Paul's thought. At the (considerable!) risk of oversimplification as someone "looking in" to the OP/NP debates of the last four decades, I wonder if a significant factor is how difficult it is to pin down the genius of Paul the "inspired reflective practitioner." The OP developed out of soteriological concerns of the Reformation period and recaptured the glorious truth of justification by faith alone. But, as is often the case, a strength (in this case a single-minded focus on justification) can also be a weakness (marginalization of other Pauline themes, particularly the Spirit and the Christian life). The NP, in various and often conflicting ways, has been wrestling with those broader questions. While details of how to hold the complexity of Paul's theological vision together will undoubtedly continue to be vigorously debated, the NP's significant contribution has been to remind us of how Paul's gospel is a rich, integrated, and hopeful narrative structured around what God has done in Christ and the Spirit. This narrative gives urgency and purpose to the "race" of the Christian life

---

121. Two studies, of a handful, are Victor Paul Furnish, *The Love Command in the New Testament* (Nashville: Abingdon, 1972), and Leon Morris, *Testaments of Love: A Study of Love in the Bible* (Grand Rapids: Eerdmans, 1981). The superb 2010 *Cape Town Commitment* of the Lausanne Movement is, to my knowledge, the first major evangelical statement of faith that is structured around the theme of love. See http://www.lausanne.org/content/ctc/ctcommitment.

(e.g., Gal. 2:2; 1 Cor. 9:24) and encourages good works (Gal. 6:9–10). It is appropriate to give the last word to Paul: "Therefore, my dear brothers and sisters, stand firm. Let nothing move you. Always give yourselves fully to the work of the Lord, because you know that your labor in the Lord is not in vain" (1 Cor. 15:58).

5

Participation in the New-Creation People of God in Christ by the Spirit

Timothy G. Gombis

The revolution in Pauline studies over the last four decades initially challenged and now has broken the dominance of a singularly Protestant reading of Paul focused on justification by faith. One result of the reconfiguration of the interpretive field is the reminder that Paul did not write a systematic theology, nor are his letters works of abstract theological reflection on the character of salvation as applied to the individual Christian. He wrote letters to churches, giving them counsel toward fruitful community dynamics, and the theological notions he brought to bear were determined by his knowledge of the situation and his relationship to that church. When we reflect on how Paul regarded topics such as the Christian life, we are reminded that we are answering this question from our reflection on Paul's letters as *contingent documents*.

Another result of the altered interpretive landscape is the space created for reading justification in the contexts of Paul's arguments and for allowing many other aspects of Paul's richly textured theology to emerge into view. Without necessarily downplaying the importance of justification, it now seems plain that it is one among a number of images and metaphors for configuring the character of Christian identity.

I will argue that the focus of Paul's reflection on the Christian life is the church, the new-creation people of God made up of individuals-in-community. Paul does not conceive of individuals living the Christian life in isolation from the community. Because these communities derive their identities (their history, language, mission, symbols, patterns of relating, and social dynamics) from the biblical storyline, I will situate the Christian life within the narrative of Scripture, stretching from creation to new creation, touching down in Israel and determined ultimately by the faithful life of Jesus.

I will then discuss how baptism into Christ by the Spirit functions as the starting point for Paul in thinking about the Christian life. The Spirit unites believers to God in Christ and unites them vitally to one another. This twofold work of reconciliation stands at the center of Paul's theological vision and is certainly the heart of his pastoral impulse. In the remainder of my essay, I will trace how Paul depicts the Christian life as participation in the new-creation people of God and participation in God himself.

Humanity in the Narrative of Israel's Scriptures

In several of his letters, Paul interprets the dynamics of Christian discipleship in terms of the larger sweep of the narrative of Scripture. In Galatians 3–4, Paul addresses community conflicts in terms of God's relationships with Abraham and with Israel through Moses. Beyond merely looking to the Scriptures for illustrations of spiritual principles, Paul regards the biblical narrative that reveals God's ways with Israel and his aim to bless the nations as the proper frame of reference for how the Galatians should pursue Christian living.

In his letter to the Roman Christians, Paul also shapes his argument in terms of the overarching narrative of Israel's Scriptures. He explicitly notes that his gospel establishes the law (Rom. 3:31), and his presentation from beginning to end is saturated with biblical allusions and quotations. Just as in Galatians, his appeals to Scripture do not indicate that Paul envisions it as something that can be set aside now that a superior divine order has arrived. The Law and the Prophets function authoritatively for Paul. They shape his thought and orient the counsel he gives his churches and the commands he issues. It will be helpful, then, to revisit how the Scriptures portray God's aims for humanity in order to set the backdrop for how Paul conceives of the Christian life.[1]

---

1. N. T. Wright develops the biblical narrative that shaped the early Christian outlook as the backdrop to Paul's theology in *Paul and the Faithfulness of God* (Minneapolis: Fortress, 2013), 475–537.

Genesis 1–2 indicates that God established creation as his temple, the place that would manifest the glory of his sovereign kingship.[2] God created humanity as "the image of God," which meant that humanity would depict the reign of the creator God in all their activity. God called humanity to reproduce over the face of the earth, to fill it and subdue it (Gen. 1:26, 28). Their overseeing the spread of *shalom* on behalf of the creator God, along with their relating to one another, was the manner in which they carried out their identity as "the image of God," a synonymous expression to "the glory of God."[3] They glorified God as they faithfully carried out God's commands. From the beginning, Adam and Eve each had a distinct identity, but essential to their identity was their relation to each other and their relation to God. Each of them was "the image of God," and together they were "the image of God." According to Scripture, the corporate obedience of Adam and Eve together faithfully represented the unseen creator God within his creation.

Genesis 3 records the fall of humanity into sin—the failure of Adam and Eve to rule over creation on God's behalf. In Paul's retelling, humanity "exchanged the glory of the immortal God for images resembling a mortal human being or birds or four-footed animals or reptiles" (Rom. 1:23).[4] That is, humanity failed to image the rule of the Creator within God's temple. Rather than glorifying God, representing his rule within creation, humanity came to image something *within* creation—the serpent in the first instance, but later other humans, or some other community's vision of the ideal human. For Paul, this is the folly of idolatry. Humans were designed to rule, to oversee the spread of God's sovereign rule of *shalom* to every corner of creation, to conduct their bodies with dignity, to relate to one another with honor and self-giving love. Such conduct would have pointed to something beyond themselves as that which is far greater.

The folly of idolatry, however, is the holistic mode of life that points to something beyond that is lifeless (a piece of wood or stone) or that God originally designed for humanity to rule over (e.g., the serpent or some other

2. John H. Walton, *The Lost World of Genesis One* (Downers Grove, IL: IVP Academic, 2009), 71–91. For the manner in which this notion works throughout Scripture, see G. K. Beale, *The Temple and the Church's Mission: A Biblical Theology of the Dwelling Place of God* (Downers Grove, IL: InterVarsity, 2004).

3. Paul links "glory" and "image" in Rom. 1:23. Humanity surrendered being "the glory of God" within creation, playing their role as the image of the transcendent God, not by setting up images of created things; rather, through their behavior they made themselves into the "image" or "glory" of such corruptible things. Paul elucidates the long human history of idolatry as absolute folly. That humanity would surrender being the glory of the creator God for being the glory of something corruptible within creation is foolish (v. 22) and dishonorable (v. 24).

4. Scripture quotations in this chapter, unless otherwise noted, are from the NRSV.

creature). Through idolatry humanity has become dishonorable (Rom. 1:24–32), no longer glorifying God or imaging him properly.

It is important to note what was lost at "the fall" so that we can see what God has set out to recover in his redemptive mission. God intended for his sovereign rule to be imaged through the gradual but persistent spread of humanity throughout the entire world. Humans would glorify the Creator through their relations with one another, their care for the creation itself, and, according to Paul, their honoring God as the Creator and giving him thanks for all good things (Rom. 1:21; 1 Tim. 4:4). The scriptural depiction of what has gone wrong is far-reaching and holistic, and God's redemptive purposes are just as holistic and comprehensive.

After their corruption, Adam and Eve no longer pursue each other's flourishing. They now too often seek to undermine each other. Rather than enjoying God's blessing alongside Abel, Cain murders his younger brother (Gen. 4:1–16). Rather than behaving honorably, humanity behaves dishonorably, shamefully relating to one another (Gen. 9:18–27). Rather than scattering to oversee the universal spread of *shalom*, humanity seeks to gather and rally around idolatrous purposes (Gen. 11:1–9).

By the end of Genesis 11, the knowledge of God has been lost. No one on earth is imaging God, glorifying him, making his name great within creation. It's at this point—at this hopeless moment—that God begins to reclaim the world through Abraham. God calls Abraham, a pagan, and makes him a series of promises. God will make him into a great nation and through him will bless the nations of the world (Gen. 12:1–3). This initial move of God is in direct continuity with his creation purposes. God had wanted humanity to spread throughout all creation, worshiping and serving him alone—imaging him and glorifying him. God called Abraham as the solution to this specific problem. The nations of the world were not worshiping the creator God, and God aimed to set this right.

Abraham's family became a great nation while in Egypt, and in the paradigmatic accomplishment of salvation, God himself made his name great (Exod. 6:1–9; 11:9; Rom. 9:17) by defeating Pharaoh and freeing God's people from slavery. God called Israel to a new vocation—they were to be the light of the world, a kingdom of priests (Exod. 19:6). They were to bring the nations to the creator God and the one true God to the nations. That is, Israel was called to teach the nations how to worship the God of Israel *as the nations*.[5]

5. The challenge of understanding how to worship the God of Israel while not being "under the law" existed from the very beginning. By God's design, Israel and the nations to which they were sent would have needed to figure out how those who weren't Israelites would follow the law while not becoming Israel.

They were to be a "holy people," a nation set apart unto God, and one that demonstrated the true character of the creator God in their nation's relational conduct, foreign and domestic policies, treatment of the poor, and waging of warfare. That is, Israel's existence and its holistic national mode of life were to image God, glorifying him and demonstrating to the nations of the world the character of Israel's God, calling out in hope that they would turn to worship the one true God.

While this was Israel's commission, they failed to be faithful to it (Ps. 78:1–72; Ezek. 16:1–52; Rom. 3:3). Rather than being a light to the nations, Israel wanted to be like the nations. They turned to idols and cultivated the national practices, relational dynamics, and social corruptions of the nations around them. They became an unholy and unjust people (Isa. 5:1–7), failing to image the God of Israel and to glorify the one who was also creator of all things. They did not love one another or care for the land as God had commanded them. According to the prophets, rather than the nations glorifying the God of Israel because of the nation's faithfulness, the name of God was blasphemed among the nations (Isa. 52:5; Ezek. 36:20; cf. Rom. 2:24). Because Israel had become a people who did not represent the God of Israel, their God said of them that they were not his people (Hos. 1:9).

Because Israel was unfaithful, God sent them into exile. But he did not do so without making promises. He would not forget about them (Isa. 43:1–28). He promised to one day restore them and make them his people once again (Hos. 1:10–11). He would pour out his spirit on them, enliven them, recall them from the lands among which he had scattered them, and make them a people of justice who would one day take their place alongside the nations in the worship of their God (Isa. 49:1–26; Ezek. 37:1–28).

The point of this all-too-brief summary of the scriptural narrative is to note that God's intentions with Israel were completely consistent with God's purposes with Abraham—to bless the nations of the world through him. And these were consistent with God's creational intentions—to have all humanity filling the earth, ruling it on God's behalf, manifesting his sovereign rule over all things by overseeing creation's flourishing. God had called Israel to be his people and to be the national agents of restoring all that was lost at the fall. They were to bring the very life of the transcendent God to the nations and be the means whereby God restored the conditions in which the nations of the earth enjoyed God's blessing, celebrated God's sovereign rule, and became nations that practiced justice and walked humbly before the God of Israel. God's design was for Israel to enjoy blessing alongside the nations, even as Israel led the nations to worship their own God, who also was the one true creator God.

Focusing more strategically on the topic of this volume, we can make some important points about the character of humanity according to Israel's Scriptures. First, humanity, created in God's image and called to rule creation on God's behalf, failed to do this. Humans have turned against God and against one another, becoming idolatrous, so that God does not inhabit creation as his temple according to his original intentions. Second, God has called one man, Abraham, to become the agent of God's reclamation of all humanity. Third, Abraham's "seed," the nation of Israel, called by God to lead the nations back to Israel's God, who is also the Creator, has also failed, turning against one another, against the nations, and against God, and has become idolatrous. God had intended to dwell with Israel in anticipation of fulfilling his original intention of dwelling with all humanity as his temple.

The Scriptures, therefore, present a scenario in which "salvation" must take place. Israel needs to be restored to God so that the nations of the world can be reclaimed and taught to worship the God of Israel. And this is necessary so that the God of Israel can truly be seen as the creator God—the one true God whose glory fills the entire creation. God's work of salvation will be complete only when the state of affairs ruined by Adam and Eve has been restored—humans worshiping God by imaging him throughout the whole of creation. Looking ahead, this narrative trajectory shapes how Paul conceives of the Christian life, both its theological orientation (restoration of worship) and its direction toward others (restoration of communal relations).[6]

The Faithfulness of Jesus Christ

It could easily pass as trite to say that Jesus Christ is the center of all of Paul's theology. Not only do all things hold together in Christ (Col. 1:17), but Paul's thought coheres in Jesus Christ, and the apostle sees him as the center and fulfillment of the Scriptures of Israel. For Paul to announce that salvation is found in Jesus Christ is to make a claim about the unfulfilled promises to Abraham about the blessing of the nations. And it is to make a claim about God's redemption of the failed narrative of Israel as God's own possession and the national agent of God's blessing of the nations. Finally, reaching back

6. That this is the narrative that shapes Paul's vision is evident in the structure of Romans. In Rom. 1:18–32, Paul expresses humanity's corruption in terms of Gen. 1–3. After narrating God's restoration project, Paul urges the Roman Christians to renew their "worship" (Rom. 12:1–2)—their embodiment of God's creational purposes for them to be the image of God. In the rhetorical climax of the letter, Paul urges the rival factions to embrace one another and sets this in terms of the restoration of the glory of God and the glorification of the God of Israel by the nations of the world (Rom. 15:7–13).

in the narrative before Abraham to the failure of Adam and Eve, Jesus is the true human who renders to the creator God a faithful obedience embodied by a life of self-giving love for others. Jesus Christ, then, and his relation to the entire range of God's redemptive purposes, becomes the context within which the Christian life takes place and the template for what it involves.

First, Jesus redeems the failed narrative of Adam and Eve. Humanity was called to faithfulness to God by ruling over creation on God's behalf. Their proper God-ward, other-oriented, and creation-directed relations represented within creation the transcendent rule of God. Where humanity failed, Jesus was faithful. He took on the sin-dominated humanity that resulted from humanity's disobedience (he came "in the likeness of sinful flesh" [Rom. 8:3]), and was obedient to God even to the point of a shameful death on a Roman cross (Phil. 2:8). His obedience to God effects the transformation of those in Christ, returning them to God's original intention for them—to "exercise dominion in life through the one man, Jesus Christ" (Rom. 5:17).

Second, Jesus is the true seed of Abraham, making good God's promises to the patriarch. Paul offers a daring argument in Galatians 3:16–18. He builds on the collective singular "seed" in order to claim that Jesus Christ is the intended recipient of the Abrahamic promises. Because the Galatian gentiles are "in Christ," united to him by the Spirit of God, they are therefore children of Abraham, beneficiaries of God's promise to bless the nations through Abraham (Gal. 3:14, 29).

Third, and related to the second point, Jesus is the true Israelite who fulfills Israel's mission to be a light to the nations, unleashing God's blessing on all humanity and drawing the nations into the praise of the God of Israel (Gal. 3:14; Rom. 15:9–12).

Fourth, Jesus's life of faithfulness to God and love for others sets the template for the Christian life. Jesus's pouring out of himself on the cross becomes paradigmatic for Paul—it is revelatory of Jesus's own character and of the character of the creator God.[7] Because of this, the pattern of Jesus's life is the template for Christian discipleship. The shape of Paul's exhortations in nearly all his letters follows this framework. Much of the balance of this essay will elaborate this claim.

Fifth, the presence of Jesus fills each church community by the Spirit of Jesus. The Spirit has been poured out, and it is the Spirit of Jesus (Phil. 1:19), filling churches with God's own life-giving presence to produce in them and among them the life of Christ embodied through corporate behaviors of

---

7. Michael J. Gorman, *Cruciformity: Paul's Narrative Spirituality of the Cross* (Grand Rapids: Eerdmans, 2001), 9–18.

self-giving love (2 Cor. 3:18; Eph. 4:15–16). Just as Jesus is the true human, the life of Jesus is being produced in these communities so that the lives of Christians and the corporate life of Christian communities resemble his true humanity. Paul speaks of Christian existence as believers being "conformed to the image of his Son" (Rom. 8:29) and participating in the renewed humanity created "according to the likeness of God" (Eph. 4:24). This language alludes specifically to God's creation intentions for humanity and indicates that the Christian life has everything to do with the recovery of God's original purposes for "the image of God."

This is why it is useful to revisit the Scriptures of Israel that narrate God's call and commission of Israel and God's pursuit of the nations. Paul's conception of the Christian life is not something completely new and unprecedented, making the rest of the Scriptures dispensable. Paul envisions the Christian life in continuity with what the creator God is doing to fulfill his original intentions, keep his promises, and pick up failed strands of the scriptural narrative. God does all of this in the effort to install on earth his own life through human agents loving one another and overseeing the spread of *shalom*.

In the death, resurrection, and ascension of Jesus Christ, and in the sending of the Spirit of Jesus, God has accomplished salvation. He is working out his purposes to reclaim humanity to manifest his sovereign rule over creation. An account of Paul's vision of the Christian life, therefore, must take account of the God-ward orientation of human identity, the fellow human-directed orientation, and how all of this has been reconfigured by what God has done and is doing in Jesus Christ and by the Spirit in the church. For it is in the church that God's purposes in calling Abraham and Israel are being fulfilled. In the church of Jesus Christ, God is creating a new body—the body of Messiah Jesus—made up of faithful Israelites and faithful non-Israelites.[8]

Baptism into Christ by the Spirit

The Holy Spirit—the Spirit of God (1 Cor. 3:16) and the Spirit of Jesus (Phil. 1:19)—is the presence of God among God's people, the agent of God's working in the church, as I've indicated above. The Spirit baptizes believers into Christ, uniting them intimately with Christ both in his death and in his resurrection

8. Paul does not envision the fulfillment of God's promises in the church as canceling out or nullifying any future restoration of ethnic Israel (Rom. 9–11). While the questions surrounding this issue are complex, fruitful discussions of post-supersessionistic readings of Paul are only beginning (David J. Rudolph and Joel Willitts, eds., *Introduction to Messianic Judaism: Its Ecclesial Context and Biblical Foundations* [Grand Rapids: Zondervan, 2013]).

into the reality of new-creation life. At least three aspects of the Spirit's action upon God's people are crucial for understanding Paul's conception of the Christian life, the latter two of which I will elucidate further in the remainder of this chapter.

First, the Spirit is the eschatological presence of God that had been promised by the prophets—the very presence of God's life-giving Spirit poured out on God's people in the coming age. That eschatological age has arrived, then, in the church—and in individual churches. The Spirit animates and brings to God's people the life of the future coming age. For Paul, believers are the ones "on whom the ends of the ages have come" (1 Cor. 10:11). In other letters, Paul imagines that his churches already inhabit that future reality called "the kingdom of God" (Col. 1:13; Rom. 14:17). Jesus-following communities experience this together, enjoying God's own presence among them in Christ by the Spirit. The identity of God's people is that they are the new-creation people of God—that eschatological reality for which the people of God had been looking (2 Cor. 5:17). The church participates by the Spirit in the new humanity (Eph. 4:24; Rom. 6:4).

It is not only the power of that coming age that has arrived among God's people, but the multinational, multiethnic reality the prophets expected is also present. That is, Jews and non-Jews are being united together in one new people in Christ (Gal. 3:28). All who are in Christ are now constituted as "God's people."

Second, churches baptized into Christ by the Spirit have their existence "in Christ." The union of church communities with God is so intimate that the corporate life of church communities is said to take place *within* God, *within* Christ (Col. 3:3; Gal. 2:20). Their identity is as full participants in that coming world over which Jesus already reigns by virtue of his resurrection and ascension (Eph. 1:3; 2:6; Phil. 3:20). Not only do believers have their existence within Christ, within God, but God in Christ dwells among them, as mentioned previously. Paul develops this at length in 1 Corinthians with his discussion of the church as God's new temple (1 Cor. 3:16–17). God's dwelling among the Corinthian church has massive implications for their corporate life together.

Third, because the Spirit intimately unites believers to Christ, believers are vitally connected to the church and to one another. Paul uses the metaphor of "the body of Christ" in several places (Rom. 7:4; 12:5; 1 Cor. 10:16; 12:12) with a variety of meanings. We partake vitally of Jesus himself, but also of the church as his body. The Spirit unites all believers to one another so that church communities are "one body," connected to one another as intimately as a person's physical arm, hands, and fingers (1 Cor. 12:12–27). Paul refers to the union of believers to God and to one another in Ephesians 2:16, seeing the work of Christ as one move—our reconciliation to God is simultaneous with our reconciliation to one another. Believers are, in fact, "members of one another" (Eph. 4:25).

For Paul, then, the baptism of believers into Christ means that they have their very existence in God and that they are vitally connected to one another. By virtue of their union with Christ, they participate in the new-creation people of God by the Spirit, and they participate in the very life of God himself.[9] Paul counsels his churches through a creative theological vision that sees Christian existence through these twin lenses. In the rest of this chapter I will discuss some of the contours of these two notions.

Participation in the New-Creation People of God

The Christian life is participation in the new-creation people of God, the church, made up of all people in Christ. God is building his new family in fulfillment of his promises to Abraham to bless the families of the earth through him and his seed. Paul refers to the church using the terminology of "new creation" (Gal. 6:15; 2 Cor. 5:17; cf. Eph. 2:10; 4:24). This language ties the church directly to scriptural promises of a renewed humanity when God restores all things in heaven and on earth. Further, Paul uses language for the church that the Scriptures use to speak of Israel. Paul calls believers in his churches "chosen," or "elect" (Rom. 8:33; Eph. 1:4).

Paul is indicating that the identity and mission of Israel sets the template and the agenda for the church, and the church is the context within which the Christian life for Paul makes sense. It is not that the church is the "new Israel," or that the church replaces Israel. The missional identity of Israel and the holistic manner in which the nation was supposed to inhabit God's redemptive purposes (including every sphere of life—economic, political, religious, familial, and agricultural, among others) point to God's purposes for the church being likewise holistic and pervasive. And Paul's conception of the Christian life cannot be extricated from his vision of the church. In fact, while much of Protestant theology has focused on the individual in abstraction from the church, we can say quite confidently that Paul would have almost nothing to say about the Christian life if he had to speak of it apart from the church.

9. By using the term *participation*, I am not smuggling in some notion of anthropological optimism, nor am I indicating that believers earn, merit, or must work for their salvation. By *participation* I mean that being Christian is a mode of existence that takes place among God's new-creation people, the church, and also within God himself.

Members of the Body

Paul's conception of being Christian is thoroughly wrapped up in and shaped by the communal experience of being the corporate people of God. At the same time, Paul doesn't diminish the individual in favor of the community, so it may be better to say that Paul conceives of individuals-in-community. This runs counter to the typical Protestant starting point of the individual as the recipient of salvation and the object in whom God is producing the character of Christ through sanctification. That is, it is somewhat typical to conceive of salvation as worked out in individuals who then must also reckon themselves part of a church made up of other individuals who are also having salvation worked out in them. This theological perspective comes not from Paul's texts, however, but from a Western tradition shaped by individualism. Paul doesn't lose the individual in the community, but when he writes his letters to give counsel on Christian discipleship, he writes to communities. And when he envisions Christian existence, his conception is communally oriented.

We can say all of this with confidence in the case of Paul because the only writings we have from him are his letters to churches. Although Paul wrote to two individuals seeking to establish churches on the island of Crete (Titus) and in Ephesus (Timothy), Paul wrote his other letters to communities. In fact, even those we call the "Pastoral Letters" are written to individuals to shape how they ought to go about leading and nurturing churches. To press the point further, the only other letter that bears an individual's name (Philemon) sets the conflict between two individuals *within a community context.* This is not merely an issue between Philemon and Onesimus, and Paul does not address Philemon by himself. Paul writes:

> Paul, a prisoner of Christ Jesus, and Timothy our brother,
> To Philemon our dear friend and co-worker, to Apphia our sister, to Archippus our fellow soldier, and to the church in your house:
> Grace to you and peace from God our Father and the Lord Jesus Christ. (Philem. 1–3)

He names himself along with Timothy as the sender of this exhortation unto reconciliation, and he addresses it to the entire community. Further, just as in many of his other letters, Paul names others of his coworkers, indicating their greetings:

> Epaphras, my fellow prisoner in Christ Jesus, sends greetings to you, and so do Mark, Aristarchus, Demas, and Luke, my fellow workers. (Philem. 23–24)

Rather than being throwaway comments at the end that can be safely filed away as "closing greetings" with no theological import, such greetings are theologically crucial. They reinforce the corporate nature of Christian identity and discipleship. To be Christian is to be a sibling in a new family, a citizen of a new *polis*, a vital organ in a new body.

It's a modern illusion that we have something called "Christian ethics" that each person can "live out" on her or his own. Paul does not envision individuals making "choices" with reference to their own behavior abstracted from a communal context. Christian behavior is thoroughly shaped by behavior with reference to "one another" and "others." Paul's prayer in Philemon 6 reflects this outlook. He prays "that your participation in the faith may become effective in the knowledge of all the good that is in you unto Christ" (AT).

Paul indicates to Philemon that because Onesimus and Philemon both share in Christian faith, they are bound together as brothers and share together in a new reality that is directed toward the corporate embodiment of Christ himself ("unto Christ"). Paul calls upon Philemon to recognize this vital bond between Onesimus and himself—that is, they are brothers in the Lord (Philem. 16)—and to act in terms of this redemptive reality.

Paul's familial language dominates his letter to Philemon, which is no surprise because it is found throughout his epistles. Reflecting a profound theological reality, Paul rhetorically shapes his churches' conceptions of themselves as God's new family and of one another as sisters and brothers.

Nearly all the commands and exhortations in his letters involve communal practices and corporate behaviors. Rather than list Paul's "one anothers," I will simply refer readers to his letters. When Paul writes to his churches, his primary aim is to shape the manner in which individuals-in-community participate in community life to reflect the reality that they are communities of the kingdom of God.

Several Pauline passages have historically been interpreted to refer to "the Spirit-filled life" of individual Christians, especially Galatians 5:16–26 and Ephesians 5:18–21. In contrast to Christians living by the flesh, understood as individuals indulging their destructive internal desires (Gal. 5:16–21), Paul commands living by the Spirit, understood as individuals drawing on divine empowerment for obedience (Gal. 5:22–23). And rather than Christians being drunk with wine, a paradigmatic fleshly practice (Eph. 5:18), Paul exhorts individuals to be controlled by God's Spirit, who will produce in them the fruits of obedience (Eph. 5:18–21).[10]

10. E.g., Harold W. Hoehner, *Ephesians: An Exegetical Commentary* (Grand Rapids: Baker Academic, 2002), 706.

When interpreters recognize the community-oriented contexts in which these two passages are situated, however, they cannot sustain such individualistic readings. In Galatians 5, "flesh" and "Spirit" represent two competing realms of power—the present evil age and its apocalyptic forces of darkness, on one hand, and the new creation that has arrived in Galatia with the proclamation of the gospel, on the other.[11] These are not two competing impulses in each individual, though each person doubtless feels the tug and pull of these cosmic realms.

Paul wants his readers to see that the community result of his opponents' influence in Galatia has been an increase in the power of the flesh, and this is seen in *the predominance of destructive corporate practices* (Gal. 5:19–21). Paul reminds them that they have been enlivened by the Spirit of God and are now animated and sustained by the Spirit, so they ought to truly inhabit the realm of the Spirit (v. 16). This is done through the cultivation of alternative corporate practices that embody the command to "love your neighbor as yourself" (v. 14). Their engagement with such practices is the fruit of the Spirit's work among them (vv. 22–23).

I have argued elsewhere that Paul's command to "be filled by the Spirit" in Ephesians 5:18 is not directed toward individuals but to the church.[12] God in Christ fills the church with his presence (Eph. 1:19–23), is building the church to be his new temple by the Spirit (Eph. 2:20–22), and has given church leaders to oversee the growth of the church so that it might grow up into the fullness of Christ (Eph. 4:13–16). The church can participate in all that God is doing among them by being that kind of gathering that is filled with God's presence by the Spirit. They do this by initiating a range of corporate practices that depict the kind of community that only the triumphant God can create in Christ (Eph. 5:19–6:9).

Much more could be said to make the point that when Paul conceives of the Christian life, he imagines individuals-in-community. The starting point for the Christian life is baptism into the body of Christ—the church—being united to other Christians in the vital bonds of God's new family by the Holy Spirit. Paul does not ponder salvation as the order of benefits applied to each individual by God. He envisions salvation as a reality that believers inhabit as bound-together communities that God animates and sustains by his Spirit.

11. Richard B. Hays, "Galatians," in *The New Interpreter's Bible*, ed. L. E. Keck et al. (Nashville: Abingdon, 1994–2004), 11:321.
12. Timothy G. Gombis, "Being the Fullness of God in Christ by the Spirit: Ephesians 5:18 in Its Epistolary Setting," *Tyndale Bulletin* 53 (2002): 259–71.

Cruciformity

Christian life for Paul takes the shape of the cross.[13] That is, the character of the corporate patterns of life in new-creation communities is "cruciform." Paul does not lay out an ethical program in his letters but rather makes exhortations to his communities so that they may faithfully meet the challenges and opportunities that face them. And these exhortations conform to the life trajectory of Jesus as faithfulness to God characterized by self-giving love to the point of death on the cross. By virtue of their being united intimately with Jesus Christ by the Spirit, believers are also co-crucified and co-resurrected with him. They share in the resurrection-powered presence of God in Christ by the Spirit, and the manner in which they enjoy this is through cruciform postures in their relationships and communal practices.

Paul counsels the Philippian church in just this way in Philippians 2:1–13. He exhorts his readers in 2:2–4 to

> be of the same mind, having the same love, being in full accord and of one mind. Do nothing from selfish ambition or conceit, but in humility regard others as better than yourselves. Let each of you look not to your own interests, but to the interests of others.

The basis for this exhortation toward unity of mind and practice, of refusing to indulge selfish ambition and arrogance toward one another, and of taking on postures of humility and self-service, is the theologically shaped narrative trajectory of Jesus Christ. Describing the mind-set that should predominate among the Philippians, Paul indicates that it is the same as that of Jesus,

> who, though he was in the form of God,
>> did not regard equality with God
>> as something to be exploited,
> but emptied himself,
>> taking the form of a slave,
>> being born in human likeness.
> And being found in human form,
>> he humbled himself
>> and became obedient to the point of death—
>> even death on a cross. (2:6–8)

13. Michael Gorman has made the singular contribution in this area. In addition to his *Cruciformity*, see his *Inhabiting the Cruciform God: Kenosis, Justification, and Theosis in Paul's Narrative Soteriology* (Grand Rapids: Eerdmans, 2009).

Even though he had all the privileges and prerogatives connected with being God, Jesus did not exploit them to gain even more. Rather, he poured himself out in self-sacrificial love toward others and in obedience to God all the way to the point of giving his life in the shameful death on the cross.

Paul continues to elaborate the theo-logic of cruciformity in 2:9–11:

> Therefore God also highly exalted him
>   and gave him the name
>   that is above every name,
> so that at the name of Jesus
>   every knee should bend,
>   in heaven and on earth and under the earth,
> and every tongue should confess
>   that Jesus Christ is Lord,
>   to the glory of God the Father.

Paul notes in verse 9 that because Jesus did this, God highly exalted him, raising him from the dead and seating him on God's own cosmic throne. Further, he bestowed on Jesus "the name"—"Yahweh"—indicating that Jesus, precisely in his life trajectory of self-giving unto death, revealed the character of the God of Israel, the one true creator God. The character of Jesus himself is cruciform, as is the character of the God who is the Father of Jesus. The mode of life, then, of the new-creation people of God, precisely because the Spirit of Jesus Christ dwells among them, is cruciformity. It must be so, since the presence of God fills and pervades the church, animating it and producing in and among its members God's own character.

Paul indicates this when he continues by exhorting the Philippians to work out their salvation with fear and trembling (Phil. 2:12). Their "salvation" is their existence as a community in whom God has begun a good work that he is also completing until the day of Christ—that final day when God saves his people fully and finally (1:6). It is their responsibility to work this out by seeing to it that their relational dynamics and their patterns of community life adopt the very same shape of self-giving love toward others and obedience to God as that of Jesus in 2:6–8. If they become this sort of community, they will share in the exaltation of Jesus at the final day. Paul reminds them that God is at work among them to produce in them the desire for this sort of community and the will to engage in cruciform community dynamics (2:13).

Paul envisioned his life and ministry in cruciform terms. He stresses this notion to the Corinthians, a community oriented by a culture of destructive competition, ambitious questing, and striving for personal advancement.

> When I came to you, brothers and sisters, I did not come proclaiming the mystery of God to you in lofty words or wisdom. For I decided to know nothing among you except Jesus Christ, and him crucified. And I came to you in weakness and in fear and in much trembling. My speech and my proclamation were not with plausible words of wisdom, but with a demonstration of the Spirit and of power, so that your faith might rest not on human wisdom but on the power of God. (1 Cor. 2:1–5)

Paul purposefully embodied the crucified Jesus Christ in his ministry practices and personal bearing while among the Corinthians. He knew that if he played into their cultural corruptions, the life-giving presence of God's Spirit would be marginalized in favor of human manipulation. According to the logic of cruciformity, however, corporate practices that embody cruciformity draw upon and radiate God's resurrection power.

Elaborating further on the cruciform character of his ministry in 2 Corinthians, Paul says:

> We always carry around in our body the death of Jesus, so that the life of Jesus may also be revealed in our body. For we who are alive are always being given over to death for Jesus' sake, so that his life may also be revealed in our mortal body. (2 Cor. 4:10–11 NIV)

Paul discerns that cruciformity is the key to experiencing the resurrection power of God. Cross-shaped relational dynamics and corporate habits unleash God's resurrection power.[14]

Paul's desire that the Corinthians become a cruciform community is seen throughout these letters. He scorns them for taking one another to court rather than allowing themselves to be wronged (1 Cor. 6:7–8). And his long discussion of food sacrificed to idols incorporates a description of his own cruciform practice of giving up freedoms for the sake of others (1 Cor. 8:15). Finally, he exhorts them: "Do not seek your own advantage, but that of the other" (1 Cor. 10:24). They are to follow Paul's example of seeking to embody Jesus's own pattern of life:

> Give no offense to Jews or to Greeks or to the church of God, just as I try to please everyone in everything I do, *not seeking my own advantage, but that of many*, so that they may be saved. *Be imitators of me, as I am of Christ.* (1 Cor. 10:32–11:1)

The renewed identity of the people of God is that they suffer with Christ (Rom. 8:17). Those who do will be glorified with Christ. The character of life in the new-creation people of God, therefore, is cruciform.

14. This is the same logic at work in Phil. 3:1–13, in which Paul reevaluates his life trajectory and the value of his privileges in light of what he says about Jesus in 2:5–11.

Unity

In the majority of his letters, Paul is primarily concerned with the unity of the churches to which he writes. Moreover, in those letters that historically have been mined for "Paul's theology"—Romans, Galatians, Philippians, and the Corinthian letters—Paul's fundamental concern is for his communities to care for one another, serve one another, and envision themselves as vital and indispensable parts of God's new family in Christ Jesus. For Paul, then, the Christian life consists of the corporate cultivation of practices that embody the pursuit of the church's unity.

Protestant, and especially Reformed, interpreters bristle at the suggestion that Paul employs the notion of justification by faith in an effort to unify Jewish and gentile Christians in Rome.[15] When one follows the grammar of Paul's argument, however, it is difficult to deny that this is what Paul is doing. He writes to a church (or network of churches) in Rome to unify them in the face of developing division. He argues in Romans 1:18–3:20 that *all* those in the Roman churches were equally condemned under sin—not just gentiles—and in 3:21–31 Paul claims that *all* Christians have been justified by faith without any reference to ethnic identity.

The force of Paul's argument can be seen in his stress of the "for" in Romans 3:22. He asserts that righteousness is now revealed apart from law, *for* there is no distinction between Jew and non-Jew. Both must be set right before God on the same basis. There is no ethnicity that has an inside track with God. Further, in 3:27, he mentions the boasting in ethnic identity that has been troubling the Roman Christian community. Some are seeking an advantage over others and are boasting in their possession of the law or their ethnic identity. Because all are united under sin and because God justifies all on the very same basis, all those in Christ in the Roman church(es) belong to one another and are siblings together in God's new family in Jesus. They must be unified and must no longer seek any advantage over one another.

There is no denying that justification by faith is crucial for Paul, as it obviously is for many Christian traditions. But paramount for Paul is the unity of the church, and he marshals his argument regarding justification in the interest of uniting disparate factions in Rome. This unity serves the purpose of vindicating the sovereignty of God, as Paul makes plain in Romans 3:29–30. Drawing on Israel's central confession—the *Shema*—Paul claims that if Jews have priority in the Roman church, then God is not the one true God over all

15. E.g., Colin G. Kruse, *Paul's Letter to the Romans*, Pillar New Testament Commentary (Grand Rapids: Eerdmans, 2012), 20–21; Stephen Westerholm, *Perspectives Old and New on Paul: The "Lutheran" Paul and His Critics* (Grand Rapids: Eerdmans, 2004), 116, 388.

the earth. He is only a regional deity like those that pagans worship. For the God of Israel to be the one true God over all the earth, *all* those in Christ must be unified and none may be seen to have an inside track with God for salvation.

Because the two factions are united in Christ, they must present their bodies as one singular sacrifice to God (Rom. 12:1–2). This is the sort of worship that is acceptable to God: a church made up of many members but having its fundamental identity as one unified body. The letter's rhetorical high point comes in Romans 15:5–9:

> May the God of steadfastness and encouragement grant you to live in harmony with one another, in accordance with Christ Jesus, so that together you may with one voice glorify the God and Father of our Lord Jesus Christ. Welcome one another, therefore, just as Christ has welcomed you, for the glory of God. For I tell you that Christ has become a servant of the circumcised on behalf of the truth of God in order that he might confirm the promises given to the patriarchs, and in order that the Gentiles might glorify God for his mercy.

Paul's purpose in writing Romans is not to lay out his theology once and for all. It is, rather, to unify the church in Rome, to exhort divided factions to embrace one another in the same way that Christ has embraced them. And the unity of God's people is not something tangential to the Christian life. It is at its very heart because the glory of God is at stake. God is glorified in his redeeming humanity in Christ from the ravages of sin, death, and hostile cosmic forces that have divided humanity along gender, ethnic, tribal, and national lines. Paul's logic in Romans is that if the church cannot be unified, God will not be glorified.

Paul argues along similar lines in Galatians. In his reported confrontation of Peter in Antioch, Paul notes that Peter was "not acting consistently with the truth of the gospel" in holding himself aloof from table fellowship with non-Jewish Christians. For Paul, this division was an offense against the gospel. In his speech to Peter (2:14) that blends into his theological exposition to the Galatian gentiles and the newly arrived "agitators" (2:15–21), Paul draws on justification by faith in order to demonstrate that all humanity is justified by faith in Christ without reference to ethnicity.[16]

The long and involved theological exposition in Galatians 3 comes to a head in the unity of all in Christ as children of Abraham, as already indicated above (3:28–29). It appears that "the agitators"—Paul's term for the newly arrived

---

16. Paul's expression "works of law" here clearly refers to deeds a person does that indicate Jewish identity. He equates "works of law" in v. 16 with the mode of life that distinguishes a person as a Jew and not a gentile in v. 15.

teachers (5:12)—have disrupted the non-Jewish Christian fellowship so that there is a division developing about how to respond. Paul is not only anxious for the church to expel those who are upsetting the Galatians (4:30), but he wants the church to be unified. The freedom in Christ that Paul wants them to inhabit involves their reengagement in communal practices of mutual service.

> For you were called to freedom, brothers and sisters; only do not use your freedom as an opportunity for self-indulgence, but through love become slaves to one another. For the whole law is summed up in a single commandment, "You shall love your neighbor as yourself." If, however, you bite and devour one another, take care that you are not consumed by one another. (Gal. 5:13–15)

Much more could be said, of course, along this line, with reference to Paul's other letters. For Paul, the Christian life involves the cultivation of social practices and community dynamics that generate and foster unity among God's people. Paul does not envision unity as something that would be nice so long as people agree on the fundamentals of doctrine. The unity of God's people is crucial because the unified community is the means whereby the proclamation of the death and resurrection of Jesus Christ is made (1 Cor. 11:26). It is the means whereby the triumph of God in Christ is made plain to the hostile cosmic powers (Eph. 3:10). It is the means whereby the death of Jesus Christ is seen not to be in vain (Gal. 2:21). If the church cannot be unified, the work of God in Christ is impotent. The unity of God's people, then, has primary place in Paul's theology and the practices that foster it are seen as central to Paul's conception of the Christian life.

Participation in God through Christ by the Spirit

Because they are baptized into Christ by the Spirit, believers have their existence within God himself. His presence pervades, envelops, surrounds, upholds, animates, and sustains new-creation communities. For Paul, churches are dwelling places—*temples*—of God. The Christian life may also be understood from another perspective—in terms of participating along with the church in God's own presence. Not only does God inhabit the earthly life of the church, but the church inhabits God's very presence in the heavenly realm. In Ephesians 1:3 and 2:6, Paul locates his churches in "the heavenly places" in Christ. They inhabit already that heavenly eschatological reality that one day will overtake this broken creation. Further, in Colossians 3:3, Paul indicates that believers are located "*in* Christ, *in* God." Paul elaborates this reality in at least two ways.

Temple

Paul writes to the Corinthians because he has heard that they have split up into factions.

> Now I appeal to you, brothers and sisters, by the name of our Lord Jesus Christ, that all of you be in agreement and that there be no divisions among you, but that you be united in the same mind and the same purpose. For it has been reported to me by Chloe's people that there are quarrels among you, my brothers and sisters. (1 Cor. 1:10–11)

He appeals to them to leave behind such fleshly behavior (1 Cor. 3:1–4) and pursue unity. He exploits their corporate identity as God's temple, his dwelling place on earth, informing them of the disastrous consequences of behaving in an unholy manner while being the habitation of the Holy Spirit.

> Don't you know that you yourselves are God's temple and that God's Spirit dwells in your midst? If anyone destroys God's temple, God will destroy that person; for God's temple is sacred, and you together are that temple. (1 Cor. 3:16–17 NIV)[17]

God dwells among this people, inhabiting the Corinthian church, and if anyone is an agent of division, they are subject to the judgment of God. These are sobering words, but they shape Paul's rebuke regarding the Lord's Supper in 1 Corinthians 11:17–34.[18]

In 1 Corinthians 11:17–22, Paul informs the Corinthians that their practice of the Lord's Supper is a sham. It is not the Lord's Supper at all (v. 20) because they eat it while factions exist (v. 19) and they do it in such a way that reflects the corrupted Corinthian social codes outside the church. The rich bring their good food and wine and eat with their social equals while excluding the poor. Then, when they are satisfied—and drunk!—they admit the poor church members, but by then the food is gone and many remain hungry. The manner in which they eat the meal reinforces the sinful social realities that God overcame in Christ.

This is unthinkable to Paul, who reminds them of what he taught them previously (1 Cor. 11:23–26). The important point comes in verse 26, where

17. Many English translations (e.g., NRSV, ESV, and NASB) fail to rightly represent the corporate character of Paul's statement. The recent NIV rendering (2011) captures it well, however.

18. Many Christians are familiar with Paul's words in 1 Cor. 11:23–26, hearing them as often as their church celebrates communion. Because of the largely individualistic manner in which it is practiced, however, the larger corporate context of this passage is neglected.

Paul states that "as often as you eat this bread and drink the cup, you proclaim the Lord's death until he comes." It's not that they should eat the meal *and* have preaching about the Lord's death. The eating of the meal *is itself* the proclamation of the Lord's death. But this is the case only if the wealthier members bring more than they need and the poor are treated with dignity and welcomed to share in the Lord's bountiful blessings along with their siblings in God's new family. Eating in this manner is the social embodiment of a radically new people created by the death and resurrection of Jesus Christ.

The Lord's Supper as a social practice informs what Paul means by eating and drinking "unworthily" (1 Cor. 11:27). If they gather to celebrate the Lord's Supper, but do so by neglecting the poor and needy, or by secretly fostering factions, they will be judged by God. Such behavior amounts to an attempt to destroy the temple of God that he has established in Christ and is building by his Spirit. It is opposition to God and can result only in judgment.

The rhetorical conclusion to this section comes with Paul's exhortation in 1 Corinthians 11:33–34:

> So then, my brothers and sisters, when you come together to eat, *wait for one another*. If you are hungry, eat at home, so that when you come together, it will not be for your condemnation.

The church inhabits God himself, a cosmically significant reality that must be embodied through social practices of unity and mutual care. Paul's harrowing words that many in Corinth have become sick and some have died (v. 30) correspond to his warning in 1 Corinthians 3:17 that if anyone destroys God's temple, God will destroy that person. For Paul, the manner in which the church embodies its inhabiting of God is a matter of life and death.

Empowerment

Because of the intimate union of believers with Christ and their mutual dwelling in and being inhabited by God, believers are empowered to live into the fullness of the new creation. Speaking of himself—and referring to the reality experienced by everyone in Christ—Paul says that because of co-crucifixion with Christ, "it is no longer I who live, but it is Christ who lives in me. And the life I now live in the flesh I live by faith in the Son of God, who loved me and gave himself for me" (Gal. 2:20). Believers are enveloped in Jesus Christ and participate in his life of faithfulness to God. This does not override or replace our lives of discipleship. This is, rather, Paul's language for Jesus's life of faithfulness empowering our lives of Jesus-oriented faithfulness embodied by love for one another and faithfulness toward God.

Paul elaborates the same notion in Philippians 2:12–13:

> Therefore, my beloved, just as you have always obeyed me, not only in my presence, but much more now in my absence, work out your own salvation with fear and trembling; for it is God who is at work in you, enabling you both to will and to work for his good pleasure.

Their lives together as a community should resemble the self-giving life trajectory of Jesus (2:5–11). As they pursue the cultivation of community habits that embody this reality, it is God himself, dwelling among them by the Spirit of Jesus, who empowers them in this endeavor.

The Christian life as the participation (along with others in Christ) in God and thus enjoyment of divine empowerment ought to relieve Protestant concerns about potential anthropological optimism. That is, many have objected to a "new perspective" approach to Paul on the grounds that it does not share a critique of works and works of law that reflects the complete inability of humans to adequately obey God or the Mosaic law. We may admit that Paul is not necessarily optimistic about humanity, but he is also not reticent about the necessity of all humanity to obey the one true God revealed in Jesus Christ. This is likely because he discerns the reality that all those who obey God in Christ can do so only because of the divine empowerment enjoyed by all those who have been united to Christ by the Spirit.

Conclusion

Much more could have been said, quite obviously, about how Paul conceives of the Christian life. The value of the revolution in Pauline studies over the last four decades is not that interpreters have preferred a "new perspective" over an "old perspective." There is no singular "new perspective," but students of Paul have returned to familiar Pauline texts with fresh eyes and have increasingly realized the wonderfully rich and multifaceted character of Paul's thought. We have been struck anew that Paul nowhere writes a systematic theology, nor does he expound on the nature of the Mosaic law, justification, or the Christian life in abstraction from the particular day-to-day issues facing the specific churches to which he writes given the unique relationship he has to each one. All these contingencies must be taken into account when thinking through any aspect of Pauline interpretation, and certainly questions such as "How does Paul conceive of the Christian life?"

6

The New Perspective
and the Christian Life

The Ecclesial Life

Scot McKnight

The American church, from the far right conservative evangelical to the far left liberal Protestant or Catholic, needs now more than ever the apostle Paul's vision of the Christian life. I say that hesitantly, having witnessed the rolling of eyes that seemingly overcomes many faces today just for mentioning the apostle Paul. My friend Daniel Kirk captured the trend of our day in the title of his book *Jesus Have I Loved, but Paul?*[1] He put into words what many think: "Some people find Paul lacking in comparison with the Master; others simply find Paul distasteful, offensive, oppressive, exclusive, confusing, arrogant, or just plain wrong."[2]

Bible readers fill in the blank, for of Jacob and Esau God says, "Jacob have I loved but Esau have I hated." Paul says this in Romans 9:13 (KJV) as

---

1. J. R. Daniel Kirk, *Jesus Have I Loved, but Paul? A Narrative Approach to the Problem of Pauline Christianity* (Grand Rapids: Baker Academic, 2011).
2. Ibid., 3.

he quotes Malachi 1:2–3. Esau became a trope of the one not-blessed as he also became a trope for being "godless" (Heb. 11:20; 12:16). For some, Paul has followed behind Esau in a train of people worth despising, not so much for godlessness but for hierarchy and authoritarianism and for his posture toward women. The attempt to rescue Paul from those texts by assigning them to post-Pauline authors, whatever you think of pseudonymity in the New Testament, doesn't delete these statements or books from sacred Scripture. The fact remains that in most churches we have a canonical Paul to deal with.

The oddest thing is that the one who is often despised today might be the one we most need, and my aim in this chapter is to see if I can reclaim the (whole canonical) apostle Paul for the American church. I believe he offers a vision of the Christian life that radically reframes how we see our lives in this world. Whether I convince you or not, I shall give my best attempt.

To do this I want in this first section to set the apostle Paul in the context of some big trends in Pauline scholarship, and here we will want to consider three major movements: the "old" perspective on Paul, the "new" perspective on Paul, and the "post–new" perspective on Paul.[3] What needs to be drawn out, but is often ignored, is that each of these perspectives or approaches to reading the apostle Paul yields a framework for understanding the Christian life.[4]

The Old Perspective

Reactions today to Paul, the sort that resonate with Daniel Kirk's title, are reactions to the "old" perspective on Paul. How to describe it?[5] In the old perspective Paul was converted from Judaism to Christianity; in the old perspective the law was (primarily)[6] an instrument of accusation, and the New

3. A very helpful and comprehensive study can be found in Magnus Zetterholm, *Approaches to Paul: A Student's Guide to Recent Scholarship* (Minneapolis: Fortress, 2009).

4. A notable exception is Michael J. Gorman, *Cruciformity: Paul's Narrative Spirituality of the Cross* (Grand Rapids: Eerdmans, 2001); Gorman, *Inhabiting the Cruciform God: Kenosis, Justification, and Theosis in Paul's Narrative Soteriology* (Grand Rapids: Eerdmans, 2009). Gorman's cruciformity could be more ecclesially shaped.

5. Among many, see Stephen Westerholm, *Perspectives Old and New on Paul: The "Lutheran" Paul and His Critics* (Grand Rapids: Eerdmans, 2004); Westerholm, *Justification Reconsidered: Rethinking a Pauline Theme* (Grand Rapids: Eerdmans, 2013); A. A. Das, *Paul, the Law, and the Covenant* (Peabody, MA: Hendrickson, 2001); Das, *Solving the Romans Debate* (Minneapolis: Fortress, 2007).

6. The distinction between Lutherans and the Reformed on law and justification cannot be explored here since the "old" perspective builds as much on its view of Judaism's works righteousness as it does on how law is understood in the Old Testament. For a good discussion of views, see James K. Beilby and Paul Rhodes Eddy, eds., *Justification: Five Views* (Downers Grove, IL: IVP Academic, 2011).

Testament and Jesus's teachings and especially life in the Spirit was now the way to live properly before God;[7] in the old perspective the human problem is sin and the human propensity to establish our own righteousness; in the old perspective the Old Testament is abrogated or at least superseded by the new covenant; in the old perspective, and here we get to the core historiography, Judaism was a religion of works righteousness that Jesus came to free us from and that Paul declared to have come to an end in justification by faith (not works);[8] in the old perspective "works of the law" refers to human attempts to establish themselves before God on the basis of works and merit building;[9] in the old perspective *grace* is much more a New Testament word, and *law* and *works* and *merit* the Old Testament words.

The old perspective came to us through Paul as interpreted by Augustine in the famous Pelagian controversies; it came to us then through Luther, who in some ways mimicked Paul's theology in his insufferably relentless demonizing of the Roman Catholic Church and its priests and popes and his own quest to find relief for a guilty conscience; it was then nuanced in important ways by John Calvin in Geneva, where law was given a more varied set of functions, including guiding the Christian, and where grace was more transformative; but it finally came to rest in the Western churches, including our American churches, through the Puritans, the revivalists of the nineteenth century, and then through theologians like Charles Hodge at Princeton and on into various segments of American evangelicalism. This view was only partially softened by American liberal theologians, whether in a social-gospel sense in people like Walter Rauschenbusch or in Reinhold Niebuhr or in Paul Tillich, and then of course by Karl Barth.[10]

The download for the American church about the old perspective's approach to Paul entails these elements: Judaism at the time of Jesus and Paul was a legalistic, works-righteousness religion; the God of the New Testament is a God of free grace, and we cannot earn our way with God since salvation

---

7. One of the elements at work in how the old perspective gained its form is the Reformed belief in a "covenant of works." See the Westminster Confession of Faith 7.2. For one discussion, see Michael Horton, *God of Promise: Introducing Covenant Theology* (Grand Rapids: Baker Books, 2006).

8. For a bold attempt to counter the portrait of Judaism in the new perspective as also a defense of the traditional view of Judaism, see D. A. Carson, Peter T. O'Brien, and Mark A. Seifrid, eds., *Justification and Variegated Nomism*, vol. 1, *The Complexities of Second Temple Judaism*, and vol. 2, *The Paradoxes of Paul* (Grand Rapids: Baker Academic, 2001–4).

9. The entire discussion about rewards and merit in Judaism has recently been shown to be a metaphorical alternative to "burden" and "sin" and not a merit-building soteriological system; see Gary A. Anderson, *Sin: A History* (New Haven: Yale University Press, 2009).

10. Christopher H. Evans, *Liberalism without Illusions: Renewing an American Christian Tradition* (Waco: Baylor University Press, 2010).

is a gift; all humans are in need of grace and salvation, which come to us through Christ's obedient life and sacrificial death; and the gospel relieves the existential crisis of guilt for the one who ceases striving and comes to rest in God's all-sufficient grace. Some old perspectivists see the ultimate and universal triumph of grace, but they are still more or less operating out of an old perspective on Judaism and Paul.

At this point I must speculate a bit because I want to synthesize the old perspective into a theory of the Christian life. The old perspective generated an *individualistic* understanding of the Christian life; the old perspective focused on *personal redemption* and thus on *happiness* now and *eternal life with God* when we die; the old perspective saw the mission of God in getting people saved, even if the word *salvation* gets expanded into the social sector for some; the old perspective saw the Christian life in terms of living out of grace (not works) and thus not seeking to please God by what we do; the old perspective tended at times (not always) to minimize social efforts because personal redemption and eternal life became the whole message; the old perspective never had ecclesiology at its center and sometimes diminished the church; the old perspective saw Judaism as the past work of God and the church as the present work of God so that it is fair to say the old perspective is inherently *supersessionist*;[11] and the old perspective framed the Christian life inside the classic *ordo salutis*— debates about order aside—in which we map the journey of the Christian to eternal life, from regeneration to final glorification. One can say then that the old perspective in most of its forms was an individualistic Augustinian anthropology, a Lutheran or Reformed or American evangelical or Protestant liberal soteriology, and more often than not a supersessionist hermeneutic. These three elements determined how one read Paul and how one lived the Christian life. I want to interrupt the more academic focus of this chapter to illustrate the implication of this individualistic Augustinian approach to the Christian life or even to American life, one in which the church's role is clearly up for grabs.[12]

Illustrations

Churches are shutting down all over the United States because lots of people think church and following Jesus are disconnected. How did this happen?

---

11. Supersessionism is a subject of intense study, but the breakthrough study is by R. Kendall Soulen, *The God of Israel and Christian Theology* (Minneapolis: Fortress, 1996). The implications of postsupersessionist readings of the New Testament for church life and mission are explored by Mark S. Kinzer, *Postmissionary Messianic Judaism: Redefining Christian Engagement with the Jewish People* (Grand Rapids: Brazos, 2005).

12. Adapted from my book *A Fellowship of Differents* (Grand Rapids: Zondervan, 2014).

America pioneered an idea that has become a Western-world assumption and law: total separation of church and state. Westerners assume freedom of religion and the "wall of separation" between church and state. No one was more responsible for the robust idea of religious freedom from state interference than the seventeenth century's Roger Williams.[13] His contribution to America—indeed, to the entire Western culture's belief in the separation of church and state—is foundational, even if many today know nothing about Williams.

In England the mutually dependent church and state had shifted at times toward the Catholic Church and finally toward a Protestant (Anglican) church. The Puritans failed in their purging England of all traces of Catholicism, so some left to become America's Pilgrims. Edwin Gaustad, one of the finest American church historians, sums up the Puritan aim: "Far from England's intruding and persecuting bishops, protected from the nation's nosy and arresting sheriffs, the Puritans, taking only the New Testament as their pattern and guide, could fashion a pure, nonpolitical, uncorrupted, uncompromised church" (and, we might add, nation).

Soon Roger Williams landed on America's shores and spotted significant failures to form a pure church, so he sought to establish a church based on the New Testament and the New Testament alone. The challenge, now well known to most of us, was beyond achievable, so he left the Boston area, moved into what is now known as Rhode Island, and created what we now know as "freedom of religion." One of his achievements was the virtual creation of a group we today call the Baptists. If I love Williams's contribution to our country, I am less sanguine about the cyclical problem he created: dream, establish the church, find problems, separate, and start the process all over again until you give up. In his puritanical desire to find the perfect church, Williams himself became the problem: no church ever got to the image in his vision. Williams formed a church of one, the first American who loved Jesus but not the church. We are given in America the power of choice, and religion has become a smorgasbord—choose your own church, choose it based on its ability to live up to your own preferences . . . I could go on with observations about the deeper American spirit by calling our attention to Henry David Thoreau,[14] but we have to get back to the old perspective with its propensity toward individualism.

13. See Edwin S. Gaustad, *Roger Williams* (New York: Oxford University Press, 2005), quotation from p. 4. See also John M. Barry, *Roger Williams and the Creation of the American Soul: Church, State, and the Birth of Liberty* (New York: Viking, 2012).

14. Hence the routine critique of Americans as individualists or narcissists and the summons to more commitment to community. Two books summoning us to individualism and

Resumption of the Argument

Individualism is one dimension of the old perspective, but we are now a little more concerned about one other element: how Judaism is understood in the old perspective. Let this be said: the old perspective is not the same as conservative evangelicalism or historic Protestantism; the old perspective ran the whole Pauline show until the discovery of the Dead Sea Scrolls. It follows that the Christian life itself was also shaped more often than not by that same old perspective on Judaism and Paul. But that all changed in the second half of the twentieth century.

The New Perspective

If it is not clear already, I shall make it clear now: the issue in the old versus new versus post–new perspectives is *how one understands Judaism* and therefore how one understands *that which gave rise to earliest Christianity.* In the old perspective Judaism was a works-based system of religion. That changes in the new perspective, and that change shifts everything—from our understanding of Paul to how the Christian life is framed.

The Dead Sea Scrolls were discovered in the late 1940s and made public not long after that, but it took three decades before their impact revolutionized Pauline studies. It got its decisive treatment in 1977 with E. P. Sanders when he wrote *Paul and Palestinian Judaism,* in which study he relentlessly rebutted particularly German scholarship on Judaism.[15] Fifteen years later he published a book on Judaism,[16] and the movement around Sanders changed *how we view Judaism* and therefore *how we view that to which Paul responded and out of which Paul emerged.* Here's the point: Judaism was no longer seen as a works-based religion, and therefore when Paul fought against "works of the law," he was not fighting against works-based righteousness. Now we will flesh this out a bit.

---

two summoning us to community are: David Riesman, *The Lonely Crowd* (New Haven: Yale University Press, 1961); William Whyte, *The Organization Man* (Garden City, NY: Doubleday, 1957); Robert N. Bellah et al., *Habits of the Heart: Individualism and Commitment in American Life* (New York: Harper & Row, 1985); Robert D. Putnam, *Bowling Alone: The Collapse and Revival of American Community* (New York: Simon & Schuster, 2000).

15. E. P. Sanders, *Paul and Palestinian Judaism: A Comparison of Patterns of Religion* (Philadelphia: Fortress, 1977). His focus was F. Weber, E. Schürer, R. H. Charles, W. Bousset, R. Bultmann, and J. Jeremias (pp. 33–59). One cannot ignore others, but it was Sanders's book that changed the playing field. Prior to Sanders, see esp. Krister Stendahl, *Paul among Jews and Gentiles and Other Essays* (Philadelphia: Fortress, 1976). We cannot fail to observe that the irony of Sanders's sketch of Judaism was that it was framed within the categories of Protestantism's system of soteriology. His study of Judaism (next note) is much better in that regard.

16. E. P. Sanders, *Judaism: Practice and Belief, 63 BCE–66 CE* (Philadelphia: SCM, 1992).

To begin with, in the new perspective Judaism is best described as *covenantal nomism*. That is, in the new perspective one became a Jew, or one found acceptance with God, on the basis of God's covenant election of Israel. The central existential anxiety of Judaism was not about personal salvation, because that matter had been settled by election. The central anxiety, if there was one, was about the condition of the people, Israel, in a world dominated by Rome. Jews were saved because they were Jews, and on that elective consciousness were on about other things, like getting a Messiah and getting the Romans back to Rome and dwelling in the land in peace and holiness.[17] Nor were Jews at all convinced that they had to be perfect, as the Reformers so often emphasized, in order to be accepted by God. The whole of the Bible spoke against that view, for, after all, they had a system of forgiveness established in the temple system. Every year, on Yom Kippur, they confessed their sins and their priests announced absolution. Perfection, it was assumed, was impossible. Torah observance then was not about getting to heaven or entering the covenant or being good enough to be approved. Rather, the law was *God's gracious instruction on how elect people were to live in the land.*

For the new perspective there is now no Judaism "other" to do battle with. Paul is not fighting Judaism per se, and he is certainly not fighting a Judaism that did not exist—the works-righteousness Judaism. What then does Paul mean by "works of the law" if not works righteousness? This is where the new-perspective scholars, especially Jimmy Dunn, paved new ground for a fresh appreciation of Judaism and Paul: works of the law refer not to general Torah observance, and neither do they refer to works done to merit favor with God.[18] Instead, as Paul's letters to Galatians and Romans especially reveal, the issue is *works Jews did that distinguished them from gentiles.* Dunn called them "boundary markers," and he was drawing on important sociological studies.[19] One of his more noteworthy contributions to this discussion was drawing attention to one of the Dead Sea Scrolls (4QMMT, or 4QHalakhic Letter).[20] In short, works of the law refer to circumcision, Sabbath observance,

---

17. A beautiful expression of this is the Benedictus of Zechariah in Luke 1:67–79.

18. Throughout James D. G. Dunn, *The New Perspective on Paul*, rev. ed. (Grand Rapids: Eerdmans, 2008).

19. James D. G. Dunn, *The Theology of Paul the Apostle* (Grand Rapids: Eerdmans, 1998), 354–71.

20. The letter is found in a number of fragments (classified now most helpfully as 4Q394–399). 4Q399 informs us that the leader has written to the community about "some of the works of the Torah which we think are good for you and for your people." Dunn has observed that language of *parash* (as in *Perushim*, or Pharisees) and that these "works" in effect separate the community from those who don't do these "works," and he parallels Paul's use of the term. However,

and food laws—that is, to the laws and practices that Jews did and gentiles did not do and that therefore distinguished Jews from gentiles. "Works of the law" then was shorthand for "become a Jew" or "be a Jew."

The old perspective framed Paul as a Christian over against Judaism. The new perspective framed Paul as a *Jewish Christian* or a *Christian Jew* over against resistant forms of Judaism, but still within Judaism.[21] A little-known statement by Paul in the book of Acts, found at Acts 23:6, is telling here. Paul, before the Sanhedrin in Jerusalem, publicly declares, "I am a Pharisee." In the old perspective he's fibbing or telling his present in light of his past or being clever by half, but in the new perspective he's telling the truth about his past *and* his present. He's a Christian all right, but he's a Christian Pharisee, a Jew through and through (Phil. 3:4b–6). To circle the wagons yet again, in the old perspective the problem was individual redemption; in the new perspective there is a shift to the people—to Israel and to the church. The old focused on the existential, and the new on the ecclesial.[22]

The tension between Paul and fellows Jews, then, is not between a Christian and a Jew but between *one vision of Judaism over against other visions of Judaism*. In the new perspective it comes down to this: Paul believed Judaism, by virtue of the death and resurrection of Jesus,[23] was big enough to expand to include gentiles in the one people of God, which he called the church, and, most important, he believed God expanded the people of God to include gentiles by exempting them from Torah observance (works of the law) and solely on the basis of faith. Thus, in one stroke of interpretation, justification by faith is not an accusation against Judaism's works righteousness but an inclusive framework for saving both Jews and gentiles. If *Abraham* was saved by faith, Jews were still saved by faith; and if Abraham was saved by *faith*, anyone with faith—including gentiles—could be included in Abraham's

---

Paul uses the term not for the whole Torah but for the special elements that create boundary markers between Jews and gentiles. On this, see "Paul and the Torah: The Role and Function of the Law in the Theology of Paul the Apostle," in Dunn, *New Perspective on Paul*, 460–67. For a longer discussion, see ibid., 339–45.

21. There is thus a residual supersessionistic dimension to the new perspective. One may call it "sectarian" supersessionism and therefore see the church as a kind of fulfilled Judaism, but over against resistant forms of Judaism it is supersessionistic. Instead of accusing Judaism of works righteousness, the new perspective accuses some of Judaism of exclusivism.

22. James D. G. Dunn, *Beginning from Jerusalem*, Christianity in the Making 2 (Grand Rapids: Eerdmans, 2009), 598–659; Kirk, *Jesus Have I Loved*, 53–72; N. T. Wright, *Paul and the Faithfulness of God*, Christian Origins and the Question of God 4 (Minneapolis: Fortress, 2013), 774–1042.

23. N. T. Wright, *The Resurrection of the Son of God*, Christian Origins and the Question of God 3 (Minneapolis: Fortress, 2003); Wright, *Paul and the Faithfulness of God*; J. R. Daniel Kirk, *Unlocking Romans: Resurrection and Justification of God* (Grand Rapids: Eerdmans, 2008).

faith. As Daniel Kirk expresses it, "[Gentiles] have been scripted into the story of Israel."[24]

This draws us now to how this new-creation theology and the new perspective frame the Christian life. Here I speak for myself, though I am a "son of Dunn" in that Jimmy Dunn was my *Doktorvater*. (We Dunn students often referred to Jimmy, a Scotsman, by the German term because, I suspect, we all were required to do plenty of work in German scholarship, as he did.) If the old perspective was driven by *personal soteriology*, the new perspective is driven by *the ecclesiology of expansion*. There is one work of God, one mission of God. That work is to form a redeemed and liberated people in this world under King Jesus, Messiah and Lord. That mission is not just for Israel but now for Israel expanded, as Paul puts it in Romans 11:11–24. In other words, the Christian life is about learning to live in an inclusive community—a new kind of fellowship of Jews and gentiles, slaves and free, male and female, barbarians and Scythians (Gal. 3:28; Col. 3:11). It is not that the old perspective has no room for ecclesiology; it just enters the game late (sometimes like subs who sit on the bench until the game has been decided); nor does the new perspective deny personal soteriology, though both Jimmy Dunn and Tom Wright have been caustically accused wrongly of such. No, the first foot in the new perspective is that God is doing the same old thing—forming a people—but now God is expanding the people to include those who were formerly excluded. Accompanying the dance of the first foot and close behind is personal soteriology.

Is there a supersessionism at work here? As you may well know, supersessionism is the one thing folks don't want to be accused of. Wright, in his book *Paul and the Faithfulness of God*, takes it on directly. Before I state his view, I want to recall a conversation I had with a well-known Jewish scholar who knows the New Testament quite well. I asked him, "If I say Jesus is Messiah and one is to believe in him for redemption, am I being supersessionistic?" He said, "Of course. All of historic Christianity's beliefs are supersessionistic." I said, "What's the alternative?" He said, "Pluralism, religious pluralism." We are at a very uncomfortable fork in the road. At some level, according to many, any firm conviction that Jesus is the world's savior, including the savior for Jews, is supersessionism. Wright admits as much and calls Pauline Christianity a kind of "sectarian supersessionism," and he says it is fully in line with the sectarian supersessionism of the Qumran scrolls.[25] Supersessionism is the driving force in the third approach to the apostle Paul and therefore frames yet

24. Kirk, *Jesus Have I Loved*, 16.
25. Wright, *Paul and the Faithfulness of God*, 806–10.

another way to live the Christian life. Before I get to how the new perspective frames the Christian life, I will sketch first the post–new perspective on Paul.

The Post–New Perspective

The post–new perspective began in some ways with Abraham Geiger in Germany in the nineteenth century, but the recent breakthroughs are not indebted so much to Geiger as they are to scholars like Mark Nanos and Markus Bockmuehl.[26] In the old perspective Paul was a Christian over against Judaism; in the new perspective Paul is a Jewish Christian or a Christian Jew, still a Jew but very much a "fulfilled, messianic" Jew. In the post–new perspective, Paul is a Jew. Paul's faith is 100 percent Jewish, and here's the big point: God saves Jews through Abraham's covenant, and he saves gentiles through the new covenant; they are one family, but there are two family origins. Two branches in the one family of God.

Jewish believers in Jesus follow the Torah; gentile believers in Jesus *follow the Torah so far as the Torah is for them*. A critical text for the post–new perspective is found in Acts 15:28–29. The probably James-shaped letter concludes with these words:

> For it has seemed good to the Holy Spirit and to us to impose on you no further burden than these essentials: that you abstain from what has been sacrificed to idols and from blood and from what is strangled and from fornication. If you keep yourselves from these, you will do well. Farewell.[27]

Some have taken this to be a rigorous set of standards that were dropped as soon as Paul got involved in the gentile mission. That is, they see Paul's real commitment to the Torah in the common chameleon-like reading of 1 Corinthians 9:19–23 where Paul says more or less that he does what it takes to get folks interested in the gospel, living in one place as a gentile and in another place like a Jew. But others, like Richard Bauckham,[28] have argued on the

26. A good sketch of Nanos's view can be found in Michael F. Bird, ed., *The Apostle Paul: Four Views*, Counterpoints (Grand Rapids: Zondervan, 2012), 159–93. In that volume, Campbell's so-called "post–new perspective" reading is as Luke Timothy Johnson describes it: "a doctrinal reading of Romans 5–8 from the perspective of the Nicene Creed that ignores Judaism altogether" (150). For Markus Bockmuehl's view, see Bockmuehl, *Jewish Law in Gentile Churches: Halakhah and the Beginning of Christian Public Ethics* (Edinburgh: T&T Clark, 2000).

27. Scripture quotations in this chapter, unless otherwise noted, are from the NRSV.

28. Richard Bauckham, "James and the Jerusalem Church," in *The Book of Acts in Its First Century Setting*, vol. 4, *Palestinian Setting* (Grand Rapids: Eerdmans, 1995), 415–80.

contrary that the four stipulations of Acts 15 are not the hoped-for morality of gentile believers but instead are specific laws shaped for gentiles living in the *Eretz Israel*. In other words, instead of modifying or toning down Torah for gentiles, this set of stipulations affirms Torah for gentiles—so far as it applies to them—but does so in a way that the Torah is never toned down for Jewish believers in Jesus.

For the post–new perspective, then, there are in effect either two quite distinct covenants or, perhaps, one covenant focused on Jews with modifications of that covenant for gentiles. What is perhaps most notable for the post–new perspective—and I'm not entirely certain this is the view of all of them, but I think it is—Paul's letters *are sent to and concern gentile Christianity and not Christian Judaism*. I was once sitting over lunch with a messianic Jew who informed me quite clearly that Romans was "not for us but for you." I had not heard this before, so I asked rather naively, "Then what in the New Testament is for you?" To which he said, "Mostly Matthew and James, with bits here and there in the other stuff, but we've got the Tanakh, you know." What he said was also a bit of a canonical reprimand when he continued, "We weren't consulted, you know, when the list of New Testament books were determined."

What I see then in the post–new perspective is the end of supersessionism, though one always has to wonder if one has to believe in Jesus to be in the covenant. And if one does, one cannot escape that term of opprobrium. For some, one does not have to believe in Jesus, and this crosses the line into pluralism: Abraham for the Jews, Jesus for the gentiles; Israel for Jews, and the church for gentile believers in the God of Abraham and Jesus. In this perspective it appears that Jews not only had precedence in the people of God but still have it.

What, then, of the Christian life? It is not unfair to say that many of us who are concerned with the niceties of early Christian history are not all that concerned with talking about the Christian life. So in some ways here I can only speak generally. For the post–new perspective, even if rarely discussed except in broad ethical categories like love and justice, the Christian life is first of all determined by who you are—Jew or gentile. If a Jewish believer, then the "Christian" life is a messianically shaped living out of the Torah. That is, Matthew 5:17–48 will serve as the template not for removing the Torah but for fulfilling it. For the Jewish believer kosher obtains, and for many today that means full kosher—no different than your typical Hasidic Jew. "Church" fellowship is more often than not seen as synagogue-like fellowship with very Jewish things going on—like reading Torah and Haftorahs, celebrating Jewish holidays like Yom Kippur and Hanukkah and Purim, circumcising baby boys properly, and learning the halakhah like any ordinary observant Jew. Gentiles are to carry on with their own believing ways, some of course opting for the creedal imperatives. But for some in the post–new perspective, gentile churches ought to follow more what is said in Acts 15 and not be so casual with either Torah or the Jewish origins of the faith. But what is perhaps most noticeable for the Christian life here is that there are in effect two fellowships, Israel and the church, or synagogues and churches. The "unity" of the one people of God is realized in separation, not in integrated fellowship, worship, and discipleship. Yes, at times a more pluralistic framework is set up in which Jews remain fully integrated into Judaism (without faith in Jesus as the Jewish Messiah), while for gentiles belief in Jesus is the way of the church.

It doesn't take genius insight to see that the post–new perspective has nearly turned the old perspective inside out and upside down. Instead of a law that had to be abrogated, we have a law that has to be followed (by Jewish and gentile believers); there is no thought here of a works righteousness but of a grace-shaped election formed through a covenant God made with Israel, and the whole Christian life is about the Torah and, for gentile believers, Paul's teaching about how gentiles who are not given the Torah are to live.

Before I offer a thicker view of the new perspective, here is a brief way of framing what we have so far contended, but this time from the angle of the *problem* the gospel resolves:

- In the old perspective, the problem is my standing before God[29]—I am guilty and under God's wrath and self-righteous and in need of a system of grace, and the gospel assaults my self-righteousness while offering consolation if I surrender in trust to God's grace in Christ.

- In the new perspective, the problem is the kind of ecclesial particularism that leads to exclusiveness and separation and ethnic privilege, so the gospel comes to reveal that God has ushered in new creation for all and loves all and justifies all in Christ (the church) through faith.

- In the post–new perspective, the problem is the need for the covenant that God made with Israel to be offered to gentiles on their own terms in a way that both preserves ethnic identity and missional privilege while at the same time expanding the people of God.

29. Or as Daniel Kirk set up alarms about this egocentric orientation: "My heart. My life. My relationship with God. My alienation from God. My repentance. My faith. My allegiance. My Lord. My justification. My sanctification. My membership added to the church. My quiet time. My closed-eye self-examination at communion. My route to heaven. My escape from the coming conflagration. My soul with Jesus forever." Thus Kirk, *Jesus Have I Loved*, 53.

The Reason I Affirm the New Perspective

In a doctoral seminar we would go patiently through each of these views and ponder the significant New Testament texts in light of Old Testament texts giving them their proper context, and we'd work toward resolutions. Here I will simply say what I think and why. I'm new perspective, neither old nor post–new, though at times I affirm postures of the post–new perspective and positions in the old. The new perspective is not wholly other but an attempt to be more historically accurate with what the New Testament teaches in the context of a fresh appreciation of Judaism.

Why do I affirm the new perspective? I could be postmodern and postliberal and say it is because of my location: I came of age intellectually with E. P. Sanders; Jimmy Dunn was my supervisor; and Tom Wright is a friend. But I came to this conviction as a non-Paul student of Dunn's when I was teaching the book of Galatians in the late '80s. This letter gets heated about Jewish believers who consider gentile believers nothing but God-fearers. They believe these gentile believers need to be fully converted, which means undergoing the blade of circumcision. That is, they believe gentiles need to become Jews to become genuine members of the people of God, here understood to be Israel.

The single text in Galatians that led me to the new perspective was Galatians 3:15–29,[30] which I will try to sort out in the remainder of this essay—a sorting out that will set the categories for understanding the Christian life for my take on the new perspective.

> Brothers and sisters, I give an example from daily life: once a person's will has been ratified, no one adds to it or annuls it. Now the promises were made to Abraham and to his offspring; it does not say, "And to offsprings," as of many; but it says, "And to your offspring," that is, to one person, who is Christ. My point is this: the law, which came four hundred thirty years later, does not annul a covenant previously ratified by God, so as to nullify the promise. For if the inheritance comes from the law, it no longer comes from the promise; but God granted it to Abraham through the promise. Why then the law? It was added because of transgressions, until the offspring would come to whom the promise had been made; and it was ordained through angels by a mediator. Now a mediator involves more than one party; but God is one. Is the law then opposed to the promises of God? Certainly not! For if a law had been given that could make alive, then righteousness would indeed come through the law. But the scripture has imprisoned all things under the power of sin, so that what was promised

---

30. James D. G. Dunn, *The Epistle to the Galatians*, Black's New Testament Commentary (Grand Rapids: Baker Academic, 1993); Scot McKnight, *Galatians*, NIV Application Commentary (Grand Rapids: Zondervan, 1995).

through faith in Jesus Christ might be given to those who believe. Now before faith came, we were imprisoned and guarded under the law until faith would be revealed. Therefore the law was our disciplinarian until Christ came, so that we might be justified by faith. But now that faith has come, we are no longer subject to a disciplinarian, for in Christ Jesus you are all children of God through faith. As many of you as were baptized into Christ have clothed yourselves with Christ. There is no longer Jew or Greek, there is no longer slave or free, there is no longer male and female; for all of you are one in Christ Jesus. And if you belong to Christ, then you are Abraham's offspring, heirs according to the promise.

It would take lots of space to unpack this, but here I make five observations. I begin at the end, at verse 28.

First, Paul thinks he has established the grounds for an inclusive church, a church made up of Jews and Greeks, slave and free, males and females. We need to keep this in mind: he's seeking to create a reading of the Old Testament that affirms one people of God in which all are mixed into one fellowship. He's landed on a reading of the scriptures that also puts the Judaizing opponents in deep water because he wants to show that gentile believers don't have to become Jews to be in the "Israel of God" (Gal. 6:16).

Second, the promise to Abraham was given, in a playful yet serious look at grammar, to the *seed*, a singular, and this leads Paul to see the promise of Abraham coming to completion in Christ and in Christ alone (3:15–16). That is, there is a pervasive *Christocentrism* in Paul's reading of Israel's Scriptures. Anything that diminishes the centrality of Christ, which at times emerges in some forms of the post–new perspective, is out of touch with how Paul thinks.

Third, the promise is first and the law is second; in fact, the law is given 430 years after the promise to Abraham (3:17–18). This sets a priority to the promise and not the Torah; Paul here lowers the Torah in the order of importance, a move not made lightly or heard easily by Paul's opponents at Galatia. The covenant's promise establishes identity, not the Torah or one's measured observance of it.

Fourth, Paul says the law was added only for a limited reason, with an inferior method, and for a limited time, and in this Paul can't be seen as post–new perspective. How so? In 3:19–24 Paul makes these very points: the law was added in order to turn transgressions into full bloom as Sin (capital letter); the law was given indirectly by God through angels, whereas the covenant was the direct, unmediated presence of God; and the law was given *only for the time between Moses and Christ*. Hence, in 3:24 we read the law was given "until Christ came." Or its disciplinarian function was until Christ came.

Fifth, the aim of the Torah was faith, and when faith came—that is, when Christ's faith and our faith in Christ came—the Torah had served its purpose. Therefore, the Torah's inevitable division of Jews from gentiles ended with Christ, and it is now time for the family of God to be established on the basis of faith, not on the basis of Israel's elective status in the mission of God in this world.

I'll put it this way: the argument here is aimed at establishing a fellowship of differents (-ts, not -ence), and these differents are Jews and gentiles and slaves and freedmen and males and females. It makes no sense to tell gentiles the law has been put aside; it was not there for them to begin with. Paul has Jews in mind, which he clearly had in mind in 2:15–21, where he reprimanded Peter and showed him that "we who are Jews by nature" had to learn that justification was by faith, not by being Jewish. So this argument about Torah is a Jew-directed statement more than it is a gentile-directed argument.

So here's the argument: Christ is the Abrahamic seed; those in Christ are in Abraham, or those in Abraham are in Christ; we are in Christ by faith not by Torah or by ethnicity; therefore, there is one body of Christ. The ecclesial focus here is the singular focus of the new perspective on Paul. The personal-redemption theme of the old perspective is not the central concern of Paul here, nor is the Torah-shaped behavior for Jews and somewhat for gentiles the focus. This passage, which forms the heart of Paul's entire theology at this point in his theological journey, has a decidedly ecclesial focus. His concern is that the church is a fellowship of differents.

The New Perspective and the Christian Life as an Ecclesial Life

My contention is that the apostle Paul can offer to us a whole new vision of the church for America, a vision that centers on the church and that centers on the church as an inclusive, social-boundary-breaking fellowship of differents. My contention is also that the Christian life is shaped by this vision of the apostle Paul: if the church is a fellowship of differents, then the Christian life is about learning to navigate this life in the company of those who are not like us. Let me put this stronger: the Christian life is learning how to love, to live with, and to fellowship with those who are not like us.

Which takes us to ecclesiology as the first move in Paul. An image: there are three ways to eat a salad. Let's get the ingredients on the table: spinach leaves, arugula, kale, chard, carrots, broccoli, dried fruit, nuts, tomatoes, purple cabbage for color and roughage, and then some cheese—I prefer Pecorino Romano. Now, there are three ways to eat the salad ingredients. First, one can take each element and put it in a separate bowl and eat each item separately. The second way is to put all the ingredients in the same bowl and drench the ingredients with your favorite salad dressing—Caesar, Thousand Island, French—and then mix it all together. The third way is to put all the ingredients in a salad bowl and put just a bit of olive oil and then toss it all together. Three images of the church, three images of the Christian life. The first is the American church path: separate all the diversity of American Christians into separate churches on Sunday morning so there is no mixing and lots of similarity. The weekly affirmation of "one, holy, catholic, and apostolic church" mocks Sunday mornings. The second is to colonize diversity by making it all taste alike: the more Caesar you pour on your salad ingredients, the less you will ever taste the ingredients. This kind of church life, in which one (cultural, ethnic, economic, or theological) culture rules, may be why we prefer the first option. The third is the way Paul saw the church: we may be different, but we need to be together—in the same bowl, mixing it up with just enough Holy Spirit oil to give each of our differences zing and taste.

Hence my claim that we need to reclaim Paul's central (new) perspective vision for the church and the Christian life for the American church. What we need is a good dose of reading Paul anew in light of what he was seeking to accomplish. First I want to explore the ecclesial focus of Paul's mission as the clue to the Christian life for Paul, and I begin with the social realities of a Pauline church, realities often ignored in our churches by assuming Paul's churches were—*voilà*—just like ours!

Ecclesial Social Realities

In his recent study of Pauline churches based on the archaeological evidence from Pompeii and adapted for other cities, Peter Oakes proposes that an early Pauline house-church, with due adjustments for Rome, would have looked something like this:[31]

Thirty people in total, comprising:

1. A craftworker who rents a workshop with separate living accommodation for his family and some male slaves, a female domestic slave, and a dependent relative

2. A few other householders who rent less space, with family and slaves and dependents

---

31. Peter Oakes, *Reading Romans in Pompeii: Paul's Letter at Ground Level* (Minneapolis: Fortress, 2009), 96.

3. A couple of members of families whose householder is not part of the house church

4. A couple of slaves whose owners are not part of the house church

5. A couple of free or freed dependents of people who are not part of the house church

6. A couple of homeless people

7. A few people who are renting space in shared rooms (migrant workers, etc.)

Unlike other attempts at this kind of sketch, Oakes constructs his model on the basis of who owned space and lived and worked in those spaces. Consequently, a clearer picture of a typical house gathering—a house church—emerges into some concrete social realities. There is an inevitable amount of speculation in this kind of historical spadework, but Oakes is far more careful than most, and I find his conclusions highly reasonable.

There is a bit of a discussion today of where on the social spectrum the earliest churches were to be located, but it seems to me that Richard Ascough and others are correct in locating the Pauline churches among the many *associations* of the Roman world.[32] Associations, it might be observed, were gatherings of the Roman nonelites, and in that they often enough mimicked the elites in their hierarchies and status alignments, it is not hard to understand why the authorities saw rebellion or at least potential disturbances brewing in the widespread growth of associations. Add to this one simple word: Paul called a gathering the *ekklēsia*, a highly political term used in the Greek world for the citizen gatherings.[33] Our churches impress us as sanitized and sanctified, whereas the first-century Pauline churches raised suspicion and the specter of sedition. To be sure, most would have seen those *ekklēsia* associations as harmless collections of mostly nobodies, but that would not have kept some from keeping an eye on them.

These social realities now need to be made even thicker. At least as early as Galatians and as late as Colossians, which I think Paul wrote, those early house churches brought together those who were not used to dining and praying and dwelling with one another. So, Galatians 3:28 and Colossians 3:9–11:

32. Richard S. Ascough, Philip A. Harland, and John S. Kloppenborg, *Associations in the Greco-Roman World: A Sourcebook* (Waco: Baylor University Press, 2012). See Richard S. Ascough, "What Are They *Now* Saying about Christ Groups and Associations?," *Currents in Biblical Research* 13 (2015): 207–44.

33. Paul Trebilco, *Self-Designations and Group Identity in the New Testament* (Cambridge: Cambridge University Press, 2012), chap. 5.

There is no longer Jew or Greek, there is no longer slave or free, there is no longer male and female; for all of you are one in Christ Jesus.

. . . seeing that you have stripped off the old self with its practices and have clothed yourselves with the new self, which is being renewed in knowledge according to the image of its creator. In that renewal there is no longer Greek and Jew, circumcised and uncircumcised, barbarian, Scythian, slave and free; but Christ is all and in all!

Take Peter Oakes's house church and give labels like Jew and Greek, male and female, ethnicity and cultural ideologies, and we peer into the first fellowships. We can complicate it further: what if one of the slaves was a woman who, at the inn where she was the slave of the innkeeper, was offered to patrons for sexual services? Now bring her into one of Paul's churches with the realization that she had few options, which she and others may have been pursuing, but until something new turned up for her we have a Roman reality impacting Paul's fellowships.

Paul's mission was churches for and composed of everyone. His gospel was that Jesus was Messiah and Lord, not just Messiah of the Jews but Messiah and Lord *of all*. If Jesus is Messiah and Lord of all, then all are invited to the table, and if all are invited to the table, then everyone has a place to sit, and that means exactly what it means: they have to talk to one another, share life with one another, give to and receive from one another. All this, regardless of one's status in the Roman world—a status-driven world.

Everywhere one went in the Roman Empire, there were very clear distinctions of status and class. Romans were obsessed with status, and it showed in clothing and in where one got to sit at public gatherings and private banquets, and it also came into full play in the legal system.[34] Martin Goodman, a leading scholar on Rome, describes it like this:[35]

On the public level, Roman society was highly stratified on the basis of birth and wealth. The social and political status of each adult male citizen was fixed at irregular censuses. . . . On the domestic scale . . . the only fully legally recognized person . . . in each family unit was its male head, the *paterfamilias*.

34. Joseph H. Hellerman, *Reconstructing Honor in Roman Philippi: Carmen Christi as Cursus Pudorum*, Society for New Testament Studies Monograph Series 132 (Cambridge: Cambridge University Press, 2005); Hellerman, *Embracing Shared Ministry: Power and Status in the Early Church and Why It Matters Today* (Grand Rapids: Kregel, 2013).
35. Martin Goodman, *The Roman World: 44 BC–AD 180*, 2nd ed., Routledge History of the Ancient World (London: Routledge, 2012), 17.

Complicate this bit on another scale, the political one—the emperor, senators, equestrians—and it gets more complex. Now we add yet another kind of scale in the Roman world of hierarchy: first men, then women, then foreigners, and then slaves. Hierarchy and status and reputation and connections are the empire. Complicate it once removed with synagogues and local Jewish communities, and status gets a twist and a challenge: Jews had their own hierarchies, and Paul, the Jew, attempted to bring together in the house churches both the Roman and the Jewish worlds. A salad all mixed up in a salad bowl that could often not contain the frisson.

Ecclesial Focus

What I want to contend is that *church* was Paul's obsession. He had nothing less than an ecclesial perception of God's mission, and we need to dwell on just this point a little more, not least because we are so madly in love with individualism and private spiritualities today. N. T. Wright once observed that if we began reading Paul in Colossians or Ephesians, we'd all be new perspective[36]—a point worth pondering, and so I shall begin with Colossians.

Paul's mission is expanding throughout the Roman Empire because the Messiah, Jesus of Nazareth, is the "firstborn over all creation" and "in him all things were created." In fact, these "all things" were created "for him," and "in him all things hold together" (1:15–17)—we dare not miss the extravagance of the claims. This Jewish Messiah, Jesus, is the fullness of God embodied in real human flesh, and God will "through him reconcile to himself all things" (1:20)—"through his blood." Most important, Paul's mission in Colossians is spelled out explicitly: he is called to "present to you the word of God in its fullness." He calls this mission the "mystery," and here's what it is: "God has chosen to make known among the Gentiles the glorious riches of this mystery" (1:25, 27 NIV). This same Christ is the "head over every power and authority" (2:10), and his cross "disarmed the powers and authorities" (2:15 NIV). At this point in the letter Paul engages the opponents, who have yet to be clearly identified. From what Paul writes, however, we can tell there is a bit of a Jewish exclusivism at work, as well as some gentile idolatries, and all of these are brought to their knees in Paul's theology. The ecclesial focus of God's redemptive work now extending to gentiles leads to the stunning statement I quoted above from Colossians 3:11–12—where "Christ is all and in all."

Because of this Christ-centered and ecclesia-centered work of God in this world, the house-church folks are to be marked by "compassion, kindness,

---

36. N. T. Wright, *Justification: God's Plan and Paul's Vision* (Downers Grove, IL: IVP Academic, 2009), 43–44.

humility, meekness, and patience," and they are to "forgive each other." But "above all" Paul underscores his letter with "clothe yourself with love, which binds everything together in perfect harmony" (Col. 3:12–14). The household regulations, which bug us today but which were a very Roman thing for Paul to bring up when associations were under suspicion, are shaped toward the church and the Lord (3:18–4:1). Notice, too, that there is for Paul an "us versus them," a sense of ecclesial identity over against the world, when he says, "Conduct yourselves wisely toward *outsiders*" (4:5). He closes the letter reminding them of their ties to other fellowships in Western Asia Minor.

I wish here to say the really important thing: there is virtually nothing about inner spirituality, about personal spiritual formation, about individual transformation, or about everything that shapes so much of how we teach the Christian life in the American church. Of course, Paul expects them to be transformed and to get sanitized from the ways of Rome, but his focus is so ecclesial that all things individual are folded into God's mission to form a new kind of community, the ecclesia. I want that to be emphasized: for Paul the church comes first, and the individual's Christian life is part of the growth and sanctification of the local church. I don't think Paul's vision entailed getting individuals sanctified and therefore improving the church. It was groupthink before personthink. It was We before Me. We hear Roger Williams and Henry David Thoreau's musical harmonies far easier than Paul's.

Ephesians could easily command more of our attention, but I want to cite one instructive passage, namely, Ephesians 2:14–22:

> For he is our peace; in his flesh he has made both groups into one and has broken down the dividing wall, that is, the hostility between us. He has abolished the law with its commandments and ordinances, that he might create in himself one new humanity in place of the two, thus making peace, and might reconcile both groups to God in one body through the cross, thus putting to death that hostility through it. So he came and proclaimed peace to you who were far off and peace to those who were near; for through him both of us have access in one Spirit to the Father. So then you are no longer strangers and aliens, but you are citizens with the saints and also members of the household of God, built upon the foundation of the apostles and prophets, with Christ Jesus himself as the cornerstone. In him the whole structure is joined together and grows into a holy temple in the Lord; in whom you also are built together spiritually into a dwelling place for God.

Notice how ecclesiocentric Paul's vision is. God's mission is to form this church. But what needs to be noticed the most is that Paul's idea of the church is a far cry from the Church Growth Movement's obsession with ethnic and social and economic segmentations (eating the individual bits of the salad separately). No, Paul's vision is that in this new age, when new creation is breaking into the Roman Empire, there is a new fellowship called the ecclesia that *mixes Jews and gentiles into one new body* (yet another political term in the Roman Empire). That is, "in Christ," an expression not that far from "in the church, the body of Christ," there is peace (yet another Roman political word), and Jew and gentile are "one," and the "hostility" is gone, and the former law is abolished, and in this church body God is "reconciling" the two into one (a subversion of Jewish politics). Gentiles are no longer "strangers" but now "citizens" (how's that for a political term!). This new body is actually "a holy temple in the Lord," that is, a "dwelling place for God." Mercy! This is a powerful new vision that is political and ecclesial to the core.

Now the point for us is this: the mission of the apostle Paul is to form fellowships in separate cities that embody a new sociopolitical and economic and spiritual order—one body made of others and unlikes, a "fellowship of differents." My contention is that for Paul the Christian life was learning how to live in this new ecclesial identity that demonstrated to Rome not its parading of power and status but instead a parade of sacrificial love and care for all. This is why I contend we need to reclaim Paul for the American church. The American church—argued by one and all—is segregated, and its witness of God's new society evaporates into a thin witness of wistful hope that someday, perhaps, but probably not, we will all be one. It does not begin at conferences and rallies; it begins when you invite a Different to your table and to the Eucharist table at your local church. I cannot think of a better statement of what God is doing than one by my professor James D. G. Dunn, who in a commentary on the book of Acts described what the Spirit can accomplish when unleashed in a group of people: "The Spirit of God transcends human ability and transforms human inability."[37] The Spirit gives us power to do things we could never do and takes what we can do and makes it even better. The Spirit transcends our abilities, and the Spirit transforms our inabilities.

Ecclesial Cohesion

I came of age in the charismatic movement, and in spite of my best efforts to experience glossolalia, it never happened when I went gape-jawed a few times in earnest prayer. But there was much chat about the Spirit and especially about identifying which spiritual "gifts" each of us had. Beside the rather laundry-list approach, and people wondering which one was theirs, and the

---

37. James D. G. Dunn, *The Acts of the Apostles* (Valley Forge, PA: Trinity Press International, 1996), 12.

weird possessiveness that seemed to overtake others, the bigger point needs constant reemphasis: each of us is gifted by God's Spirit. But the gifting is for a purpose, and the new perspective's ecclesiocentric focus draws our attention to the purpose of gifts.

Ask yourself why God chose to give to the church spiritual gifts. Then ask how Paul saw them. If, as Dunn says, the Spirit of God transcends human ability and transforms human inability, then perhaps the most significant strategy for building unity in the salad bowl is to let the Spirit guide the whole body of Christ in its gift assignments. In the midst of his missionary work, when his churches were cracking and creaking with disunity, Paul reminded them of the gifts of the Spirit. Paul's question is this: *Why* the gifts? His answer: unity. As each person's body has different parts, so the body of Christ has different parts. Why? "So in Christ we, though many, *form one body*, and each member belongs to all the others" (Rom. 12:5 NIV). Later in his ministry Paul will say the gifts are given to *create unity in the church* (Eph. 4:16). The unity Paul envisioned for the social realities he knew in the house churches springing up in the Roman Empire was a unity achieved *only* because of the gifting of the Spirit. The more Spirit, the more unity; the less unity, the less Spirit.

There are four lists of gifts in the New Testament, the most complete one being in 1 Corinthians 12:8–10, 27–28 (NIV):[38]

> To one there is given through the *Spirit* a message of wisdom,
> to another a message of knowledge by means of the same *Spirit*,
> to another faith by the same *Spirit*,
> to another gifts of healing by that one *Spirit*,
> to another miraculous powers,
> to another prophecy,
> to another distinguishing between spirits,
> to another speaking in different kinds of tongues,
> and to still another the interpretation of tongues.
> . . . .
> Now you are the body of Christ, and each one of you is a part of it.
>   And God has placed in the church
> first of all apostles,
> second prophets,
> third teachers,
> then miracles,
> then gifts of healing,

38. The list from 1 Corinthians is here formatted differently than in the NIV. The other lists are found at Rom. 12:3–8; Eph. 4:11; and 1 Pet. 4:10–11.

of helping,
of guidance,
and of different kinds of tongues.

When the Spirit comes, the Spirit assigns everyone a responsibility in the church, and in so doing the Spirit takes us away from our selfishness and individual life and tosses us in the salad bowl. In addition, the four lists of the spiritual gifts differ, leading me to an observation: *these are representative examples of the Spirit's assignments.* Some tally the gift lists into about twenty spiritual gifts, but a preoccupation with the list turns things inside out. Instead of looking at the list and wondering which one is me, a better approach is to ask, what is the Spirit gifting me to *do* in the fellowship? The answer to that is your "gift."

To repeat our point, the gifts are *for (unto) the good and unity of the body of Christ.* In one of Paul's last letters he said this with utter clarity (Eph. 4:12–13 NIV); Paul gives the *eschatology* of spiritual gifts: "until we all reach unity in the faith and in the knowledge of the Son of God and become mature, attaining to the whole measure of the fullness of Christ."

Now we need to pause yet again to consider the Christian life in light of Paul's *ecclesiocentric* and *pneumacentric* understanding of the Christian life. For him the Christian life is an assignment in the local body of Christ—not so much an opportunity for growth in personal intimacy with God but an assignment designed to make the local ecclesia more than anything one could imagine in the Roman Empire. This assignment is our contribution to local church unity across all known boundaries: ethnicity, race, gender, culture, and socioeconomic status. We are assigned a gift in order to help the church become one and so witness to the world that God's work unleashes a whole new creation.

Ecclesial Ethics

It is not uncommon to hear the liberalizing of the Christian tradition to be an ethicizing of the tradition; that is, to become liberal is to turn everything into politically aligned social ethics like justice and peace.[39] One might counter with a rather bold, "Well, aren't those *biblical* ethics through and through?" What, then, we ask, is Paul's ethic? In two words I'd say Paul has an *ecclesiocentric* ethic that derives from *the Spirit*. That is, his ethic is the pneumatic life in the church. This is altogether clear if we take a look at what Paul says about the *fruit* of the Spirit, which once again reveals our

39. Evans, *Liberalism without Illusions*, 117–39.

penchant for individualism over against Paul's steadfast heading toward an ecclesial ethic.

A person exposed to the Spirit is filled with the Spirit and manifests the fruit of the Spirit. Here they are from Galatians 5:22–23 (NIV):

> But the fruit of the Spirit is
> love,
> joy,
> peace,
> forbearance,
> kindness,
> goodness,
> faithfulness,
> gentleness and
> self-control.

When the Spirit takes root in our life, the Spirit brings forth fruit. Which is to say, the Spirit transforms, and I could appeal yet again to Dunn's words about transcendence. That's the big idea for Paul: the Spirit is in us to make us more Christlike, more godly, more loving, and wiser. But we are wrong if we think this is going to lead to the Spirit as our "life coach" or "personal spiritual trainer" so we can become more healthy or fit. No, Paul's list here is not about intimacy with God or the *via contemplativa*. Notice how other-oriented, or ecclesiocentric, his list is. The first fruit, love, is first because for Paul love is the heart of the Torah, it is the central Christian virtue, and it is the singular bond that brings peace in the church. Jews and gentiles, slaves and free, males and females are one in Christ, and that oneness is sustained when they love one another through the Spirit. Try mixing churches and you will see why love was so prominent to Paul.

Love, which deserves more attention—and I will turn to it immediately below—is but one of the "fruits."[40] What deserves our attention more than we can give it here, except in passing, is that the fruit of the Spirit is fundamentally other-oriented and not self-oriented. The same is immediately visible in the list of the "works of the flesh"; such items as enmities, strife, jealousy, anger, quarrels, dissensions, factions, and so on, pertain to communal problems. So the fruit of the Spirit becomes marks of a community shaped by God's cohesive Spirit. As J. Louis Martyn says so well,

40. I find it either a category mistake or anachronistic to equate the fruit of the Spirit with the system of virtue ethics. In the first, virtue ethics is decidedly Greek and Aristotelian, employing categories not used by either Jesus or Paul, and in the second, a system of ethics developed far later and therefore is a considerable development from what Paul says here. It is not that virtue ethics is wrong but only that it is not how Paul operates.

The effects of the Flesh are developments that destroy community—outbursts of rage, etc.—and the fruit of the Spirit consists of characteristics that build and support community—love, joy, peace, etc. Thus, in the apocalyptic war of the end-time, vices and virtues attributable to individuals have lost both their individualistic nature and their character as vices and virtues. They have become marks of community character, so that if one speaks of "character formation," one adds that it is the community's character that is being formed by the Spirit (cf. [Galatians] 4:19).[41]

Love is at the top of Paul's community-building list. Over and over Paul *explicitly claims* that love is the center of the whole Christian life. Please read these verses carefully, and you will see that the first item on Paul's prayer list in his last recorded prayer in Philippians[42] is love, because it was central to the Christian life:

For in Christ Jesus neither circumcision nor uncircumcision has any value. *The only thing that counts is faith expressing itself through love.* (Gal. 5:6 NIV)

For the entire law is fulfilled in keeping this one command: "*Love your neighbor as yourself.*" (Gal. 5:14 NIV)

But the fruit of the Spirit is *love*. (Gal. 5:22 NIV)

Do everything in love. (1 Cor. 16:14 NIV)

And over all these virtues put on *love, which binds them all together in perfect unity*. (Col. 3:14 NIV)

Love, he says, is the "only thing that counts," much more than circumcision (big round of applause from the males in the house churches). And in a deft, revolutionary claim, Paul radicalizes love when he says loving your neighbor is the "entire law." Response from the right side of the synagogue: "There are 613 commandments in the Torah, so how can one of the commandments be the *entire* law?" Paul's response: "Because love expresses the totality of God's will for us." For Paul love is central. It was central because he knew the challenges of the Christian life for those who were now in fellowship with one another in

41. J. Louis Martyn, *Galatians: A New Translation with Introduction and Commentary*, Anchor Bible 33A (New York: Doubleday, 1997), 532–33.
42. Phil. 1:9–11 (NIV): "And this is my prayer: *that your love may abound more and more* in knowledge and depth of insight, so that you may be able to discern what is best and may be pure and blameless for the day of Christ, filled with the fruit of righteousness that comes through Jesus Christ—to the glory and praise of God."

house churches across the eastern parts of the Roman Empire. The *only* way they would make it was if each person learned to love the others. Roman slaves and workshop owners were not used to sitting down at table and praying with Torah-observant Jews, and kosher Jews were not used to reading Scripture with prostitutes or migrant workers—and Paul thought this was the greatest vision of God's way of living! We're back to the need to love one another.

Love, Finally

But what is love? Ah, so glad you asked. Four points.[43]

One. The Bible begins telling us what love is when God formed a rugged commitment with Abraham, then with David, then promised a whole new covenant prophecy in Jeremiah 31, and then fulfilled the new covenant in Jesus. Love, then, is a rugged covenant commitment to someone. I use this word *rugged* with the word *commitment* in reexpressing what a covenant is for obvious reasons. American theologian Stanley Hauerwas once said that no two people are really compatible.[44] If he's right—and who would argue with a Texan—then love commits to another person who is changing and growing and not the same as she or he was yesterday. Love decides in advance to be committed to someone wherever they are.

Two. The central covenant promise to Israel was that God would be *with* them. "I will be your God and you will be my people" forms the wording.[45] How was God *with* humans? In a smoking pot, in a pillar of cloud and fire, in a "tabernacle," in a temple, and all along God's presence was known through leaders, like kings and priests and prophets. But God's deepest act of being "with" is the incarnation. Matthew tells us Jesus was "Immanuel, . . . God *with* us" (Matt. 1:23 NIV). The theme of with-ness goes on: Jesus, after his resurrection, sends the Spirit to be *with* us. And the final book of the Bible sketches the new heavens and the new earth in the new Jerusalem where "God's dwelling place is now *among* the people [of God], and he will dwell *with* them" (Rev. 21:3 NIV). God's covenant is a commitment to be *with* us.

Three. Love in the Bible is also a rugged commitment to be *for* a person. Advocacy forms the heart of love. There is a standard covenant formula in the Bible: "I will be their God and they will be my people," which means "I've got your back." And Revelation 21:7 says, "I will be their God and they will be my children."

---

43. Adapted from McKnight, *Fellowship of Differents*.
44. Stanley Hauerwas, "Sex and Politics: Bertrand Russell and 'Human Sexuality,'" *Christian Century*, April 19, 1978, 417–22.
45. See Lev. 26:12; Jer. 7:23; 11:4; Ezek. 14:11; Zech. 8:8.

We learn love by watching God love, and God loves in a rugged covenant commitment to be with us and for us, so that—and here is the fourth element of love—we will fulfill God's perfect design for us. He loves us *unto* our end. This unto-ness is the principle of direction. God loves us and dwells with us *in order to make us loving and holy and fit for God's kingdom*. How does this happen? God's gracious presence transforms us because it is, to use the words of Leslie Weatherhead, a "transforming friendship."[46] Genuine friendships, which are always two-way, are transformative because we permit others inside our innermost existential circle of being. The inevitability of transformation in genuine loving relationships explains in part why church people sit in separate churches on Sunday mornings—the fear of change leads us to push others away.

Now perhaps the most important thing I have to observe about love.

Order Matters

The order of these prepositions matters: first, *with*; second, *for*; and third, *unto*. Or, presence, advocacy, and then direction. The reality of presence communicates to the one we love our advocacy, and that combination of presence and advocacy empowers the one we love to internalize us and be transformed. Wanting the transformation of direction without presence or advocacy is experienced by the child or friend as *coercion*. In other words, pastors behind pulpits and parents on the other side of the table and serious friends sometimes have not earned the connection required to be people whose presence is close enough to be transformative.

Back to the Church and the Christian Life

The divine codes for love teach us clearly that love is a covenant, a commitment to be with someone, to be for someone, and to be with and for unto the kingdom. These divine codes for love drove the apostle Paul to a new kind of people of God, the church, and we have compared the church to the salad in a bowl. Just a short time spent in the salad bowl reveals that God's kind of love is not bliss. It's far harder than bliss, in fact. It's easy to love people just like us (actually, even that can be challenging), and it's hard to love people unlike us or who don't even like us. The gospel calls us to love everyone in the fellowship. Paul's mission is for those fellowships to be formed, and in the context of that fellowship of love we learn what it means to live the Christian life.

46. Leslie Weatherhead, *The Transforming Friendship* (New York: Abingdon, 1929).

7

A Symphonic Melody

Wesleyan-Holiness Theology Meets New-Perspective Paul

TARA BETH LEACH

H oliness unto the Lord" is the banner and passion for many Wesleyan-Holiness churches in America. Wesleyan-Holiness churches are a people and a group of denominations who desire a life of holiness uniquely set apart from the rest of the world by the power of the Holy Spirit and a life of self-denial.[1] What is more, the holiness heartbeat of the Holiness tradition can hear a renewed challenge from some recent developments in Pauline studies called "the new perspective on Paul" in a way that both confirms its emphasis on holiness while pushing it to expand its emphasis into the fellowship of the church itself. It is the concern of this chapter to explain both the Holiness tradition and this new perspective while showing also the challenge of the latter on the former. The new perspective has been

1. See especially Donald Dayton with Douglas Strong, *Rediscovering an Evangelical Heritage: A Tradition and Trajectory of Integrating Piety and Justice*, 2nd ed. (Grand Rapids: Baker Academic, 2014); William C. Kostlevy, ed., *A Historical Dictionary of the Holiness Movement* (Lanham, MD: Rowman and Littlefield, 2001); also David Hempton, *Methodism: Empire of the Spirit* (New Haven: Yale University Press, 2006).

percolating in academic circles for nearly four decades, but not often enough have those academics sought to show the significance of the new perspective for church life today. This chapter, then, is an exploration of the new perspective for the Holiness tradition, and it is my hope that a conversation can be started among leading thinkers in the Holiness tradition.

The Wesleyan-Holiness tradition takes its cues from the teachings of John Wesley (1703–91). Wesley, a passionate preacher and scholar, was an ordained pastor in the Church of England but was later called a "Methodist" due to his rigorous methods for spiritual discipline.[2] At its heart, the message of John Wesley pushed the life of Christian holiness to love God with all one's heart, mind, soul, and strength and to love one's neighbor as oneself (from Mark 12:28–32). Wesley believed that above all else, holiness of heart and life was of central importance.[3] To better understand the holiness teachings of John Wesley, we must first take a look at his doctrines of original sin, prevenient grace, and justification.

Original Sin

Intimately connected to Wesley's doctrine of holiness is his doctrine of original sin, which is fairly similar to the classical doctrine that the Protestant Reformers taught.[4] In Wesley's doctrine of original sin, each human is born with a *corrupt nature* because of Adam's disobedience. Sin entered the world through the freedom and act of disobedience of Adam and Eve. Therefore, "no one is born without the taint of sin, the reality of guilt, the mark of death upon him," as Wesleyan theologian J. Rodman Williams says.[5] As Romans 5:19 puts it: "Through the disobedience of the one man the many were made sinners."[6]

The Creator did not make humanity sinful; rather, sin is transferred to humankind because of Adam's disobedience. Because of its freedom to obey or disobey, humanity chooses to follow the ways of this world that lead to slavery and death.[7] Sin is the turning away from God; the consequence of sin, then, is a profound separation between God and humanity. Kenneth J. Collins writes, "No longer did God look upon humanity with approval; no

2. See Henry D. Rack, *Reasonable Enthusiast: John Wesley and the Rise of Methodism*, 3rd ed. (London: Epworth Press, 2014).
3. See John Wesley, *A Plain Account of Christian Perfection* (Kansas City, MO: Beacon Hill Press of Kansas City, 1966).
4. Alan Jacobs, *Original Sin: A Cultural History* (New York: HarperOne, 2009).
5. J. Rodman Williams, *Renewal Theology* (Grand Rapids: Zondervan, 1992), 1:269.
6. Scripture quotations in this chapter are from the NIV.
7. Williams, *Renewal Theology*, 1:262–67.

longer did men and women enjoy the rich blessings of the Most High in an uninterrupted fashion."[8] Because of the corruption resulting from the fall, humanity is now infected. Flowing from the corrupted nature is our actual sin, which impacts our words, tempers, and actions.[9] Wesley writes this about the dimensions and effects of sin:

> [Our sins], considered in regard to ourselves, are chains of iron and fetters of brass. They are wounds wherewith the world, the flesh, and the devil, have gashed and mangled us all over. They are diseases that drink up our blood and spirits, that bring us down to the chambers of the grave. But considered . . . with regard to God, they are debts, immense and numberless.[10]

Although Wesley maintained that all are born with a disposition toward sin, it is not the disposition toward sin that makes the sinner guilty; rather, it is the voluntary sins committed that bring guilt. Guilt is located in the individual's choice to sin rather than in the inherited corrupt nature; therefore, God deals with each sinner individually.[11] H. Orton Wiley writes this about guilt:

> The consequences of sin are to be found in guilt and penalty, which should be carefully distinguished in thought. Guilt is the personal blameworthiness which follows the act of sin, and involves the twofold idea of responsibility for the act, and a liability to punishment because of it. Penalty carries with it the thought of punishment which follows sin, whether as a natural consequence or a positive decree.[12]

Sin seeps into the entire being; it violates the spirit, soul, and body like a sickness. The human is under the reign and force of sin. "The affections are alienated, the intellect darkened, and the will perverted."[13] It is in our sin that we see the depth of pride, the intensity of anger, the perversion of sexuality, the pain of hatred, and the illumination of violence. Therefore, humans are totally incapable of saving themselves and of coming to God except by God's prevenient grace. As J. Rodman Williams writes, "For the human situation is not only one of exile from Paradise but also one of human bondage. Any and

8. Kenneth J. Collins, *The Scripture Way of Salvation: The Heart of John Wesley's Theology* (Nashville: Abingdon, 1997), 29.
9. Randy Maddox, *Responsible Grace: John Wesley's Practical Theology* (Nashville: Kingswood, 1994), 82.
10. *John Wesley's Sermons: An Anthology*, ed. Albert C. Outler and Richard P. Heitzenrater (Nashville: Abingdon, 1991), 233.
11. Maddox, *Responsible Grace*, 75.
12. H. Orton Wiley, *Christian Theology* (Kansas City, MO: Beacon Hill, 2011), 2:88–89.
13. Ibid., 129.

every attempt on the part of man to restore what has been lost only meets with failure."[14] Sin, or as Galatians 5:19 and 5:24 call it, "acts of the flesh," must be "crucified." Indeed, sin must be crucified. But if any attempt on the part of men and women is met with failure, are we eternally doomed? This creates a conundrum. Since sin is the ultimate problem and all are sentenced to death, what are men and women to do? Is there any hope for cleansing and restoration to God? Yes, says the Wesleyan. It begins with prevenient grace, God's loving activity that comes prior to and makes possible a creaturely free response.[15]

Prevenient Grace

Yes, there is good news. "Who shall separate us from the love of Christ?" (Rom. 8:35). Nothing will. As we have discussed, the result of the original sin of Adam and Eve is that humans can neither change sin by their own strength nor call upon God by their own strength. Wesley preached the doctrine of prevenient grace: that is, God's grace goes before faith, and this grace enables and empowers humans to turn from their sins to righteousness to follow Jesus Christ. It is, as Wiley says, "the gracious purpose of God to save mankind from utter ruin."[16] It is the beginning, the initial step toward salvation where God calls, pursues, awakens, and convicts.[17] Prevenient grace, then, comes first and makes possible salvation as humans respond properly to this love (John 6:44; 12:32; Rom. 2:4; Titus 2:11).

Prevenient grace cannot be confused with the Calvinist understanding of predestination. Calvin believed that God predestines those who will be saved and those who will not be saved.[18] Calvin writes on predestination, "We call predestination God's eternal decree, by which He determined with Himself what He willed to become of each man. For all are not created in equal condition; rather, eternal life is foreordained for some, eternal damnation for others."[19] Wesley, however, believed that God's saving grace was available to *all people*. He believed that "God permits a measure of freedom, through the Holy Spirit, which is sufficient for people to act responsibly."[20] Saving grace is

14. Williams, *Renewal Theology*, 1:266.
15. For more, see J. Gregory Crofford, *Streams of Mercy: Prevenient Grace in the Theology of John and Charles Wesley* (Lexington: Emeth Press, 2010).
16. Wiley, *Christian Theology*, 337.
17. Ibid., 337–43.
18. Don Thorsen, *Calvin vs. Wesley: Bringing Belief in Line with Practice* (Nashville: Abingdon, 2013), 33–35.
19. John Calvin, *Institutes of the Christian Religion* (Peabody, MA: Hendrickson, 2008), 184.
20. Thorson, *Calvin vs. Wesley*, 35.

not limited, then, to a select few as it is for the Calvinists; rather, through the doctrine of prevenient grace, grace is extended to every human being, and each person can therefore willfully respond to God's offer of grace, embrace that offer, and find redemption. Although prevenient grace is for all who accept the invitation, grace does not guarantee that someone will decide to follow Christ. Grace is God's free gift to all, but all have the capacity to accept or deny this grace.

In the Holiness tradition there is a divinely ordained order from the exercise of saving faith to final glorification.[21] God's grace prompts and attends each element in the order while humans are responding to this grace. This order, often called the *ordo salutis*, or the "order of salvation," is constructed from Romans 8:28–30:

> And we know that in all things God works for the good of those who love him, who have been called according to his purpose. For those God foreknew he also predestined to be conformed to the likeness of his Son, that he might be the firstborn among many brothers. And those he predestined, he also called; those he called, he also justified; those he justified, he also glorified.

It is not inaccurate to contend that in the Holiness tradition the Christian life is entrance into and progress in the *ordo salutis*, with the implication that justification leads to the distinctive emphasis of sanctification.

Justification

As we have discussed, humanity is under the reign of sin as a result of the fall of Adam. People are unable, acting alone, to restore themselves to God; every effort will end in failure. As John Wesley says, "Thus 'through the offence of one' all are dead, dead to God, dead in sin, dwelling in a corruptible, mortal body, shortly to be dissolved, and under the sentence of death eternal. For as 'by one man's disobedience all were made sinners,' so by that offence of one 'judgment came upon all men to condemnation' (Rom. 5:21)."[22] We are all accused, guilty, and condemned because of our sinful actions. Is there any hope for pardon? While humanity was in this sinful state, Jesus—the substitute for us all—died for us (Rom. 5:8). Wesley continues,

21. Maddox, *Responsible Grace*, 157–58. Maddox sketches the debate of "*ordo salutis*" and preference for "way" among some Wesleyan scholars. Some argue that "way" or "*via salutis*" better conveys the gradual dynamics of Wesley's "way of salvation."
22. John Wesley, "Justification by Faith," in *John Wesley's Sermons*, 113.

And as such it was that "he bore our griefs," the Lord "laying upon him the iniquities of us all." Then "was wounded for our transgressions, and bruised for our iniquities." "He made his soul an offering for sin. He lay on the tree," that "by his stripes we might be healed." And by that one oblation of himself once offered he "hath redeemed me and all mankind"; having there by "made a full, perfect, and sufficient sacrifice and satisfaction for the sins of the whole world."[23]

As Paul writes in 2 Corinthians 5:19, "God was reconciling the world to himself in Christ, not counting people's sins against them." By the original sin of Adam, all "fall short of the glory of God" (Rom. 3:23). Jesus, the Second Adam (1 Cor. 15:45–49), was a sacrifice for sin on our behalf. "Therefore, there is now no condemnation for those who are in Christ Jesus" (Rom. 8:1). Humanity is therefore declared righteous, "not by legal fiction, but by judicial action, and stands in the same relation to God through Christ, as if he had never sinned," says Wiley.[24]

Since humanity is doomed for accusation, justification is "the clearing us from accusation" from not only Satan but also the law.[25] But because of the work of Jesus Christ, Wesley says, "God will not inflict on that sinner what he deserved to suffer, because the Son of his love hath suffered for him. And from the time we are 'accepted through the Beloved,' 'reconciled to God through his blood,' he loves and blesses and watches over us for good, even as if we had never sinned."[26]

Justification, then, is not necessarily the act of being made right in one's life; Wesley contends that that is actually the doctrine of sanctification.[27] Rather, justification is what God does for us through Jesus Christ. It is important to note that it is *what God does for us*. "Works" are defined by Wesley, as with many in the Protestant tradition and which is challenged in some ways in the new perspective on Paul, as any attempt made by human effort alone to "earn" God's forgiveness and gift of salvation. No matter what we do, we will always fall short. In his sermon "Salvation by Faith," Wesley declares, "Wherewithal then shall a sinful man atone for any the least of his sins? With his own works? No."[28] Faith is the key component for justification. In fact, Wesley says, "faith is the *only condition* of justification."[29] It would be

---

23. Ibid., 114.
24. Wiley, *Christian Theology*, 383.
25. Wesley, "Justification by Faith," 114–15.
26. Ibid., 115.
27. Ibid., 114.
28. Wesley, "Salvation by Faith," 40.
29. Wesley, "Justification by Faith," 119.

tempting for sinners to try to fix themselves through good deeds, charity, and works of the law. However, any attempt is futile.

In Wesley's understanding of justification, Ephesians 2:8 is an important verse, much as it was for the early Reformers. For Wesley, justification is the "clearing us from the accusation brought against us by the law."[30] Therefore, we are pardoned and forgiven for our sins by the blood and atoning death of Jesus Christ. Wiley describes this as a "forensic or judicial act." He writes,

> A forensic proceeding, therefore, belongs to the judicial department of government; and a judicial act is a declaration or pronouncement, either of condemnation or justification. The act of justification in a theological sense, is judicial, for God does not justify sinners merely of his own good pleasure, but only on account of the righteousness of Christ.[31]

For most in the Wesleyan-Holiness tradition, the moment the sinner turns to God and chooses to believe, that sinner is saved, and, it ought to be observed, in Wesleyan theology God does not deny anyone who turns to him. Salvation comes only by the infinite mercy and grace of God, the death of Christ,[32] and faith through a heartfelt trust in Christ. Wesley continues in "Salvation by Faith,"

> Ye are saved from sin. This is the salvation which is through faith. This is that great salvation foretold by the angel before God brought his first-begotten into the world: "Thou shalt call his name Jesus, for he shall save his people from their sins." And neither here nor in other parts of Holy Writ is there any limitation or restriction. All his people, or as it is elsewhere expressed, all that believe in him, he will save from all their sins: from original and actual, past and present sin, of flesh and of the Spirit. Through faith that is in him they are saved both from guilt and from the power of it.[33]

Therefore, by the infinite mercy and grace of God, while we were still sinners, Christ died for us. As a result, we are saved—but not by works. We are saved by the prevenient and justifying grace of Jesus Christ through faith. But justification is but one element in the *ordo salutis*, and the distinctive emphasis in this tradition is on a justification that by God's grace leads to genuine sanctification in this life.

30. Ibid., 115.
31. Wiley, *Christian Theology*, 389.
32. Maddox, *Responsible Grace*, 106–9. Maddox, exploring Wesley's view of atonement, writes, "One is tempted to describe [Wesley's view] as a penalty satisfaction explanation of the atonement which has a moral influence purpose, and a ransom effect!"
33. Wesley, "Salvation by Faith," 42.

Holiness and Sanctification

Wesleyan-Holiness people rely deeply on the promises of holiness found in Scripture.[34] In Ezekiel 36:25 God promises, "I will sprinkle clean water on you, and you will be clean; I will cleanse you from all your impurities and from all your idols." This cleansing is also described in 2 Corinthians 7:1: "Therefore, since we have these promises, dear friends, let us purify ourselves from everything that contaminates body and spirit, perfecting holiness out of reverence for God." Not only does God promise to cleanse his people and make them holy, but God also commands his people to be holy. In Matthew 5:48 Jesus declares, "Be perfect, therefore, as your heavenly Father is perfect." Not only does Jesus command it, but Peter reminds his readers of this important command in 1 Peter 1:16: "For it is written, 'Be holy, because I am holy.'"

Founder of the Church of the Nazarene Phineas F. Bresee believed holiness to be the goal of the redemptive process.[35] But what exactly *is* holiness? There are several positions on this subject.[36] In general, for Wesley, holiness is a partnership with the Holy Spirit that transforms the sinner to become more holy, more loving, and more Christlike. Subsequent to the moment of conversion is the second work of grace, or entire sanctification. Entire sanctification, Christian perfection, and holiness are terms used in the Wesleyan-Holiness tradition to describe the breadth and divinely ordained goal of progress in the Christian life.

What is sanctification? We have discussed justification, where God declares us righteous because of the work of Jesus Christ. Now, in sanctification the restored believer is made free from original sin and is able to live a cleansed life in obedience to God. In Wesley's *Plain Account of Christian Perfection*, he describes sanctification:

> That habitual disposition of soul which, in the sacred writings, is termed holiness; and which directly implies the being cleansed from sin, "from all filthiness both of flesh and spirit"; and, by consequence, the being endued with those virtues which were in Christ Jesus; the being so "renewed in the image of our mind," as to be "perfect as our Father in Heaven is perfect."[37]

34. Al Truesdale, ed., *Global Wesleyan Dictionary of Theology* (Kansas City, MO: Beacon Hill Press of Kansas City, 2013), 591–605.
35. Wiley, *Christian Theology*, 440.
36. Wiley (ibid., 441) describes four general positions on this subject: (1) holiness is concomitant with regeneration and completed at that time; (2) holiness is growth extending from the time of regeneration until death of the body; (3) man is made holy only until the hour of death; (4) the Wesleyan view, which will be discussed below. See also Thorsen, *Calvin vs. Wesley*, 80–86, for a comparison of Wesley and Calvin on the view of holiness and the Christian life.
37. Wesley, *Plain Account*, 12.

The entirely sanctified person is cleansed of any hostility to God, is delivered from the bondage of sin, and is no longer a slave to the sinful nature.[38] H. Orton Wiley quotes a definition from a "Mr. Watson": "A complete deliverance from all spiritual pollution, all inward depravation of heart, as well as that, which, expressing itself outwardly by the indulgence of the senses is called filthiness of flesh and spirit."[39] This is the greatest hope of entire sanctification; the *power of sin* is removed. In his sermon "The Great Privilege of Those That Are Born of God," Wesley says:

> God in justifying us does something for us; in begetting us again, he does the work in us. The former changes our outward relation to God, so that of enemies we become children; by the latter our inmost souls are changed, so that of sinners we become saints. The one restores us to the favour, the other to the image, of God. The one is the taking away the guilt, the other the taking away the power, of sin.[40]

Not only is the grip of sin removed, but because of the presence of the Spirit we live a life of holiness. Wesley declares:

> The Spirit or breath of God is immediately inspired, breathed into the newborn soul; and the same breath which comes from, returns to, God: As it is continually received by faith, so it is continually rendered back by love, by prayer, and praise, and thanksgiving; love and praise, and prayer being the breath of every soul which is truly born of God.[41]

The Spirit of the living God breathes life into those who are spiritually dead. As a result, the new believer breathes out acts of love, prayer, praise, and thanksgiving. This illuminating analogy illustrates the once-sinner-now-saint daily breathing in of the grace of God and breathing out of love and thanksgiving.

Although the believer is set free from the grips and power of sin, entire sanctification is not based on perfect performance and flawlessness; rather, it is based on growth, maturity, and love for God and can only be accomplished by the power of the Holy Spirit. Wesley writes, "[Holiness] is not perfect in knowledge," and it is "not free from ignorance, no, nor from mistake." He

38. "Sinful nature" is common language in classic Holiness writings; however, Wesleyan-Holiness scholars today might use language such as "reoriented away from a life of sin to live a life of love" or being delivered from the "propensity" to sin.

39. Wiley, *Christian Theology*, 468 (quoting Richard Watson, *Theological Institutes* [Eaton, NY: Phillips & Hunt, 1880], 2:450).

40. John Wesley, "The Great Privilege of Those That Are Born of God," in *John Wesley's Sermons*, 184.

41. Ibid., 187.

continues, "We are no more to expect any living man to be infallible, than to be omniscient."[42] He emphasizes that no one is perfect in the sense of "sinlessness" by pointing out 1 John 1:8: "If we claim to be without sin, we deceive ourselves and the truth is not in us." Because Christian perfection has everything to do with maturation in the Christian life, Wesley did believe that it is achievable in this life. By the infusing of the Holy Spirit, the believer is transformed from the inside out and therefore is inclined to live a life of holiness.

Although this second work of grace is an instantaneous "crisis" moment for some, Wesley also believed it to be a process and a linear movement of growth toward God. Christian holiness is a constant gradual growth and movement toward the divine, empowered by the Holy Spirit. The believer is often becoming aware of sin that wasn't known before. The path of growth should never end: "By this kind of spiritual respiration, spiritual life is not only sustained, but increased day by day."[43] As the human is daily shaped and transformed, he or she begins to reflect God, and sin is less and less experienced in the believer's life. When the saved person is cleansed by the Holy Spirit from the inside, he or she is inclined to be changed in his or her outward actions. Suddenly the Christian has a desire to grow in grace and holiness. It is a life away from sin and toward the divine. The following quotation, which comes from his sermon "On Working Out Our Own Salvation," encapsulates Wesley's understanding of this linear process:

> Salvation begins with what is usually termed (and very properly) "preventing grace"; including the first wish to please God, the first dawn of light concerning his will, and the first slight transient conviction of having sinned against him. All these imply some tendency toward life, some degree of salvation, the beginning of a deliverance from a blind, unfeeling heart, quite insensible of God and the things of God. Salvation is carried out by "convincing grace," usually in Scripture termed "repentance," which brings a larger measure of self-knowledge, and a farther deliverance from the heart of stone. Afterwards we experience the proper Christian salvation, whereby "through grace" we are "saved by faith," consisting of those two grand branches, justification and sanctification. By justification we are saved from the guilt of sin, and restored to the favour of God: by sanctification we are saved from the power and root of sin, and restored to the image of God. All experience, as well as Scripture, shows this salvation to be both instantaneous and gradual. It begins the moment we are justified, in the holy, humble, gentle, patient love of God and man. It gradually increases from that moment, as a "grain of a mustard seed" . . . and becomes a great tree; til in another instant the heart is cleansed from all sin,

42. Wesley, *Plain Account*, 23.
43. Wesley, "Great Privilege," 185.

and filled with pure love to God and man. But even that love increases more and more, til we "grow up in all things into him that is our head," "til we attain the measure of the stature of the fullness of Christ."[44]

The Heart of Holiness: Love

At the heart of the doctrine of holiness is love. It is the ultimate fruit that should emerge from the Christ follower's life. The hope in the holiness life is that a person may have the ability to love God fully and love his or her neighbor fully. Deuteronomy 30:6 says, "The Lord your God will circumcise your hearts and the hearts of your descendants, so that you may love him with all your heart and with all your soul, and live." In entire sanctification, our hearts are circumcised, transformed, and set apart to love God with all we are and propelled to live a holy life. In Mark 12:30–31, Jesus declares the greatest commandments for the Christ follower are to "love the Lord your God with all your heart and with all your soul and with all your mind and with all your strength.' The second is this: 'Love your neighbor as yourself.'"

First John 4:18 says, "There is no fear in love. But perfect love drives out fear, because fear has to do with punishment. The one who fears is not made perfect in love." Wesley believed holiness to be "perfect love." He writes, "An instantaneous change has been wrought in some believers; none can deny this. Since that change they enjoy perfect love; they feel this, and this alone; they 'rejoice evermore, pray without ceasing, and in everything give thanks.' Now, this is all that I mean by perfection; therefore, these are witnesses of the perfection which I preach" (1 Thess. 5:16–18).[45]

In their book *Relational Holiness*, Thomas Jay Oord and Michael Lodahl write, "Divine love outpoured through Jesus Christ in the power of the Spirit can so fill our hearts that in this very moment—and in the next—we can truly love God, our neighbors, and God's creation, including ourselves." They go on to say, "Christian perfection is, in its essence, *perfection in love*."[46] The way to holiness is love, divine love that comes from the indwelling of the Holy Spirit that gives us the ability to become colaborers of God's love to a world that so desperately needs it.

We can conclude, then, that the mark of the Wesleyan-Holiness tradition is transformation and love. God's gracious action goes before us and propels

44. Wesley, "On Working Out Our Own Salvation," in *John Wesley's Sermons*, 488–89.
45. Wesley, *Plain Account*, 115.
46. Thomas Jay Oord and Michael Lodahl, *Relational Holiness: Responding to the Call of Love* (Kansas City, MO: Beacon Hill Press of Kansas City, 2005), 107.

us into a character change that makes us *more like God*. Holiness is a divine participation between God and humanity where God declares us righteous (justification), and we are being made righteous (sanctification). Here we see the classic emphasis of the elements in the *ordo salutis*.

While holiness is of upmost importance and is a rich biblical concept, it can be rooted in a very individualized spirituality. The ultimate goal for some is personal salvation and personal holiness to fit the individual for heaven. Many sermons are focused on the individual's walk with Christ, and in an increasingly individualized society, holiness too easily becomes a private or personal matter. As a result, the proclivity to focus on salvation and holiness in an individualized manner loses what it means to be a holy *people*. Many scholars in recent years have blamed this line of thinking on what is called the "old perspective on Paul," which focuses on the classic *ordo salutis* of Protestant soteriology.

Before we can push ahead, we must first grasp some of the basic differences between old-perspective and new-perspective readings of Paul. The differences in old- and new-perspective Paul are directly linked to how one understands Judaism, which impacted earliest Christian thinking.[47] Those of the old perspective argued for centuries that Judaism was inherently a works-based religion, which is what Paul had in mind when he spoke against "works of the law." Paul's phrase "works of the law," then, refers to any individual's attempt to earn God's grace through "works." Furthermore, grace is seen as a word rooted only in the New Testament, and "works" is simply an Old Testament concept. Anything connected to Judaism in Paul's time was works righteousness, and the New Testament understanding of grace could not be earned; salvation was a gift. Therefore, the law reveals the brokenness of humanity and accuses humans of their sinfulness.

The focus here is on individual redemption. The goal for the Christian life in this framework is similar to the *ordo salutis*, which we have discussed above. Personal redemption, personal sanctification, personal experience, personal growth, and personal intimacy with God become the chief emphases for the Christian life. We can conclude, then, that the old-perspective framework has a predisposition toward individual spirituality.

---

47. N. T. Wright, *Paul and the Faithfulness of God*, Christian Origins and the Question of God 4 (Minneapolis: Fortress, 2013), 1487–516. It is perhaps not observed by many that Wright's own index (p. 1657) refers to reconciliation "as the ultimate meaning of Paul's thought." Also see James D. G. Dunn, *The New Perspective on Paul*, 2nd ed. (Grand Rapids: Eerdmans, 2007), and E. P. Sanders, *Paul, the Law, and the Jewish People* (Minneapolis: Fortress, 2009). I would like to thank Dr. Scot McKnight for interacting with me on this essay. As a younger student of Dr. McKnight's, I am new to Pauline studies, and I am grateful for the insight he gave me on "new perspective" Paul.

The new-perspective framework dramatically impacts how one understands the Christian life. While the old perspective has a propensity toward individualism, the new perspective has an inclusive and ecclesial framework.

In the new-perspective framework, simply put, "works of the law" does not mean works righteousness or a human attempt to earn merit before God. So, then, if "works of the law" does not mean works righteousness, what exactly does it mean? A deep dive into Paul's letters to the Galatians and Romans reveals that "works" is anything that distinguished Jews from gentiles. "Works of the law" in a new-perspective framework describes behaviors and religious practices that are designed to separate Jews from gentiles. Therefore, Paul was focused on building an inclusive framework, which included gentiles in *the people of God*.

In the new perspective, God has been doing what God has always been doing—forming a people of God—but this time the flood gates have been opened, and it is no longer an exclusive community of Israel's elect but an inclusive community of Jew, Greek, gentile, male, female, slave, and free. In *Paul and the Faithfulness of God*, N. T. Wright sees the primary aim of Paul's gospel in terms of *reconciliation*, both of persons with God and of persons with one another so that a new-creation community marked by love of God and love of one another is created.[48] This new perspective does not eliminate the individual, though some have unfairly criticized the new perspective for that, but instead locates the individual in the larger plan of God. Reading Paul afresh puts the *ordo salutis* and the individual in the context of the larger ecclesial mission of God in this world. Allow me to illustrate.

For most of my life I have played the cello. The sound radiating from the instrument when the bow is drawn across the strings is exquisite. I enthusiastically admit my bias, as I claim the cello to be the most beautiful instrument in the world. As a solo performer, the cello has no equal, but as incredible as it is on its own, there is nothing as captivating as an entire symphony orchestra with all types of strings, woodwinds, brass, and percussion contributing to the mosaic of sound. When the conductor raises his or her hands and the instruments are pulled up and into position, magic begins.

When I was a senior in high school, our symphony orchestra entered into a statewide competition. Our conductor carefully selected a piece that he believed suited our orchestra well, the *Overture from Egmont* by Ludwig van Beethoven. Never before had I played something so profound . . . so poetic . . . so magical. The first time I heard Beethoven's masterpiece, I could not hold back my tears.

48. Wright, *Paul and the Faithfulness of God*, 1487–516.

Sheet music was distributed to our ensemble, and we went to work. I practiced day and night, but performing alone never had the same impact on my emotions as when we played together. The cello role, while exciting, seemed incomplete when played by itself. The first time we played it together as an entire symphony orchestra was unlike anything I had ever experienced as a young musician. I laughed with joy during some movements and wept in others. The magic was created by the simultaneous contribution of eighty musicians moving at the same pace, creating the music that Beethoven created in his head, generated by his heart. If the cello was removed, we would have lost the haunting melody that sang underneath the violins. If the wind section was taken away, we would have lost the joyful melody that only wind instruments can bring. Remove any part and it destroys the whole.

Beethoven did not write the overture with one instrument in mind, but he also didn't create it so that every instrument would sound exactly the same. The mystique of it all is that Beethoven wrote the symphony with all the instruments in mind and for each instrument to sing and to shine in the way that only it can. The beauty of music happens when the ensemble comes together in one unifying voice.

God *is love*—love lived out through the power of the Holy Spirit in a community of gifted individuals playing one musical piece in different parts, a *holy* symphony. Holiness is life lived by people in the fullness of the Holy Spirit who are empowered to offer a drastic alternative to the world around them. Love is the melody running through the community, underneath the community, and all around the community. The Christian community is not a place of jarring instruments singing different songs, or a place of gossip, conflict, rejection, pain, strife, and hatred. It is a place where the Spirit's fruit is present in abundance, so much so that the world around the Christian community can't help but join the melody. It is a community that is so unified, so melodious, so beautiful that it stops others in their tracks. Those on the outside can't help but peer in, and watch with awe and wonder, and notice the unity of the symphony. Instead of the emphasis being on the solo Christian striving to live a holy life, it is on *a holy people, a symphony*. It is a collection of individuals all uniquely gifted, sometimes polarizing opposites, yet unified in the same symphony.

In what follows I want to expound for the Holiness tradition what is found in Wright's fine study of reconciliation in his *Paul and the Faithfulness of God*, but I will do so by giving more attention to the work of Gordon D. Fee, a scholar whose work is not as prominent in Wright's study of ecclesial reconciliation as it should be.

Walk by the Spirit

The apostle Paul speaks often of holiness being the work of the Spirit in God's people.[49] In Galatians 5:16 Paul implores the community to walk by the Spirit. He writes, "So I say, walk by the Spirit, and you will not gratify the desires of the flesh." This command is central to the Christian life and is to infiltrate the lives of the Christian community. It is by following the Spirit that Christians live in obedience to God; by doing this the people of God fulfill the Torah.[50] Fee writes this about the new kind of obedience:

> Israel was to be instructed in the law so that they could be shown "the way in which they are to walk" (Exod. 18:20); indeed they were to "walk in obedience to all . . . the Lord has commanded" (Deut. 5:33). Since the Spirit is God's own sufficiency for "obedience" among the new covenant people of God, the primary new covenant imperative is "walk by the Spirit." With this imperative Paul has shifted the emphases from the arena of obedience (the law) to the means of obedience (the Spirit). It is through the enabling of the Spirit that one will fulfill the entire law in loving one's neighbor as oneself (v. 14).[51]

Furthermore, this command is not directed so much toward *just* the individual; rather, Paul is encouraging the entire Christian community to walk in the presence of the Spirit. The Holy Spirit shapes, transforms, and molds the Christian community to live a life in unison, a life of fellowship, and, most important, a life of *inclusion*. Paul writes in Ephesians 2:14–22 about what it means to be *one inclusive* body:

> For he himself is our peace, who has made the two groups one and has destroyed the barrier, the dividing wall of hostility, by setting aside in his flesh the law with its commands and regulations. His purpose was to create in himself one new humanity out of the two, thus making peace, and in one body to reconcile both of them to God through the cross, by which he put to death their hostility. He came and preached peace to you who were far away and peace to those who were near. For through him we both have access to the Father by one Spirit. Consequently, you are no longer foreigners and strangers, but fellow citizens with God's people and also members of his household, built on the foundation of the apostles and prophets, with Christ Jesus himself as the chief cornerstone. In him the whole building is joined together and rises to become a holy temple

49. For example, see 1 Thess. 5:23; 2 Thess. 2:13; 1 Cor. 3:16–17; Eph. 4:24.
50. Michael J. Gorman, *The Death of the Messiah and the Birth of the New Covenant: A (Not So) New Model of the Atonement* (Eugene, OR: Cascade, 2014), 80.
51. Gordon D. Fee, *Galatians*, Pentecostal Commentary (Blandford Forum, UK: Deo Publishing, 2007), 208.

in the Lord. And in him you too are being built together to become a dwelling in which God lives by his Spirit.

Here Paul paints a picture of what it means for both Jews and gentiles to live in God's family. Although Jews and gentiles were once strangers, they now have a bond in Christ Jesus that cannot be broken. Gentiles, although once aliens, are now bonded together with the Jews; they are one body. Those who were once excluded are now included; inclusion and unity bring about holiness.

The shared experience of God's Spirit among Christians isn't a stagnant presence of the Spirit but an empowering one. The Spirit ministers in the community of believers to reorient them to live a Spirit-empowered, transformed, holy life. This reorientation affects how we live in community and how we treat one another. By loving God, that is, living in the divine presence of the Spirit, we obsess over unity. As we are in the presence of the divine, our lives are radically transformed to put others before ourselves, welcome the broken, pursue the outcast, do life with those who are "unlike us," and fellowship at an inclusive table.

Fruit of the Spirit

When we look at the fruit of the Spirit, each one has to do with how we live life in community. The fruit is a product of the people of God living in the shared presence of the Spirit. Paul writes in Galatians 5:22–26,

> But the fruit of the Spirit is love, joy, peace, forbearance, kindness, goodness, faithfulness, gentleness and self-control. Against such things there is no law. Those who belong to Christ Jesus have crucified the flesh with its passions and desires. Since we live by the Spirit, let us keep in step with the Spirit. Let us not become conceited, provoking and envying each other.

We must be careful not to overemphasize the individual and underemphasize the corporate life of the community when it comes to understanding the fruit of the Spirit. Fee notes this about the fruit of the Spirit:

> Most of these items have to do not with the internal life of the individual believer but with the corporate life of the community. While it is true that individuals must love, work toward peace, express forbearance, kindness, and goodness, and be characterized by gentleness, in Pauline ethics these virtues characterize God's relationship toward his people. The Spirit bears fruit in

our individual lives for the same purpose, to be toward one another the way God is toward us.[52]

It is in the fruit of the Spirit, *love*, that we are propelled to live in fellowship with those who are radically different than us; it is in the fruit of the Spirit, *joy*, that a community celebrates a victory in the life of another in the fellowship; it is in the fruit of the Spirit, *peace*, that the community experiences calmness and ease even when in dark and difficult times; it is in the fruit of the Spirit, *patience*, that we learn how to live better in close community; it is in the fruit of the Spirit, *kindness*, that we treat others in the ways that we want to be treated; it is in the fruit of the Spirit, *goodness*, that we care deeply about the benefit of others who are in our fellowship; it is in the fruit of the Spirit, *faithfulness*, that we have a radical allegiance and commitment not only to God but to those we are in community with; it is in the fruit of the Spirit, *gentleness*, that we speak to one another in grace and love instead of anger and bitterness; it is in the fruit of the Spirit, *self-control*, that we restrain ourselves from doing anything that might exclude anyone from the fellowship or cause division and strife. When the Spirit of the living God propels a community into the new world order that King Jesus established, it is marked with the fruit that brings nothing less than a unified symphony that sings a melody for all the world to hear, so that all people will stop and notice the radical alternative to what they have been living.

The Dying of Exclusiveness

Not only does the Spirit propel us to life in unity, but we are also empowered to *put to death* anything that might exclude others from the fellowship. In Galatians 5:17–18 Paul contrasts the Spirit and the flesh: "For the flesh desires what is contrary to the Spirit, and the Spirit what is contrary to the flesh. They are in conflict with each other, so that you are not to do whatever you want. But if you are led by the Spirit, you are not under the law."

In the old perspective, the struggles of the "flesh" are considered to be an individual's struggle between right and wrong. While that might be partially true, this passage has more to do with how individuals are living together in community. Yes, the Spirit and flesh are in battle with one another, but how we understand flesh can dramatically impact the way we view this passage. The Greek word *sarx* is most often used to describe humanity rather than

52. Gordon D. Fee, *Paul, the Spirit, and the People of God* (Grand Rapids: Baker Academic, 1996), 115.

one's own body.[53] Fee writes, "The Spirit-flesh conflict in Paul has to do not with an internal conflict in one's soul, but with the people of God living the life of the future in a world where flesh is still very active."[54] When we look at verses 13–15 in Galatians 5, we get a clue that Paul believes a life that is contrary to the Spirit involves "biting, devouring, and destroying" one another. Scot McKnight notes, "The flesh destroys fellowship, unity, and holiness."[55] In other words, life in the flesh, or a life that is contrary to the Spirit, has everything to do with how the community is living in fellowship. Fee says, "The way of the flesh is to fight back in order to get even, or to oppose someone who sees things different."[56] Likewise, he says, "The way of the Spirit is to love one's neighbor in any and all such circumstances, and only the Spirit can enable fallen people like ourselves to love."[57] Holiness is an entire *people* reoriented toward the cross, toward the divine, toward love, toward unity, toward inclusion—but also away from strife, hatred, exclusion, prejudice, divisiveness, division, gossip, slander, lying, cheating, and so on. Paul writes in Galatians 5:19–21,

> The acts of the flesh are obvious: sexual immorality, impurity and debauchery; idolatry and witchcraft; hatred, discord, jealousy, fits of rage, selfish ambition, dissensions, factions and envy; drunkenness, orgies, and the like. I warn you, as I did before, that those who live like this will not inherit the kingdom of God.

This list, which contrasts the list of the fruit of the Spirit, highlights the world in which the community used to live.[58] The community of believers is now part of the "new creation" in Christ (2 Cor. 5:17); therefore, they must put to death the ways of the old world. The acts of the "flesh" must be avoided, by the power of the Spirit, as these actions only turn people away from one another. Division, strife, and prejudice make a holy people virtually impossible.

As a holy people, not only are we concerned with our own individual actions, but we care deeply about the lifestyle of those in our fellowship. Paul writes in Galatians 6:1–3,

> Brothers and sisters, if someone is caught in a sin, you who live by the Spirit should restore that person gently. But watch yourselves, or you also may be tempted.

53. Ibid., 129.
54. Ibid., 126.
55. Scot McKnight, *Galatians*, NIV Application Commentary (Grand Rapids: Zondervan, 1995), 270.
56. Fee, *Galatians*, 209.
57. Ibid.
58. Ibid., 211.

Carry each other's burdens, and in this way you will fulfill the law of Christ. If anyone thinks they are something when they are not, they deceive themselves.

John M. G. Barclay, a respected New Testament scholar—likely influenced by old-perspective Paul—emphasizes the individual with this passage. Of course, this passage includes individual believers—"Be careful not to fall into the same temptation yourself"—but we can see that the point of this passage is for the whole of the community too. Barclay writes, "While supporting and correcting others, the individual believer must look to himself, test himself and bear his own responsibility."[59] To Barclay's point, we could very easily overcook the corporate aspect and undercook the individual aspect of the Christian life. The Christian life does require personal responsibility and obedience to the Spirit, so we do not need to jettison the old perspective's individual themes. But for Paul, personal holiness is not the end goal; therefore, we must always remember the weak ones in the community.

Again, allow me to illustrate. Before there was Michael Phelps there was Tom Jager, "the Bullet." In his day, Tom was the fastest swimmer in the world and held the record for the 50-meter freestyle. When I was fifteen years old, I was accepted into the Tom Jager International Swim Camp in Albuquerque, New Mexico. This swim camp was only for the fastest emerging swimmers; I wasn't one of them. I was accepted into the camp because of my brother, a swimmer on the Olympic training swim team.

Swim practice after swim practice, set after set, I was always the last to finish; I was the slowest. But still at the forefront of my mind was the most prized opportunity for all of the campers: a one-on-one swim lesson with Tom Jager. When the day came to hike a local mountain with all one hundred campers, I was, of course, the last in line. Dead last. The altitude and intensity of the climb were more than my lungs could handle, and I found myself hyperventilating every ten minutes and consequently holding up the rest of the campers. Nearing the end of the climb, thinking I was about at the end of my rope, I collapsed on a rock with nothing left to give. Ready to throw in the towel, I looked up to a line of about a hundred frustrated campers and saw the six-foot-three Tom Jager making his way down the mountain to the end of the line.

With his hand held out, he said, "Come on, Tara Beth, we will do this together." Suddenly, I had motivation; I was no longer alone. I had confidence that maybe I could do it after all. And we did just that. I was stunned that

59. John M. G. Barclay, *Obeying the Truth: Paul's Ethics in Galatians* (New York: Regent College Publishing, 2005), 162.

Tom Jager chose to walk with me. I was the least likely to succeed, the least likely to be chosen, the last in line, and clearly the weakest.

In our churches, we have spiritual climbers at the front of the line "leading" the way. But at times it seems like all of us are focused on our solo paths, so much so that we fail to notice the weak ones falling behind. When the Christian life is viewed as an individual climb with occasional Sunday "check-ins," we fail to notice those who are falling behind, and most times we don't realize or even care. But when we begin to understand that Christian holiness was always about *a people* and that we weren't meant to climb on a solo path, we quickly catch the weak ones; we throw them over our shoulders and carry them together until they are able to stand again on their own two feet. Paul thinks it is imperative that Christians face difficulties in community. He writes in 1 Thessalonians 5:14, "And we urge you, brothers and sisters, warn those who are idle and disruptive, encourage the disheartened, help the weak, be patient with everyone." Paul desires that the whole community help the weak and disheartened. Fee makes an illuminating point regarding this passage and the "American way":

> It is easy for the typical "American" reader of this letter to read past these staccato imperatives, since they pose special problems for people who have been raised on the "gospel" according to Ben Franklin, that God helps those who help themselves. Instead of "helping" the weak, one should admonish them to "get with it" and "carry their own weight." But the God of scripture is fortunately not a "typical American"; rather, he has revealed himself, both in the Old Testament and especially in the Incarnation, as the "God of the humble," the God who pleads the cause of the poor and indigent. Thus at this point Paul, by the Spirit, has placed himself in the long line of biblical authors who "plead the cause of the needy." Since these come by way of imperative, they should probably be taken much more seriously than many are wont to do.[60]

Love

Above all, holiness is love. In 1 Corinthians 13 the centrality of love in Paul's theology is more than evident. He writes,

> If I speak in the tongues of men or of angels, but do not have love, I am only a resounding gong or a clanging cymbal. If I have the gift of prophecy and can fathom all mysteries and all knowledge, and if I have a faith that can move mountains, but do not have love, I am nothing. If I give all I possess to the poor

60. Gordon D. Fee, *The First and Second Letters to the Thessalonians*, New International Commentary on the New Testament (Grand Rapids: Eerdmans, 2009), 213.

and give over my body to hardship that I may boast, but do not have love, I gain nothing. (1 Cor. 13:1–3)

Paul is clear: in this life there are many good things, but without love, it is nothing. In fact, here is just a fraction of verses in which the centrality of love is expressed in Paul's letters:

And hope does not put us to shame, because God's *love* has been poured out into our hearts through the Holy Spirit, who has been given to us. (Rom. 5:5)

Be devoted to one another in *love*. Honor one another above yourselves. (Rom. 12:10)

Let no debt remain outstanding, except the continuing debt to *love* one another, for whoever *loves* others has fulfilled the law. (Rom. 13:8)

The commandments, "You shall not commit adultery," "You shall not murder," "You shall not steal," "You shall not covet," and whatever other command there may be, are summed up in this one command: "*Love* your neighbor as yourself." (Rom. 13:9)

Love does no harm to a neighbor. Therefore *love* is the fulfillment of the law. (Rom. 13:10)

Now about food sacrificed to idols: We know that "We all possess knowledge." But knowledge puffs up while *love* builds up. (1 Cor. 8:1)

Love is patient, *love* is kind. It does not envy, it does not boast, it is not proud. (1 Cor. 13:4)

Do everything in love. (1 Cor. 16:14)

For in Christ Jesus neither circumcision nor uncircumcision has any value. The only thing that counts is faith expressing itself through *love*. (Gal. 5:6)

For the entire law is fulfilled in keeping this one command: "*Love* your neighbor as yourself." (Gal. 5:14)

Be completely humble and gentle; be patient, bearing with one another in *love*. (Eph. 4:2)

Then make my joy complete by being like-minded, having the same *love*, being one in spirit and of one mind. (Phil. 2:2)

My goal is that they may be encouraged in heart and united in *love*, so that they may have the full riches of complete understanding, in order that they may know the mystery of God, namely, Christ. (Col. 2:2)

And over all these virtues put on *love*, which binds them all together in perfect unity. (Col. 3:14)

May the Lord make your *love* increase and overflow for each other and for everyone else, just as ours does for you. (1 Thess. 3:12)

For Paul, love is at the core of what it means to be in the body of Christ. In a community of Jews, gentiles, Greeks, men, women, slaves, free, children, poor, and rich, love is the glue that binds the fellowship together.

Fee notes this about love:

To act lovingly means, as in the case of Christ, actively to seek the benefit of someone else. For Paul it is a word whose primary definition is found in God's activity in behalf of his enemies (Rom. 5:6–8), which was visibly manifested in the life and death of Christ himself. To "have love," therefore, means to be toward others the way God in Christ has been toward us. Thus, in the Pauline parenesis, for those who "walk in the Spirit" the primary ethical imperative is "love one another." This is found at the heart of every section of ethical instruction, and other exhortations are but the explication of it.[61]

Love is the essence of God and God's relationship with his people. In Romans 5:5–8 Paul writes,

And hope does not put us to shame, because God's love has been poured out into our hearts through the Holy Spirit, who has been given to us. You see, at just the right time, when we were still powerless, Christ died for the ungodly. Very rarely will anyone die for a righteous person, though for a good person someone might possibly dare to die. But God demonstrates his own love for us in this: While we were still sinners, Christ died for us.

The love of God has been lavishly expressed in Christ's death on the cross. As Fee says, "God's love, played out to the full in Christ, is an experienced reality in the 'heart' of the believer by the presence of the Spirit."[62] As the people of God know and experience the love of God through his promises, in the

61. Gordon D. Fee, *The First Epistle to the Corinthians*, New International Commentary on the New Testament (Grand Rapids: Eerdmans, 1987), 631.
62. Gordon D. Fee, *God's Empowering Presence: The Holy Spirit in the Letters of Paul* (Grand Rapids: Baker Academic, 2009), 496.

faithfulness of Jesus Christ, and in the life-giving presence of the Spirit, they then embody it toward one another. The love that the people of God have toward one another is a direct result of the love of God that is lavished on God's people. It is the fundamental fruit that should emerge in the fellowship.

Again, the centrality of love in holiness is expressed in 1 Thessalonians 3:12–13:

> May the Lord make your love increase and overflow for each other and for everyone else, just as ours does for you. May he strengthen your hearts so that you will be blameless and holy in the presence of our God and Father when our Lord Jesus comes with all his holy ones.

Paul prays that the community's love for one another will increase and overflow as the Spirit of Christ strengthens their hearts for holiness. As the local community is daily shaped and transformed, it begins to reflect God, and God is, after all, love. Love is the music that the symphony sings; it is the notes that fill our words; it is the conduits that unify us; and it is the source that impels us to offer the world a new way. Love is the distinctive characteristic of the people of God. It is embodied in the way the people of God give themselves up for one another; it is seen in the way they submit to one another; it is seen in the way they care for the marginalized, sick, widow, and orphan; it is seen in the way they walk with one another in times of grief; it is seen in the way they pray for one another; it is seen in the way they share one another's possessions. Love is the embodiment of holiness that is sourced by the Spirit of the living God himself.

Edification

As a holy people, we must tune our instruments and tune them often. Tuning is the process of transformation and edification. While acts of personal devotion to God, such as prayer and study, are important, the tuning essentially happens in the rhythm of the weekly gathering. Paul writes in 1 Corinthians 14:26,

> What then shall we say, brothers and sisters? When you come together, each of you has a hymn, or a word of instruction, a revelation, a tongue or an interpretation. Everything must be done so that the church may be built up.

The very purpose for the gathering is to strengthen *one another* and build *one another up*. The weekly gathering should have transformative disciple-making power with a distinct way of eating, drinking, and talking as a fellowship. It is a time in which the redemptive narrative is told through the structure and actions of worship. As Christians, we are called to engage our entire selves in this story as active participants instead of viewers of a feature presentation. In Colossians 3:16 Paul writes,

> Let the message of Christ dwell among you richly as you teach and admonish one another with all wisdom through psalms, hymns, and songs from the Spirit, singing to God with gratitude in your hearts.

And again in Ephesians 5:18–19,

> Do not get drunk on wine, which leads to debauchery. Instead, be filled with the Spirit, speaking to one another with psalms, hymns, and songs from the Spirit. Sing and make music from your heart to the Lord.

The weekly gathering, which includes singing hymns of praise, community prayer, confession, proclamation, giving, and breaking bread together, is the tuning of our instruments and nourishment of our bodies so that we as a community might be holy and loving. Paul implores the people of God to admonish one another in teaching through hymns and psalms and to sing Spirit-filled songs. It is at the gathering that the people of God are tuned and transformed into holiness. Holiness cannot and will not happen outside of the gathering.

Not only do the people of God gather weekly for the prayer, praise, and breaking of bread, but it is also in the gathering that the sharing of gifts harmonizes to edify the body of Christ. As Paul says in 1 Corinthians 14:12, "So it is with you. Since you are eager for gifts of the Spirit, try to excel in those that build up the church." These gifts include teaching, admonishing, prophesying, knowledge, exhortation, healing, miracles, and guidance. See 1 Corinthians 12:4–11, for example:

> There are different kinds of gifts, but the same Spirit distributes them. There are different kinds of service, but the same Lord. There are different kinds of working, but in all of them and in everyone it is the same God at work. Now to each one the manifestation of the Spirit is given for the common good. To one there is given through the Spirit a message of wisdom, to another a message of knowledge by means of the same Spirit, to another faith by the same Spirit, to another gifts of healing by that one Spirit, to another miraculous powers, to another prophecy, to another distinguishing between spirits, to another speaking in different kinds of tongues, and to still another the interpretation of tongues. All these are the work of one and the same Spirit, and he distributes them to each one, just as he determines.

Fee notes that Paul's list "illustrate[s] the *diversity* of the Spirit's activities/ manifestations in the church."[63] It is in the gathering that the people of God are empowered by the Spirit to build one another up through these gifts. They are gifted toward one another, not as a solo performance, but in a symphonic harmony. In this mutual edification, the people of God are more and more transformed into a holy people.

Conclusion

So, then, is this really *any* different than the old perspective? Yes . . . but also no. When we speak of the Christian life through the lens of a new perspective on Paul, the individualistic emphasis isn't thrown out at all; it is simply expanded. For example, a verse that is near and dear to many Christians today is Romans 3:23–24: "For all have sinned and fall short of the glory of God, and all are justified freely by his grace through the redemption that came by Christ Jesus." Tom Holland writes the following about this passage in his commentary on Romans: "[The] final act of justification is not the result of the community being punished for her sin, but of her representative taking the guilt of his fellow men."[64] At the heart of the old perspective is the need for God to take on the guilt of sinners, hence the focus on personal redemption. Humanity is saturated with the guilt of sin and has therefore fallen short of God's glory. While this is in so many ways true, when this becomes the starting point or the whole message, there arises an incredible propensity toward individual soteriology. When the emphasis is on individual soteriology, ecclesiology is only an afterthought.

As mentioned earlier, Beethoven did not write his *Overture from Egmont* with one instrument in mind, but he also didn't create it so that every instrument would sound exactly the same. Beethoven wrote the symphony with all the instruments in mind and for each instrument to shine in its unique way. It is exactly as Paul says in 1 Corinthians 12:12–26:

> Just as a body, though one, has many parts, but all its many parts form one body, so it is with Christ. For we were all baptized by one Spirit so as to form one body—whether Jews or Gentiles, slave or free—and we were all given the one Spirit to drink. Even so the body is not made up of one part but of many.
>
> Now if the foot should say, "Because I am not a hand, I do not belong to the body," it would not for that reason stop being part of the body. And if the ear should say, "Because I am not an eye, I do not belong to the body," it would not

63. Ibid., 264.
64. Tom Holland, *Romans: The Divine Marriage*, A Biblical Theological Commentary (Eugene, OR: Wipf & Stock, 2011), 97.

for that reason stop being part of the body. If the whole body were an eye, where would the sense of hearing be? If the whole body were an ear, where would the sense of smell be? But in fact God has placed the parts in the body, every one of them, just as he wanted them to be. If they were all one part, where would the body be? As it is, there are many parts, but one body.

The eye cannot say to the hand, "I don't need you!" And the head cannot say to the feet, "I don't need you!" On the contrary, those parts of the body that seem to be weaker are indispensable, and the parts that we think are less honorable we treat with special honor. And the parts that are unpresentable are treated with special modesty, while our presentable parts need no special treatment. But God has put the body together, giving greater honor to the parts that lacked it, so that there should be no division in the body, but that its parts should have equal concern for each other. If one part suffers, every part suffers with it; if one part is honored, every part rejoices with it.

The beauty of music happens when the ensemble comes together in one unifying voice. In the very same way, our Creator and King did not create the redemptive narrative with one person in mind, but the goal has always been for a holy people. The beauty of it all is when the people gather as one voice; this is when holiness happens.

8

Paul and Missional Hermeneutics

N. T. WRIGHT

What Is Missional Hermeneutics?

Paul's theology is widely agreed to be *missional* theology; that is, it is theology in service of his vocation as a *missionary*, specifically, as "the apostle to the gentiles." That was not a hobby, as though he were a missionary some of the time and the writer of theologically dense letters the rest of the time. His missionary mandate shaped the rest of his life, his writing included. At the same time, most Pauline scholars would agree that in some sense his theology is *hermeneutical*; that is, he thinks and writes (and, we should add, prays) in constant dialogue with Israel's Scriptures, drawing on them, engaging with them, selecting and arranging quotations and allusions from them to further his theological, and hence also his missionary, purposes. Thus—since for Paul these two aspects of his work belonged tightly together—we may say that Paul's *mission* was *hermeneutical* and that his *hermeneutics* were *missional*. It would be interesting to explore both halves of that balance, but my task here is to focus on the latter, and to expand it so that we are talking not just about Paul's own "missional hermeneutics" but also about our own in relation to his.

The phrase "missional hermeneutics" was new to me not many years ago, and it was a surprise to find that some of my friends and readers—in many cases the same people—seemed to think that whatever "missional hermeneutics" was, that was what I was doing. At first I was alarmed. I had thought I was simply trying to understand the world of the New Testament and to offer fresh readings of the Gospels and Epistles in ways that avoided anachronisms or the dangers of subjectivity. I had thought, in other words, that I was doing that rather complicated thing we call "history." Hence my alarm: if my work belonged in a different subspecialization, did that mean that it was thereby being shunted off into a siding? Might my books turn up, not on reading lists about Jesus and Paul, about Christology, soteriology, or eschatology, but simply in the sort of elective taken by a handful of bored students who don't know what missional hermeneutics is either but hope it might be less dull than the other available options?

I have put those fears aside and have come to embrace the category for three reasons, closely connected to my work on the New Testament in general and Paul in particular. Let me explain those three reasons before I turn to Paul himself.

First, I have been trying to think through the implications of what I think of as the *Surprised by Hope* agenda.[1] In that book I outlined the biblical teaching, which does indeed surprise many people, that the aim of Christianity is not to get disembodied souls to heaven but to bring about "new heavens and new earth." What you believe about the ultimate future has considerable impact on your view of the church's mission. When Christians slide off into Platonic hope, they try to save a few more souls for heaven. When they slide the other way into secular humanism or even Epicureanism, they try to bring justice and peace to the world with no sense that they are thereby anticipating God's new creation. The biblical hope refuses these two (apparently) "missional" applications and insists instead that since we live between the resurrection of Jesus and the renewal of all things, our task, in the Spirit, is to plant signs of God's coming kingdom even in the present time. We recognize that these will be partial and sometimes puzzling, but we believe with Paul in 1 Corinthians 15:58 that "in the Lord . . . the work [we're] doing will not be worthless."[2] I take it that the phrase "missional hermeneutics" is meant to denote a reading of Scripture with this new-creational horizon, and its consequent mission, in mind. One could of course imagine a "missional hermeneutic" from either a Platonic or an Epicurean reading of Scripture, the one screening out all

1. N. T. Wright, *Surprised by Hope: Rethinking Heaven, the Resurrection, and the Mission of the Church* (New York: HarperOne; London: SPCK, 2008).
2. New Testament quotations in this chapter, unless otherwise noted, are from N. T. Wright, *The Kingdom New Testament: A Contemporary Translation* (New York: HarperOne, 2011). Old Testament quotations are from the NRSV.

present-kingdom reference and the other having nothing else. Indeed, both such readings would, in some sense, be "missional hermeneutics," readings of Scripture with those kinds of "mission" in mind. But I suspect, though I cannot be sure, that the phrase "missional hermeneutics," referring to what I see as a reading of Scripture in line with the larger narrative of creation and new creation, has come to apply to that, rather than to either of the other options, because those who use it perceive the whole of Scripture as having to do with "the mission of God" in a way which is not true of the others.

Second, to cite another of my books, I see the idea of a missional *hermeneutic* belonging with the proposals I have made in *Scripture and the Authority of God*.[3] I have there argued that the phrase "authority of Scripture" can avoid incoherence only if we take it as a shorthand for "the authority of God *exercised through* Scripture," and that God's authority is not the sort of "authority" in which you look up correct answers to tricky questions—though you might sometimes do that too—but the kind of authority which *gets things done*. It is not ultimately about correct ideas but about transformative action (which of course requires true ideas to energize and shape it). That is why I have proposed (back in *Surprised by Hope*) the initially unlikely trio of justice, beauty, and evangelism as the church's central missional tasks. When people work on new creation, even in temporary and provisional form, they are more likely to be heard when they speak about the new creation which arrived in Jesus. Thus, whereas some kinds of hermeneutics treat the Bible rationalistically (as the book from which you can cull true propositions about how people get saved and how they should live as a result), I am arguing for a more dynamic hermeneutic in which the reading, praying, studying, and teaching of the New Testament transforms communities into missional bodies. This way of reading the text, I believe, goes with its grain. This is what the texts themselves were doing, and what the authors wanted their hearers to be doing.

Third, as a result, when I began writing the Christian Origins and the Question of God series, I asked myself whether I was really writing a kind of "New Testament Theology" and concluded that I wasn't. What I think I am writing is a kind of "New Testament Missiology." The New Testament was written to build up and energize the church to be God's people in God's world, living between Jesus's resurrection and the final renewal. A properly contextualized historical account of the New Testament would therefore give priority to explaining how the text was meant to serve that function. Of

3. N. T. Wright, *Scripture and the Authority of God: How to Read the Bible Today* (New York: HarperOne, 2011).

course, theology matters enormously as well, otherwise mission degenerates into ideologically driven pragmatism. Part of the point of the mission is that it is, so to speak, taking the battle to the enemy, confronting the principalities and powers with the news that in Jesus their power has been nullified. But the principalities and powers have ways of fighting back, and one of those ways is to distort the underlying theology so that the mission, too, goes off at a drunken angle. If I am spared to finish this series of books, I would like the final volume to be about mission, with theology as its reinforcing scaffolding, rather than about theology, with mission as its possible outflowing. We shall see.

All that is why, to come at last to my recent work *Paul and the Faithfulness of God* (PFG),[4] the central argument is not for this or that particular construal of Paul's theology, though obviously that is how it all works out. The central argument is that we should understand *how Paul invented Christian theology in the first place* or, to be more specific, how Paul was teaching his communities the vocational task of learning to work with Scripture in hand, prayer as the energy, Jesus as the focus, the church as the matrix, and God's future as the goal. That is why from a missional point of view the really important part of the book is the fourth and final one, where all the theology of part 3 "lands" in the worlds of empire, religion, philosophy, and even, by reflex, the Jewish world of Paul's day. That is where the missional implications really start to come out. When we see what the theology might mean in the wider pagan world, the missional reading becomes clear. In the final chapter of the book I explore the ways in which Paul's missionary plans, as outlined in Romans 15, have a special shape which is often missed, a shape which ties back in to some of the other themes I am exploring.

There is a puzzle here. In the section on Paul's worldview (part 2), I have emphasized that the central symbol for Paul's work is the church itself. When we ask what symbol encapsulates Paul's worldview (what people would see on the street, in the public world, that would express and summarize what Paul thought he was all about), it wouldn't be coins or inscriptions or special buildings or flags or uniforms. The early church had none of those. It would be a community, of a sort previously unimagined. Now here is the puzzle. I would love to have been able to argue that for Paul the central features of this symbolic community included something called "mission," but I find it impossible. I grew up in churches which assumed that the early church was always being encouraged to "do mission" in some way or another, because that's what *we* were all trying to do, usually in the Platonic form I mentioned

4. N. T. Wright, *Paul and the Faithfulness of God* (Minneapolis: Fortress, 2013).

earlier. We were all supposed to be telling our neighbors about Jesus; and it was assumed that the early church did that as well. But Paul, perhaps to our surprise, gives us no direct warrant for that.

What he does say, over and over again, is that the church, this symbolic community, must be *united* on the one hand and *holy* on the other. The unity across traditional boundary lines—Jew/Greek, slave/free, male/female—is well known; Paul insists on it in more or less every letter, often in great detail. Church unity looms much larger for him even than justification. One of the great benefits of some kinds of "new perspective" reading (note that there are many different kinds of reading which come under that umbrella) is that, without losing the importance of every person having a living faith (as some wrongly imagine), we can grasp Paul's constant emphasis on unity, starting (for instance) with Galatians, where it is absolutely central. In addition, without going soft on Paul's insistence on "faith alone" as the marker of justification, we can leave behind the threat of antinomianism that comes from a low-grade, would-be Reformational reading of that doctrine. For Paul, justification by faith is the demarcation of the sin-forgiven people of God. People in this category are, on the one hand, the "circumcision of the heart": though not having the law, they keep it because the Spirit has written it on their hearts (Rom. 2:25–29). They are, on the other hand, the inaugurated new creation, living from within the resurrected Messiah. They stand under the *mē genoito* of Romans 6:2, and their lives are to embody before the watching world the signs of new creation, including kindness, generosity, abstention from anger and malice, and not least sexual purity, whether in marriage or in celibacy. This kind of a way of life, of community, was more or less unknown in the ancient world. This is why the church was, for Paul, the sign and symbol of the new covenant and the new creation.

But Paul does not mention mission—except perhaps in one passage to which we will come presently. This has worried me, because as a bishop I used to tell people that the church should be shaped by mission, and that mission should be shaped by eschatology. We used to warn against imagining that the first task was to sort out the church and only then, if there was any time left, which often there wasn't, one might get around to some mission. But the more I have studied Paul, the more I have become convinced that for him the fact of this symbol—of the united and holy community in the Messiah—was itself the mission, or at any rate the heart of it. Paul knows of other "evangelists" like himself; that was a specific commission. He never suggests that all Christians possessed that calling (another puzzle for some traditional readings). But he sees the church itself as the powerful sign to the watching world, and for that matter to the watching principalities and powers, that a new way of being human has been launched upon the world, and that this is because there is a new *kyrios*, a new *sōtēr*, embodying the power and love of the God of Abraham, Isaac, and Jacob. So, as I ask myself what it might mean to have a "missional hermeneutic" in the reading of Paul, my provisional answer is that a historical analysis of Paul's letters indicates that these documents were written in order to keep the church focused on the central task of learning to think Christianly—the task of theology, in other words—so that the vocation to unity and holiness might be sustained, *and so that the world would see the signs of the lordship of Jesus at work.*

There is one other element which in my work to date I have mentioned but not highlighted: suffering. For Paul, sharing in the Messiah's sufferings was not simply an incidental or accidental occasional by-product of following the Christian way. It was a necessary part of it. "Sharing the sufferings of the Messiah" was not an optional extra (Rom. 8:17–18; Phil. 3:10; 1 Thess. 3:3–4; and elsewhere). What is more, Paul can sometimes speak of suffering in instrumental terms, for instance when he indicates that his own sufferings are "on behalf of his [the Messiah's] body, which is the church" (Col. 1:24). The patient sufferings of the church can function in this way, too, as a sign from God (Phil. 1:28). And with that, we move straightaway to my first key passage.

Philippians 2:1–18

I said that Paul never speaks of the missional task of the church. The only Pauline letter which might be an exception is Philippians, specifically in 2:14–16 (cf. 1:12–18):

> There must be no grumbling and disputing in anything you do. That way, nobody will be able to fault you, and you'll be pure and spotless children of God in the middle of a twisted and depraved generation. You are to shine among them like lights in the world, clinging to the word of life. That's what I will be proud of on the day of the Messiah. It will prove that I didn't run a useless race, or work to no purpose.

In that translation I took a firm position on the disputed meaning of *epechontes* in verse 16. I see it as "clinging to," "holding fast to," rather than, as some have it, "holding *forth*," which would have the implication that the church was to present the word of life (presumably, the word of the gospel) to the surrounding world. My objection to that view isn't simply that this would then be the only passage where Paul says that sort of thing. It is that the evidence about *epechō*, from the Septuagint and the classical world, seems to point toward "clinging to." But actually I don't think it makes much difference. Paul's point is still *the missiological impact of the united, holy, and suffering community.* Whether the word means "holding fast" or "holding forth," what matters is "you are to shine like lights in the world." Within Philippians, this goes very closely with 1:27 ("your public behavior must match up to the gospel of the king") and also 4:5 ("Let everybody know how gentle and gracious you are"). Philippians is concerned with the public perception of the church, the impact of this strange new community, people whose lives shed light, and run straight and true, in a dark and twisted world.

There is little explicit scriptural quotation in Philippians. But there is a great deal of implicit Scripture just under the surface, and the three passages that resonate behind Paul's words tell us a great deal about how his missional hermeneutic is working—that is, his own missional reading of Israel's Scriptures, the missional hearing of his words in Philippi, and perhaps also our own missional reading of such a text.

First, the warning against grumbling and questioning (Phil. 2:14) is regularly lined up with the idea of the church as the new-exodus community. The point is clear: let's get it right this time! Paul gives the same warning in 1 Corinthians 10:10, where the Exodus context is more explicit. Here it simply gives his warning the flavor of new covenant, of the people who were called to be the royal priesthood, the holy nation.

Second, there is Daniel 12, where the wise will shine like lights in the sky, "and those who lead many to righteousness, like the stars forever and ever" (v. 3). This is a prediction of the resurrection, often quoted as such by later Jewish writers. It is also an echo of Isaiah 53:11, not exact but audible. What we have here (Phil. 2:15), in Paul's own missional reading of Daniel and Isaiah, is the sense of *inaugurated eschatology* in which the new life of resurrection has begun already, and the church, even in the present time, is to shine like lights in a dark sky, visible to the world around, carrying forward the servant-promise of Isaiah.

This is clinched, third, by one of Paul's frequent applications of Isaiah 49 to himself. He will (he says) be proud not to have run a useless race or worked to no purpose (Phil. 2:16). Isaiah 49 was one of Paul's most-quoted texts, always, I think, in relation to his own commission and ministry; and this negative side of it—the anxiety about working in vain—seems to have haunted him quite a bit. It turns up in Galatians, Thessalonians, and elsewhere. In Isaiah 49 we have not only the original call of the servant, not only the complaint about laboring in vain, but the famous extension of the mandate: "It is too light a thing that you should be my servant to raise up the tribes of Jacob and to restore the survivors of Israel; I will give you as a light to the nations, that my salvation may reach to the end of the earth" (v. 6). The passage goes on to speak of the time of favor, the day of salvation, and the fact that the servant has been given "as a covenant to the people" (v. 8), bringing people in from far away and causing all creation to rejoice.

So what is Paul doing by joining together Exodus, Daniel, and Isaiah 49? (As often, we note, he is drawing on the three sections of Israel's Scriptures: Torah, Prophets, and Writings.) He is saying that the communities he has founded are the people through whom the Servant's missionary mandate is now being effective—if they are indeed united and holy, as they must be, and, as the Servant-people must be, suffering also. This is his own missional hermeneutic of his Scriptures, and as the Philippians read his letter, a new hermeneutic takes place as those passages find a new focus in the Messiah—just as another new missional hermeneutic takes place whenever later Christians, including today's church, hear what Paul was saying and work out its implications for themselves.

At the heart of this missional hermeneutic in Philippians 2 we have, of course, the famous poem of 2:6–11. I sometimes wonder if Paul at least, though clearly knowing that the poem is what it is, thought of what we call verses 12 and 13 as part of the center of this passage. Verses 1–5 and verses 14–18 form balanced sides, sixty-eight words in the former, and sixty-nine in the latter. Perhaps that is only coincidence. But I do think we should take verses 12 and 13 more closely with verses 6–11 than we are accustomed to doing. The passionate and detailed appeal for a unity of heart and mind in verses 1–5 is undergirded by the fact of the Messiah's self-abnegation and crucifixion in the poem, *and* by the fact of the *hōste* clause which follows: *Therefore*—work out your own salvation!

That is not, of course, a command to do a bit of Pelagianism on the side. That, indeed, is ruled out by the insistence that the one at work within them is God himself. The poem's strong implication is the contrast between *kyrios Kaisar* and *kyrios Iēsous*. Since Caesar offers the Roman world (not least a colony like Philippi) his own brand of *sōtēria*, the church must think through, and put into practice, the form of "salvation" proper to itself, the form expressed in the poem just cited. All this I have of course written about at much more length elsewhere.

When we stand back for a moment from the whole passage, what do we see? Obviously, the poem of verses 6–11 is one of the most striking christological and also theological statements in all Christian literature. It embodies the missional hermeneutic Paul is expounding, drawing together the great strands of Scripture, from Adam to the Servant, focusing them on Jesus and his shameful death, then broadening out, just as the Servant Songs themselves do, to embrace the world, and thereby celebrating Jesus as its rightful sovereign. And in the context of Philippians, the meaning for a missional hermeneutic is clear. The dark world in which the church must shine like the stars through unity, holiness, and suffering is the world which Caesar claims for his own. This is exactly what we should expect from Isaiah itself, not to mention the echoes of Exodus and Daniel. We are not just talking about moral example. We are talking about confronting the powers, temporal and spiritual (if we can make that distinction), with the news of their own demise and of the rescue by the true God of a new people who embody the new covenant and the new creation before the unsuspecting imperial world. The redefinition of power in the great poem, cognate with Jesus's own redefinition of power in the Sermon on the Mount and passages like Mark 10:35–45, is a key part of this missional rereading of Israel's Scriptures. Jesus himself is the mission of God in person, and Paul's work is to proclaim him as Lord and to watch and work as the community figures out in practice what this new type of "salvation" will mean.

So much of Philippians is about this same theme: from Paul's imprisonment making the gospel known to the whole Praetorian guard (1:13) to the public celebration, as I take it, in 4:4. This passage, then, and the whole letter, is best read with the grain of a missional hermeneutic in which Paul is rereading his Scriptures as having come to full flowering in the gospel and generating a community which embodies God's mission. When we read or pray or study or teach Philippians, this is the most natural way to understand it.

The Larger Context: Paul's Missional Reading of Israel's Scriptures

Let me take a step back to look at Paul's overall missional reading of Scripture. The allusions to Isaiah, to Exodus, and to many other passages are not mere random gestures toward a distant text assumed to be authoritative. They fall within an implicit narrative upon which Paul draws at various points. It is precisely, in his hands, a missional narrative: the story of how the creator God called a people through whom he would undo the plight of the world, and of the human race, rescuing the creation rather than abandoning it. This story runs from Genesis to Exodus and on, with highlights such as the close of Deuteronomy and the promises to David and the shocking fact of covenant disloyalty and subsequent exile, and the strange, unfulfilled promises of a glorious return, of God overthrowing the pagans and coming back to Zion to be king, of covenant renewed and creation renewed. I know, of course, that all this is now routinely set aside by those for whom the mid-century German critique of a Hegelian doctrine of progress somehow applies to Israel's covenant narrative as well, or those for whom speaking of "covenant" at all is impossibly restrictive when in the gospel God throws his arms open to welcome the world. To all that I reply that this is a radical and sometimes willful misunderstanding of the missional hermeneutic of Israel's Scriptures which we find right through the New Testament, which is not at all about progressive revelation or a steady crescendo of Israel's story leading up to a natural climax. Nor is the covenant restrictive: it is precisely the way God addresses the whole world. The gospel is, of course, a radical reversal, a shocking and unexpected fulfillment; but as in all the Jewish apocalypses it is a reversal which takes place in fulfillment of ancient promises, at the divinely appointed time, in the proper place, in a sequence which, though it cannot be read off *from* history, nevertheless takes place *within* history. I suppose you could generate a kind of missional hermeneutic out of the currently popular "apocalyptic" reading of Paul. But it will not be Paul's missional hermeneutic. For Paul, what matters—as he sums it up at the end of the argument of Romans—is that "the Messiah became a servant of the circumcised people in order to demonstrate the truthfulness of God—that is, to confirm the promises to the patriarchs, and to bring the nations to praise God for his mercy" (Rom. 15:8–9). Paul sees the gospel as unveiling the covenant faithfulness, the truthfulness, of the promises to the patriarchs.

What were those promises, and how are they explained in, and developed through, Paul's missional reading of Scripture? I have for many years been fond of quoting *Genesis Rabbah*, which puts into God's mouth the words, "I will make Adam first, and if he goes wrong I will send Abraham to sort it all out" (14:6). That, it seems to me, is a proper reading of Genesis in its own terms where the commands to Adam become promises to Abraham, with the obvious link between Adam being fruitful and multiplying and looking after the garden and Abraham being promised a family and a land. The exile—Abraham's family being finally ejected from the land—is then the direct parallel to the expulsion from the garden in Genesis 3. Somehow the stories fit together. Paul's own Messiah-shaped and Spirit-driven rereading takes its place among other Second Temple readings, claiming as its validation the resurrection and the power of the Spirit. For Paul the promises to Abraham had been radically widened through the Davidic psalms. The "inheritance" which, for Abraham, is the holy land has been extended: "Ask of me," says YHWH to the Messiah in Psalm 2:8, as the pagan nations are raging all around, "Ask of me, and I will make the nations your heritage, and the ends of the earth your possession." Psalm 2, developed further in Psalm 72 and elsewhere, including Second Temple texts, is basic. Paul's vision of Jesus as the Davidic Messiah, to whom the title "Son of God" would apply from that angle, while being also the natural linguistic vehicle to express Jesus's identity with, and sending from, the Father—this vision was of the Messiah as the Lord of the whole world.

All this means that we can leave behind the older idea, which owed much to the nineteenth-century love of "isms" and to a hatred of the Jewish "ism" in particular, that Paul abandoned the Jewish notion of Messiah and used instead the Hellenistic notion of lordship in order to leave behind the law-bound Jewish world and address the law-free Hellenistic one. Against that, Paul himself replies regularly that it is precisely as the Jewish Messiah that Jesus claims the nations as his inheritance. This entire sequence of thought makes excellent sense of the two great Abraham letters, Romans and Galatians. In Romans in particular Paul expounds both the covenant with Abraham (chap. 4) and the extension of the covenant through the Messiah (chap. 8), though he backdates the latter to Abraham's time by saying in 4:13 (and this is foundational for his missional hermeneutic) that the promise to Abraham and his seed was that they would inherit *the world*, the *kosmos*. Abraham has routinely been downgraded into a mere example of someone who believed a promise and had "righteousness" reckoned to him. But for Paul Abraham was promised a *family* and an *inheritance*—hence the miracle of grace, since he was at the time a childless nomad. Paul expounds the family, the "seed," in terms of the Messiah and his people; and he expounds the inheritance as the whole world—with the Spirit as the down payment, the advance guarantee of the final inheritance.

The notion of a worldwide inheritance was developed by various Jewish thinkers through the Second Temple period. Philo of Alexandria explored the idea that, with Jewish settlements all around the known world, this might be a sign of the coming day when God's people would become the true empire through which justice and peace would come at last. We cannot tell whether Saul of Tarsus might have thought like that too. What we can be sure of is that he plugged in to the implicit narrative of Adam, Abraham, and David, aligned with the historical sense of exile and return, and not least YHWH's abandoning of the temple and his own promised return. Paul expounded enough different bits of this narrative here and there for us to be able with some security to reconstruct the entire implicit story as he understood it. I know some people object strongly to this approach, but its heuristic value is immense, and it relies not upon guesswork but on careful study of actual texts.

Here we meet two of the great objections to any missional reading of Paul himself, or any hypothetical Pauline missional reading of Israel's Scriptures. First, some object on principle to narratival readings, though usually substituting an implicit narrative of their own—namely, the older Protestant one of sinful humans, Jesus as substitute, and heaven after all. That is not a narrative we find in the New Testament, but it remains powerful. The objection then comes at various points, not least against any suggestion of God's kingdom coming "on earth as in heaven," though that is what the New Testament intends.

The second objection comes from the other end and mocks any narrative of promise and fulfillment, or of a mission which grows out of such a thing, as simply an ecclesial power trip. Of course, it is possible to use it that way, and perhaps—I don't know—that was part of the perceived problem to which Käsemann and others were objecting. But that has nothing to do with Paul's vision, in which the church is designated as co-inheritor with the Messiah on the strict provision that it must suffer with him if it wants to be glorified with him. The messianic reapplication of inheritance in Romans 8 is tied directly to holiness, suffering, the groaning of uncomprehending prayer, and the assurance of God's love despite the principalities and powers. This is hardly triumphalism. And if it generates a missional reading, which it ought to do, that mission will be characterized by Sermon-on-the-Mount living, not by a kind of neo-imperialism.

Conclusion

Let me conclude by highlighting two features of *Paul and the Faithfulness of God* which might be taken up elsewhere, and then pointing to an obvious though controversial conclusion.

First, in chapter 14 of *PFG* I outlined what seems to me a fruitful way of lining up Paul's implicit engagement with ancient philosophy. I am particularly interested in what Paul might have had to say to the three normal categories of philosophical discourse: physics, ethics, and logic. Physics describes what is there in "nature"—including the gods. Ethics is about thinking through how to live in accordance with that "nature." Logic is about the act of knowing and the techniques of reasoning. Paul, as he himself tells us, saw his own mission to the pagan world, energized and shaped by his missional reading of Israel's Scriptures, as including the bold attempt to "take every thought prisoner and make it obey the Messiah" (2 Cor. 10:5). He says a lot which relates to "physics" in the ancient sense, though of course his God is not an object in the world, whether far distant as with the Epicureans or suffusing all things as with the Stoics. The world is, rather, the object of God's generous love and care, a very different thing. But, in particular, Paul believes that new creation has come into being—a new kind of *physics*, a new reality. It has begun in Jesus, but the Spirit brings it into reality in human lives. Paul's ethics, therefore, are not to be seen simply as the manufacture of some new rules out of bits and pieces left over from his Jewish background, or a potpourri of street-level philosophical maxims picked up here and there. Paul's ethics are about *living in tune with the new creation*. His missional hermeneutic has the cross and resurrection at its heart. Since his vision of the united, holy, and suffering community is the spearhead of this missiology, this idea of lived-out new creation is central. One of its obvious results is the command to "remember the poor" (cf. Gal. 2:10), which (as has recently been argued) may well not be simply referring to the poor church in Jerusalem but may indicate the launching of a new vision of human society, economics included.

In particular, Paul has a different kind of logic, of epistemology. There is a new mode of knowing let loose upon the world. This is where the advocates of a so-called apocalyptic are on to something vital. Paul's knowing takes place within the world of new creation—but the point of new creation is that it is new *creation*, not absolutely discontinuous with what has gone before but transforming it. The new sort of knowing is a kind of three-dimensional version of the old two-dimensional one: there is both continuity and discontinuity. This discussion, central (I think) to any missional hermeneutic, needs to be mapped on to the larger theological discussions, not least those associated with Karl Barth, from the last century. I merely flag the matter here for further consideration.

The second major point for now comes in the final chapter of *PFG*. There I argued that Paul's missionary plans in Romans 15 are specifically related to the Roman Empire. His desire to go to Spain was not random. Spain was the far west outpost of Rome's domain; and Paul's apocalyptic vision, like that of Daniel or *4 Ezra*, was that the fourth monster who had tyrannized the world should be faced down by the one like a son of man, by the lion of Judah. Here again the political focus of Paul's missiological understanding of the great scriptural narrative comes to the fore. Again, I merely flag this for further thought.

My final point is controversial because it takes us to Ephesians. As I have said in *PFG*, I regard the prejudice against Ephesians as just that, a prejudice, growing out of an older liberal Protestantism of which there are few surviving representatives, yet kept in place by our nervous scholarly traditions which normally parrot the tradition rather than investigating it or—heaven help us!—challenging it. But much that I have said finds a strong echo in Ephesians, whether it was written by Paul or a good friend of his who understood his mind (and may even have had the same name). Whatever: the scriptural vision of a new creation, of all things in heaven and on earth brought together in the Messiah (1:10), fits exactly with Paul's vision of new creation in Romans 8 or 1 Corinthians 15. The fact that this is instantiated through the coming together of Jew and gentile into a single body, a new temple, is exactly in line with Romans, Galatians, and 1 Corinthians. (The theme of the temple is a major part of Paul's missional hermeneutic which I haven't had time to explore here.) But then, in Ephesians 3, we have a statement of precisely that missional understanding of the church for which I was arguing in Philippians 2. The coming together of Jew and gentile in the Messiah means that "God's wisdom, in all its rich variety, was to be made known to the rulers and authorities in the heavenly places—through the church!" (Eph. 3:10). This, indeed, was the unveiling of the secret plan, the "apocalypse" of what the creator God had in mind all along (3:9). And Ephesians 4, 5, and 6 likewise emphasize the unity and holiness of the church as the necessary characteristics if the church is to be the sign and symbol of the mission of God in the world, equipped with the whole armor of God to withstand the attacks that will come from the principalities and powers.

There are many themes, many strands of thought that I have not even mentioned, let alone developed, but which would be important for a full account. But I hope I have said enough to indicate at least some ways in which my recent exposition of Paul points directly and, I hope, fruitfully toward not only a fresh understanding of Paul's missional reading of his Scriptures but also a fresh missional reading, for the church, of the Scriptures which now include Paul's writings themselves. If—to revisit one of my opening points—the Scriptures are there not simply to convey true information but to energize and refocus the church for its multiple tasks, then to understand the ways in which Paul retrieved and refocused his Scriptures around Jesus and the Spirit ought to help us toward a mature understanding of how we can work with the grain of his text, rather than against it. The imperatives toward unity and holiness, and the mission which follows from a vision of new covenant and new creation, seem to me as urgent in the early twenty-first century as they were for Paul himself.

Selected Bibliography

An asterisk (*) denotes a seminal work.

Bird, Michael F. *The Saving Righteousness of God: Studies on Paul, Justification, and the New Perspective*. Eugene, OR: Wipf & Stock, 2007.

Dunn, James D. G. *Jesus, Paul, and the Law: Studies in Mark and Galatians*. Louisville: Westminster John Knox, 1990.

*———. *The New Perspective on Paul*. Rev. ed. Grand Rapids: Eerdmans, 2008.

———. "A New Perspective on the New Perspective on Paul." *Early Christianity* 4 (2013): 157–82.

Garlington, Don. *In Defense of the New Perspective on Paul: Essays and Reviews*. Eugene, OR: Wipf & Stock, 2005.

Kim, Seyoon. *Paul and the New Perspective: Second Thoughts on the Origin of Paul's Gospel*. Grand Rapids: Eerdmans, 2001.

*Moore, George Foot. "Christian Writers on Judaism." *Harvard Theological Review* 14 (1921): 197–254.

Sanders, E. P. *Judaism: Practice and Belief, 63 BCE–66 CE*. Philadelphia: Trinity, 1992.

*———. *Paul and Palestinian Judaism: A Comparison of Patterns of Religion*. Philadelphia: Fortress, 1977.

———. *Paul: The Apostle's Life, Letters and Thought*. Minneapolis: Fortress, 2015.

———. *Paul, the Law, and the Jewish People*. Minneapolis: Fortress, 2009.

*Stendahl, Krister. "The Apostle Paul and the Introspective Conscience of the West." In *Paul among Jews and Gentiles*, 78–96. Philadelphia: Fortress, 1976.

Thompson, Michael Bruce. *The New Perspective on Paul*. Cambridge, UK: Grove, 2002.

Wright, N. T. *Justification: God's Plan and Paul's Vision*. Downers Grove, IL: IVP Academic, 2009.

———. *Paul and the Faithfulness of God*. Christian Origins and the Question of God 4. Minneapolis: Fortress, 2013.

———. *Paul: In Fresh Perspective*. Minneapolis: Fortress, 2009.

*———. "The Paul of History and the Apostle of Faith." *Tyndale Bulletin* 29 (1978): 61–88.

———. *What Saint Paul Really Said: Was Paul of Tarsus the Real Founder of Christianity?* Grand Rapids: Eerdmans, 1997.

Yinger, Kent L. *The New Perspective on Paul: An Introduction*. Eugene, OR: Cascade, 2010.

List of Contributors

Lynn H. Cohick (PhD, University of Pennsylvania, Philadelphia) is professor of New Testament at Wheaton College in Wheaton, Illinois. Her books include *Philippians* (The Story of God Bible Commentary) and *Women in the World of the Earliest Christians: Illuminating Ancient Ways of Life.*

James D. G. Dunn is Emeritus Lightfoot Professor of Divinity at the University of Durham, where he taught from 1982 to 2003. He has authored over twenty monographs, including *Unity and Diversity in the New Testament*; *The Theology of Paul the Apostle*; *The New Perspective on Paul*; *A New Perspective on Jesus*; *Jesus, Paul and the Gospels*; and commentaries on Romans, Galatians, Colossians and Philemon, and Acts. He recently completed his trilogy on *Christianity in the Making*: volume 1, *Jesus Remembered*; volume 2, *Beginning from Jerusalem*; volume 3, *Neither Jew nor Greek: A Contested Identity*. He is married to Meta, has three children, and served as a Methodist local preacher for forty years.

Timothy G. Gombis (PhD, University of St. Andrews) is associate professor of New Testament at Grand Rapids Theological Seminary. He is the author of *Paul: A Guide for the Perplexed* and *The Drama of Ephesians: Participating in the Triumph of God.*

Tara Beth Leach is finishing her master of divinity degree from Northern Seminary. She lives in the western suburbs of Chicago with her husband, Jeff, and her rambunctious boys, Caleb and Noah. A Nazarene pastor, Tara Beth has served churches in upstate New York and Naperville, Illinois, and now serves as pastor of women's ministry at Christ Church of Oak Brook. She contributed the essay "Perfect Love" to the book *Renovating Holiness* and also blogs for Missio Alliance.

Bruce W. Longenecker (PhD, University of Durham) is professor of early Christianity and the Melton Chair of Religion at Baylor University in Waco, Texas. He previously taught in Britain at the universities of Durham, Cambridge, and St. Andrews. His books include *Remember the Poor: Paul, Poverty, and the Greco-Roman World* and (coauthored with Todd Still) *Thinking through Paul: A Survey of His Life, Letters, and Theology.*

Scot McKnight (PhD, University of Nottingham) is professor of New Testament at Northern Seminary in Lombard, Illinois. He is the author of *The Epistle of James* (New International Commentary on the New Testament), *Jesus and His Death*, *The King Jesus Gospel*, *Kingdom Conspiracy*, and *The Jesus Creed* and hosts the widely influential blog *Jesus Creed.*

Patrick Mitchel (PhD, London School of Theology) is principal of Belfast Bible College. Previously he was director of studies and lecturer in theology at the Irish Bible Institute in Dublin. He is author of *Evangelicalism and National Identity in Ulster 1921–1998.*

Joseph B. Modica (PhD, Drew University) is university chaplain and associate professor of biblical studies at Eastern University. He is the coeditor, with Scot McKnight, of *Jesus Is Lord, Caesar Is Not: Evaluating Empire in New Testament Studies.*

N. T. (Tom) Wright was Bishop of Durham in the Church of England from 2003 to 2010 and is now Research Professor of New Testament and Early Christianity at the University of St. Andrews. He has written over seventy books, including the popular "Everyone" series of commentaries and the academic series Christian Origins and the Question of God, and has appeared as a guest on the BBC and on American shows such as *Fresh Air* and *The Colbert Report*. He is married to Maggie, and they have four children and four grandchildren. He lists among his hobbies music, poetry, hill walking, and golf.

Index of Subjects

Abba, cry of, 13
Abraham
  Adam and, 188
  Christ and, 9, 86–87, 109,
    138–39, 188–89
  the church and, 120–21,
    132–33
  Israel and, 30, 106
  the Spirit and, 11–12, 15,
    91–92
Adam, 105–7, 109, 154–55, 188
adoption, 29–34
advocacy, love and, 150
agency, salvation and, 77–80
agitators, 14–15, 64–65, 120–21
alms, 42–45, 54
anthropology. *See* humanity
Antioch, incident at, 5–6,
  11n23
apocalyptic, 35, 38–40. *See*
  also eschatology
"Apostle Paul and the
  Introspective Conscience
  of the West, The"
  (Stendahl), xii, 73
apostleship, Paul's, 2–6
associations, Roman, 141
astrology, identity and, 23–24
Augustine, 127
authority, 2–4, 181

badge, law as, xiii
baptism, 9–10, 110–12

Bardaisan of Edessa, 23–24
Bible, the. *See* Scripture
body, Christ's, 39–40, 111–15
body, physical, 96
boundary marker, law as, xiii,
  77–80, 131–33
burdens, ethics and, 54

causality, the Spirit and, 51–52
centrism, ethical, 66–70
Cephas. *See* Peter (apostle)
character, moral, 51–52
charity, 42–45, 54
children, Christians as, 12–13
Christ
  Abraham and, 138–39,
    188–89
  baptism into, 110–12
  the church and, 39–40, 60,
    121–24, 142, 143
  the cross and, 116–18
  faith and, 7–10, 11–12, 30n23
  justification and, 157–59
  the law and, 17n34, 49–50,
    138–39
  love and, 53
  monotheism and, 84–86
  salvation and, 42–43
  Scripture and, 86–89, 108–10
  the Spirit and, 51, 83–84, 91
church, the
  community and, 36–40,
    112–21, 139–51

individualism and, 74,
  171–72
the new perspective and,
  133, 135–36
the old perspective and,
  128–29
the Spirit and, 90–94, 99–
  101, 111–12
circumcision, 7, 14–15, 64–65
commitment, rugged, 150
Communion, Holy, 122–23
community, 36–40, 68, 74,
  99–101, 116–21
convention, epistolary, 2–4
conversion, Paul's, 4–6
cosmic powers, 56–60, 67
covenantal nomism, xii, 131
covetousness, ethics and,
  54–60
creation
  the church and, 105–8, 143
  new, 90–91, 112–21, 133,
    180–81, 190–92
cross, the, 85–86, 96–97, 109,
  116–18
custodian, law as, 9

darkness, human wisdom
  and, 37–38
David, Jesus and, 188–89
Dead Sea Scrolls, 130–31
death, ethics and, 56–57, 60
debt, sin as, 42, 44–45

Index of Authors

Index of Scripture
and Other Ancient Sources

205

Colossians

1:1 2nn4–5
1:3–6 3n7
1:4 100
1:8 100n120
1:10 89n81
1:13 111
1:15–17 143
1:17 108
1:20 143
1:24 184
1:25 143
1:26–27 84n59
1:27 143
2:2 84n59, 100, 174
2:10 143
2:13–14 44
2:15 143
3:3 111, 121
3:5 44n55
3:9–11 141–42
3:11 89, 133
3:11–12 143
3:12 93, 100
3:12–14 144
3:13 99
3:14 100, 149, 174
3:16 176
3:18–4:1 144
3:19 100
4:3 84n59
4:5 144

1 Thessalonians

1:2–3 3
1:4 93, 100
1:5 64
2:8 100
2:12 89n81
3:3–4 184
3:6 100
3:12 99, 100, 174
3:12–13 175
3:13 97
4:9 100
4:19 99
5:8 100
5:11 99
5:14 172
5:14–15 60

5:15 49, 99
5:16–18 163
5:23 167n49

2 Thessalonians

1:3 99, 100
1:3–4 3n7
1:5 89n81
1:11 89n81
2:8–10 58n13
2:13 93, 100, 167n49
2:16 100
3:5 101

1 Timothy

1:1 2n4
3:16 84n59
4:4 106
5:8 32
6:6–19 43

2 Timothy

1:1 2n4
1:7 64
1:14 52

Titus

1:1 2n4
2:11 156
2:14 93

Philemon

1–3 113
4–7 3n7
5 100
7 100
9 101
16 114
23–24 113

Hebrews

11:20 126
12:16 126

James

1:27 33

1 Peter

1:16 160
4:10–11 146n38
4:16 1n2

1 John

1:8 162
4:18 163

Revelation

21:3 150
21:7 150

Old Testament Apocrypha

Sirach

24:1–12 22

Old Testament Pseudepigrapha

2 Baruch

82:5 66

1 Enoch

93:10 22

4 Ezra

6:56 66

Jubilees

22:16 66
23:24 66
47:5 30

Psalms of Solomon

1:1 66
2:1 66
17:5 66

Pseudo-Philo

Liber antiquitatum biblicarum

7.3 66
12.4 66